THE PASSION FOR
Pelargoniums

THE PASSION FOR

Pelargoniums

*How they found their
place in the garden*

ANNE
WILKINSON

FOREWORD BY
*CHRIS
BEARDSHAW*

SUTTON PUBLISHING

First published in the United Kingdom in 2007 by
Sutton Publishing Limited · Phoenix Mill
Thrupp · Stroud · Gloucestershire · GL5 2BU

British Library Cataloguing in Publication Data
A catalogue record for this book is available from the British Library.

Hardback ISBN 978-0-7509-4428-1
Paperback ISBN 978-0-7509-4429-8

Typeset in 11.5/14.5pt Photina MT.
Typesetting and origination by
Sutton Publishing Limited.
Printed and bound in England.

Contents

	List of Illustrations	vii
	Foreword	xi
	Acknowledgements	xiii
	A Pelargonium Chronology	xv
	Introduction	1
1.	Splendid Curiosities	13
2.	Delights for Aristocrats	33
3.	The Impudent Frenchman	57
4.	'The First Practical Botanist in Europe'	79
5.	The Quest for the Perfect Pelargonium	95
6.	The Age of Bedding	123
7.	Flights of Fancy	147
8.	Flowers for the Million	175
9.	The Final Flowering of the Nineteenth Century	197
10.	Demise and Renaissance	213
11.	Regaining the Treasures of the Past	239
	Appendix 1 Botanical Classification of Pelargonium Species	251
	Appendix 2 Horticultural Classification and Glossary	257
	Appendix 3 List of Suppliers and Organisations	267
	Notes and Sources	269
	Bibliography	289
	General Index	295
	Index of Pelargoniums	300

To
Isabelle and Florence

List of Illustrations

Colour Plates

1. Mrs Delany's 'paper mosaic' of *P. fulgidum*
2. *P. caffrum*
3. *P. oblongatum*
4. *P. triste*
5. Bedding at Bowood House
6. *P. × rubescens*, the Countess of Liverpool's Storksbill
7. *P. × daveyanum*, Davey's Storksbill
8. *P. × involucratum*, the Large-bracted Storksbill
9. Beaton's 'Indian Yellow'
10. Coloured-leaved Zonals
11. *Young Lady in a Conservatory*
12. 'Duchess of Sutherland' Nosegay
13. French or 'Spotted' pelargoniums
14. Zonal pelargonium and hybrids
15. Fancy, Show and Decorative pelargoniums
16. Catalogue of Caledonian Nurseries

Black and white illustrations

	page
1. Zonal pelargonium	3
2. Geranium and pelargonium flowers compared	5
3. Seedpod from *Pelargonium capitatum*	7
4. John Tradescant's house in Lambeth	15
5. William Bentinck, Earl of Portland	28
6. The Duchess of Portland	38

		page
7.	Dr John Fothergill	43
8.	Excerpt from Kew record book	53
9.	William Curtis	61
10.	*P. × striatum*	81
11.	Sir Richard Colt Hoare	85
12.	'Large-flowered' pelargonium	101
13.	Florists' flower diagram	104
14.	Captain Thurtell's 'Pluto'	105
15.	Edward Beck	111
16.	Beck's 'Harlequin'	117
17.	George W. Hoyle	118
18.	French or 'Spotted' pelargonium, 'La Belle Alliance'	121
19.	Donald Beaton	127
20.	*Ciconium crenatum*	137
21.	Francis Rodney Kinghorn	139
22.	Diagram for a 'panel garden'	141
23.	Design for a flower bed	142
24.	Design for Liverpool Botanic Garden	143
25.	The 'geranium pyramid' at Stoke Newington	145
26.	The parterre at Eythrope	149
27.	Peter Grieve	150
28.	Leaf of 'Sophia Cusack'	152
29.	Leaf of 'Princess of Wales'	153
30.	Diagram showing Peter Grieve's pelargoniums	154
31.	Leaf of 'Crimson Nosegay'	157
32.	Henry Cannell	158
33.	Ivy-leaved pelargoniums in hanging basket	163
34.	Victor Lemoine	166
35.	Wilmore's Surprise	173
36.	J.R. Pearson's Chilwell Nursery	176
37.	John Royston Pearson	177
38.	'Rienzi' – florists' Zonal pelargonium	179

		page
39.	Pelargonium Society certificate	182
40.	Charles Turner	185
41.	Victorian plant seller	188
42.	Victorian paper collage	190
43.	*Pelargonium album*, an early Regal pelargonium	191
44.	William Bull	192
45.	Bull's catalogue showing 'Beauty of Oxton'	193
46.	Bruant's pelargoniums 'de grand bois'	203
47.	Gardener with a potted pelargonium	205
48.	Advertisement for Zonate pelargoniums	206
49.	*Cannell's Floral Guide* for 1910	210
50.	Bedding display, 'basket of flowers'	215
51.	Inside an amateur's greenhouse, 1904	224
52.	Victorian pressed pelargoniums	249
53.	Poster for Liverpool International Garden Festival	250

Plant profiles

	page
P. triste	14
P. cucullatum	21
P. zonale	22
P. peltatum	23
P. capitatum	26
P. inquinans	29
P. gibbosum	34
P. papilionaceum	35
P. odoratissimum	36
P. fulgidum	37
P. betulinum	51
P. echinatum	54
P. tricolor	55
P. panduriforme	68

List of Illustrations

	page
P. tomentosum	73
P. × ardens	76
P. × ignescens	87
P. × fragrans	90
'Rollisson's Unique'	126
'Mrs Pollock'	155
'Mrs Quilter'	156
'L'Elegante'	165
'New Life'	168
'Freak of Nature'	169
'A Happy Thought'	170
'Apple Blossom Rosebud'	171
Regal 'Geoffrey Horseman'	195
'Red Black Vesuvius'	198
'Madame Salleron'	200
'Scarlet Unique'	209
'Catford Belle'	221
'Patricia Andrea'	228
Stellar 'Arctic Star'	229
'Deacon Lilac Mist'	230
'Rouletta'	231
'Reticulatum'	233
'Sparkle'	234
'Variegated Lady Plymouth'	242
'Lady Scarborough'	244
'Clorinda'	246

Foreword

If one were to write a character profile of a fantasy plant, a genus that exhibited a palette of favourable and admirable attributes, how might it read? For me it would be essential that the plant had a history, a convoluted and often mysterious past that demonstrated a strong heritage, a blood line of diverse personalities resulting in offspring with gravitas. Apart from the historical facts there is folklore, shrouded in mysterious whispers spoken by learned tongue, telling tales of adventure, magic, medicine and myth. It almost goes without saying that this plant would require an unrivalled beauty, a delicacy of form, diversity of structure and a chameleon-like ability to flush with a million tints. Such an extraordinary palette would facilitate the blending and weaving of the blooms through timeless designs and countless generations. And while presenting a truly exotic face this plant would possess an appetite and enthusiasm for life and an amiability of spirit that offers a hand to novice and expert alike.

This is my recipe for a fine plant, one that touches generations of gardeners and whose character permeates social and cultural divides. However, far from being a theoretical flight of fancy, this is a perfect description of the pelargonium, whose charm and poise I first encountered as a young boy helping my grandfather to pinch out his crop. It is, therefore, entirely appropriate that this extraordinary genus should be celebrated in a book.

Chris Beardshaw
Spring 2007

Acknowledgements

This book evolved over fifteen years or more, during which time my own pelargonium collection was built up and lost three times during house moves. The reading and research continued, however, and the information came from many sources. I could not have written the book without the painstaking work of Richard Clifton of The Geraniaceae Group, whose Checklists, Notes and Commentaries were essential for reference, and I very much appreciate his help and encouragement. I was inspired to start the book by Penelope Dawson-Brown who, like Richard Soar, whom I met much later, made me realise how little I knew about Robert Sweet and Richard Colt Hoare, early 'pelargonistes' whose legacy is still with us today. I thank them both for their encouragement and interest. I also thank Jaqueline Mitchell and all at Sutton Publishing who had faith in the subject matter.

Most of my research took place in the RHS Lindley Library, old and new, and the expert advice from Brent Elliott and all the staff never ceased to amaze me. I also had considerable help from The Museum of Garden History, whose curator, Philip Norman, and volunteers spent more time than I deserved hunting out material. I also thank the following libraries and archives who provided extra information or pictures: Hackney Archives, British Library, British Museum, Southend Museum, Hounslow Library, Natural History Museum, Bridgeman Art Library, The Harley Gallery, The National Trust, Dickens House Museum, Guildhall Library, The Curtis Museum and Kew Herbarium.

Acknowledgements

Special thanks also go to those who helped me find plants, particularly Jack Gaines and Jane Partridge at Southend Parks Nursery, who were generous with their time and, I think, genuinely surprised that anyone should want to see their plants. They hardly knew what little gems they possessed! I thank the Stourhead gardeners and Charles Stobo of the Chelsea Physic Garden for showing me their collections, and the Vernon Geranium Nursery, Bill Pottinger, The Geraniaceae Group, *Amateur Gardening* and the British Pelargonium and Geranium Society for allowing me to use their pictures. I especially thank Jean-Patrick Elmes for helping me with the technicalities of photography, for the use of his pictures and for replacing plants I lost from my first collection. It's true what they say: the best way to keep a plant is to give it away.

Finally, I would not have succeeded without the support of my daughters, Isabelle and Florence, to whom I dedicate the work.

A Pelargonium Chronology

1621–35   The 'night-scented Indian geranium' known in
           Europe and described by Thomas Johnson when he
           sees it in Tradescant's Lambeth garden; first
           illustrated by Jacques Cornut in *Canadensium
           Plantarum*.

1672   Paul Hermann sends *P. cucullatum* specimens from
           the Cape of Good Hope to Holland.

1690   *P. Zonale* depicted in J. Moninckx's *Hortus Botanicus
           Amsterdanensis*. *P. cucullatum* and *capitatum* in the
           garden of William and Mary in England, believed to
           have been brought from Holland by William
           Bentinck.

1700   Adriaan van der Stael sends seeds of a *P. peltatum*
           from the Cape to Holland.

1713   *P. inquinans* included in list of plants in Bishop
           Compton's Fulham garden.

1732   John Jacob Dillenius suggests the name
           'pelargonium'(storksbill) for the seven 'African
           geraniums' in *Hortus Elthamensis*, and includes
           P. fulgidum.

1773–7   Francis Masson collects fifty different pelargoniums
           at the Cape.

1780   *P. fothergillii* recorded as having been hybridised at
           Upton, Essex.

1787–1801 William Curtis depicts eighteen pelargoniums,
           inconsistently calling them pelargoniums,

	geraniums or cranesbills, but using the Linnean system, in his *Botanical Magazine*.
c. 1789–92	Charles-Louis L'Heritier de Brutelle depicts forty-four pelargoniums, named as such, in *Compendium Geranologia*, establishing twenty-one species, and further figures are used in Aiton's *Hortus Kewensis*.
1797–1814	Henry Andrews's *Botanist's Repository* includes about sixty figures and descriptions of pelargoniums, but still names them geraniums.
1800	Carl Ludwig Willdenow divides geraniums and pelargoniums in *Species Plantarum*.
1805–29	Henry Andrews's *Geranium* monograph, depicting 194 plants, still called geraniums.
c. 1818	Richard Colt Hoare breeds *P.* × *ignescens* at Stourhead.
1820–30	Sweet's *Geraniaceae* describes and depicts 500 varieties, but divides them into ten new genera.
1820s	Colvill's nursery in Chelsea contains 400–500 varieties of pelargonium. Collections of Colt Hoare and Jenkinson contain most of the known species and are producing early hybrids.
1841	*Gardeners' Chronicle* lists criteria for the pelargonium as a florists' flower, based mainly on hybrids of *cucullatum* and *fulgidum*.
1842	'General Tom Thumb' is thought to be the best bedding pelargonium of its day.
1844	'Golden Chain' is one of the earliest variegated pelargoniums used for bedding.
1847	Edward Beck publishes his *Treatise* on the pelargonium and improves the quality of seedling pelargoniums.
1857	'Stella' is described as best Nosegay pelargonium.

1860–1	Chiswick trial for best pelargoniums, instigating the mystery of the origins of Uniques.
1862	John Wills hybridises Ivy-leaveds and Zonals to produce *Willsii rosea*.
1863	Peter Grieve starts to produce coloured-leaved Zonal pelargoniums.
1864	Victor Lemoine produces first double Zonals.
1866	*Gardeners' Chronicle* classifies pelargoniums into twelve classes. L'Elegante, variegated Ivy-leaved, is exhibited in Birmingham.
1868	Henderson's sell Lilliputian varieties from Saxony.
1869	Pelargonium Congress in London.
1870s	Rosebud/Noisette varieties are developed.
1874	Pelargonium Society established; florists' Zonal recognised as a class. Bruant's plants of 'grand bois' developed in France.
1877	König Albert, first double-flowered Ivy-leaved. New Life – striped sport from Vesuvius. 'Decorative' pelargoniums first described as Regals.
1878	'Fringed' or 'frilled' petalled flowers appear.
1884	Le Nain Blanc (Mme Salleron) sold by Bruant.
1889	Black Vesuvius – first 'black-leaved' plant.
1890s	Paul Crampel produced by Victor Lemoine.
1896	H. Dauthenay describes and classifies Zonal pelargoniums in *Les Geraniums*.
1898	Bird's Egg varieties in Cannell's catalogue.
1899	Fire Dragon first cactus-flowered pelargonium.
1908	Fiat strain developed from Bruant's 'grand bois' plants.
1930s	Arthur Langley-Smith develops what become known as Angel pelargoniums, using *P. crispum* and Regals.
1942	Behringer produces Irenes in USA.

1951–3	Zonal pelargoniums repopularised as bedding plants for the Festival of Britain and the Coronation, with particular emphasis on Gustav Emich.
1951	John E. Cross, *The Book of the Geranium*. British Geranium Society founded; later becomes British Pelargonium and Geranium Society.
1957	The Crocodile, first commercially produced mesh-leaved pelargonium.
1958	Derek Clifford's *Pelargoniums, including the Popular Geranium*.
1960s	Francis Hartsook produces 'modern' Uniques from Uniques and Regals.
1964	'Formosum' or fingered-flowered pelargoniums produced in USA.
1966	Tulip-flowered pelargoniums produced in USA. Ted Both's 'Staphs' produced, later called Stellar pelargoniums.
1967	'Carefree' F1 hybrids produced in USA.
1970	British and European Geranium Society formed. S.T. Stringer's Deacon strain of pelargoniums shown at Chelsea.
1977–88	J.J.A. van der Valt's *Pelargoniums of Southern Africa* in three volumes provides a comprehensive guide to species of Southern Africa.
1981	Geraniaceae Group formed to further information on species and early hybrids. They start to produce *Pelargonium Species Checklist*, *Decadic Cultivars* and *Commentaries* on Sweet, Andrews and L'Heritier.
1988	National Collection of Pelargoniums started by Hazel Key at Fibrex Nurseries.
1994	Peter Abbott, *Guide to Scented Geraniaceae*.
1996	Diana Miller, *Pelargoniums*.
2000	Hazel Key, *1001 Pelargoniums*.

Introduction

This book is a celebration of pelargoniums, and the people who loved them. Passion is not too strong a word. Through three and a half centuries pelargonium growers have been driven by an obsession for this brightly coloured plant, brought from the warmth and sunshine of the southern hemisphere to the dull damp climate of northern Europe.

Little could the aristocratic enthusiasts of the eighteenth century or the commercial nurserymen of the nineteenth imagine how this interesting, but sometimes wayward, plant would become the mainstay of our summer gardens, and so apparently ordinary and mass produced that it is despised by many gardeners as just too dull to bother with. Or perhaps they could. There must have been something that drove them on to constantly hybridise the plants until they found that elusive colour or special markings that became the successive holy grails of the pelargonium world.

Modern gardeners who are tempted to reject the pelargonium as too much of a cliché and too 'municipalised' to put into their own gardens should pause for a moment and consider its ancestors or its cousins. The richness of the genus will surprise and delight them, and then they too will be captivated by its charm and versatility. This book explains how the garish, stiff, compact plants of today were in effect manufactured from the pliable, pungent, beautiful, vivid, delicate species discovered centuries ago by pioneer plant collectors and travellers, and adopted by marquesses and earls, medical men and ladies of leisure, humble gardeners and painstaking horticulturalists.

The joy of discovering the real pelargonium is that it is not too late to rescue it from extinction. Although many of the hybrids are lost, the species are very much alive and well, and there is nothing to stop anyone trying to re-create the old hybrids and bring back the glories of the past.

Whether you call it a geranium or a pelargonium, you will know the plant. It is grown in the majority of cultivated gardens in Britain and Europe, and many in the United States, New Zealand and Australia. It is predominantly bright red, but also appears in pinks, purples and white. In fact it is so common that most people never give it a second thought. It is picked up from the garden centre at the beginning of the summer, used to adorn the pots and window boxes on the patio, and seen laid out in rows in every public park and garden. But why? Perhaps the answer is obvious: it is colourful, easy to grow, easily available, and stands up to a considerable amount of neglect. The more expert gardeners would also say that it comes in infinite variety, is easy to propagate and even to hybridise. This is a clue to its success: throughout history it has been a hybridiser's dream, and it can be commercially produced on a massive scale with few problems, so it is eminently marketable. It is also popular among flower show exhibitors, who love to create and try out new varieties. However, even experts often struggle to explain the history of the plant or have much knowledge of the old sorts that our ancestors once grew. Most people have no idea what an impact it had on gardeners in the nineteenth century.

First, an explanation of the name. Although most gardeners know perfectly well the difference between the so-called 'hardy geranium' and the 'Zonal or bedding geranium', they often seem reluctant to call the plants by their proper names. This is probably because writers and nurseries continue to use the wrong name, probably in the belief that if they call the 'Zonal' or bedding plants pelargoniums, people will be confused and not buy them.

1. A Victorian Zonal or bedding pelargonium, generally thought of as typical of modern plants. *(Shirley Hibberd,* Familiar Garden Flowers, *c. 1880/Author's Collection)*

Why they should think so is difficult to understand. The names of plants are often changed and people accept the changes without much complaint. Could it be that because the pelargonium is so well known and so popular it has almost become an institution, and therefore it is thought that the whole fabric of the gardening establishment would collapse if it is challenged? Surely it cannot be that important! Some people believe that names do not matter; yet few serious gardeners would dispute the fact that using botanical names instead of common names is more accurate and informative, and should be encouraged. There is absolutely no need ever to call a pelargonium a geranium: they are distinct plants, separately named over 200 years ago. Unfortunately, however, many writers did not accept the difference, and throughout the nineteenth century certain groups of pelargoniums were still referred to as geraniums. But in the twenty-first century we have grown used to calling 'horseless carriages' cars or automobiles, we generally call the 'wireless' the radio, and we have ceased to wonder how aeroplanes stay in the air. There is really nothing difficult or confusing about calling a pelargonium by its proper name.

The confusion came about in this way. When the pelargonium, a tender plant native to southern Africa,[1] was first seen in Europe, it was thought by the herbalists of the time to be a type of cranesbill, or geranium, a familiar hardy plant native to northern Europe. In the seventeenth century botany was in its infancy and plants were generally described by likening them to another plant that had already been named. The botanists or herbalists of the time little imagined how many more plants of the same type were to appear in Europe in the following century and so at first they saw no need to invent a new category to put them in. Even when the name pelargonium had been introduced and was widely used by some botanists and gardeners, others were slow to accept it. By the nineteenth century certain types of

2. Geranium and pelargonium flowers compared. The geranium (left) has five identical petals, whereas the pelargonium's top two petals are often strikingly different, or more marked or feathered. *(Author's Collection)*

pelargoniums were being hybridised, but others were not, so gardeners and writers felt it was convenient to use the name pelargonium for the specialised group and geranium for the others. At the time the true geranium was only seen as a wild flower of the hedgerows and barely considered a garden plant at all, so the term 'hardy geranium' was never used. Presumably, as 'hardy' geraniums were never red and the bedding pelargonium usually was, the term 'scarlet geranium' conveniently distinguished the two. Since those days, however, geraniums have been hybridised into popular herbaceous perennials, and should be given back their true name with no qualification.

Geraniums and pelargoniums are easily distinguishable from each other, even by the layman. The geranium's five-petalled flowers are symmetrical and appear in many shades of blue, purple and pink, as well as white. They are never red or yellow, however, and are barely, if ever, scented. They can withstand temperatures below freezing and so thrive in northern gardens throughout the year. Pelargoniums, on the other hand, are not frost hardy. They are also five-petalled, but the top two petals are different from the lower three, sometimes quite strikingly, sometimes not. Even the pelargoniums that seem at first sight to have five identical petals, on closer inspection show darker markings on the top two. This distinction in petals is not the botanical way of identifying the plants, but serves well in most cases for ordinary gardeners trying to learn the difference. The pelargonium flower colours range from bright red to shades of magenta and purple, lilac, pink, white, even black and yellow, but never blue. The foliage can be green, variegated with white or cream, or can have a distinctive dark zone, giving one group the name 'Zonal pelargonium'. In some hybrids the leaves exhibit both zoning and variegation, producing fantastically vivid patterns that include reds and browns where the zone overlaps the white or green part of the leaf. Added to this, many pelargoniums have strongly scented leaves, found pleasant by most people, but not always. Some scents are like fruit, others like spices or chemicals; a few might be described as goatlike or catlike. Some species even have the fascination of night-scented flowers, similar to jasmine or honeysuckle. They are the gems of any collection.

One final plea for the use of the correct name. If pelargoniums are seen as one coherent group of plants, all bearing the same name, the range of the genus can really be appreciated. The main cultivated groups are the Zonal or bedding pelargoniums, the Ivy-leaved, trailing pelargoniums, the beautifully marked Regal pelargoniums and the interesting Scented-leaved pelargoniums. Consider them all as brothers and sisters of the same family, and look at their common features rather than their differences. It will be seen that the pelargonium is a versatile plant, and can be developed both for its flowers and its foliage: an attribute not found in many other plants.

The pelargonium is closely related to the geranium. In botanical classification they are two genera in the family Geraniaceae,

3. Seed pod of *P. capitatum*. The shape gave the plants the name 'storksbill'. *(Geraniaceae Group Slide Library)*

which has three other members: erodium, sarcocaulon and monsonia. Erodiums look like small versions of geraniums, and are useful plants for rockeries and alpine gardens. These three groups are known as storksbills (pelargoniums), cranesbills (geraniums) and heronsbills (erodiums), from the shapes of their seedpods, which are supposed to resemble the beaks of those birds. Geranium has by far the largest number of species: about 400; while pelargonium has about 250. By contrast, there are about 60 erodium species, 30 monsonia and only 15 sarcocaulon. However, the number of varieties of plants available in the pelargonium and geranium genera is on a completely different scale: there are about 300 known cultivar names of geraniums, while the number of known cultivar names of pelargoniums was estimated in the year 2000 to be anything up to 25,000.[2] This may be misleading, as it is not known whether the names are all valid, and most of the plants certainly no longer exist, but it shows how much hybridisation has gone on over the last 200 years.

Pelargoniums first appeared in Europe in the seventeenth century, brought back by Dutch traders from their settlement at the Cape of Good Hope in southern Africa. They returned with whatever they thought could be useful, which included plants that might be eaten or used as medicinal herbs. They were grown in botanical gardens and sent to other European countries, particularly France and Britain. As they became more sought after for their decorative value, pelargoniums became popular with collectors for the same reason they have always been popular: they were attractive and easy to grow. However, because they needed to be kept under cover in the winter in northern Europe, only wealthy collectors had the opportunity to grow them for more than one season, and this gave them the status of exotics.

By the 1840s pelargoniums were cheap enough to be taken on by competitive flower growers, known as florists, who competed with each other to produce better novelties and more variety in colour and patterning. By the middle of the century they became recognised as the perfect plant for the bedding craze that was invading every garden, following their use in parks. They developed further as outdoor decorative plants when the mania for the coloured-leaved varieties hit the gardening population, and then there was no going back. By the end of the century, with small conservatories on the back of every middle-class house, they became known as indoor plants and yet more classes were developed. Throughout this time, however, the species plants continued to be grown by minorities, and interest was shown sporadically in using them for hybridising. By the twentieth century the attraction of pelargoniums had reached Australia and the United States as well. In temperate climates pelargoniums could be kept outside all winter, which meant they could be planted as permanent shrubs along streets and in gardens. They were also popular with flat dwellers in Europe, as they would happily cascade down balconies from window boxes. In each country, pelargonium enthusiasts developed their own breeding programmes, producing characteristically different groups of plants, which were eventually exported abroad and again used to hybridise with plants developed there.

To understand the variety in this huge family, and see how interesting and enjoyable they can be to grow, we must go back to the beginning of the gardeners' love affair with the plant and see what delights appeared along the journey from the seventeenth century to the twenty-first. Few gardeners in the early days could have imagined how the straggly, weedy specimens they saw flowering sporadically in northern gardens could be turned into the universally useful plant we have today. But there was a germ of an idea in the minds of the wealthy plant collectors and nurserymen of the eighteenth century. They recognised the potential in the very brightness of some of the flowers: the vivid red is a colour not often seen in nature; and other species have pink, white or lilac flowers with magnificent feathering in magenta or purple on the top two petals. Very soon it was discovered that the number of different species was in scores rather than dozens, and eventually proved to be hundreds. But it was the gardeners of the nineteenth century who recognised the commercial potential of the plants, leading to an explosion in the number of varieties, and producing a legacy for the gardeners of the twentieth century, who wanted low maintenance and high colour.

In essence, the pelargonium has established itself as one of the ideal plants for all gardeners. It has greater variety than the fuchsia or carnation, blooms longer than the chrysanthemum or dahlia, is perfect in a greenhouse or conservatory, and is easier than the rose to grow to perfection. It could hardly be better known, but how well do we know it? This book came about because when I started growing pelargoniums in the early 1990s I wanted to find out more about the old varieties and how they were used to produce the modern ones. There was no book that told me this. Some nursery catalogues purported to give dates when a plant was introduced, but it was difficult to verify these, and information in some books did not always corroborate the 'facts' in others. Most perplexingly, they all gave the same basic historic origins of the plants, but then left the history dangling somewhere about 1700, referred to books on 'geraniums' in the 1820s and never tied this information to the modern plants that seemed to 'spring up fully formed' in the 1990s. I therefore ploughed my way back through Victorian gardening magazines and trawled the libraries for books written in the 1950s and 1960s, in order to piece the information together.

The genus pelargonium is greatly varied; that is its beauty, its fascination and its usefulness. Some species have been used for hybridising much more than others, for reasons that will be explained. This book concentrates on them because it is a book for gardeners and those with a general interest in garden history. The classification of pelargoniums has always been in dispute and is still not universally agreed. The text will explain the reasoning behind the different attempts at classification, but the technical details can be found in the appendices. The botanical classification, however, is one thing; the gardeners' and nurserymen's grouping is another. Zonals, Regals, Angels, Scented-leaved, Uniques, miniatures, dwarfs, Ivy-leaved, coloured-leaved and of course the species are some of the names known in Britain. In Europe, Australia and the United States, other names are used too. Many plants will fall into two or more groups. Names may be Latinised and sound like species, but may be hybrids; other names have been used for several different plants over the course of three centuries, and there will probably be no proof that a modern plant sold under a particular name will be the same as a plant with that name in an old nursery catalogue. Show secretaries maintain their own listings, which are only useful for their own members. Nurseries classify their plants into groups, generally according to purpose. A glossary is therefore provided to explain the terminology, but not a classification of cultivars, as none exists that will satisfy everyone.

Throughout the text there are 'Plant Profiles' which appear in boxes. These are a selection of pelargoniums, featuring the main species used in hybridising and therefore the ancestors of the familiar modern plants, as well as examples of some of the groups of pelargoniums grown today. Most plants are still obtainable now from specialist nursery catalogues. They therefore provide a living history of the pelargonium and would be a good base for anyone starting a collection.

I hope this book will provide a link between botany, history and horticulture, and that in reading it gardeners, horticulturalists and botanists may be more inclined to appreciate the work and enthusiasm that has gone into producing modern pelargoniums and so may understand their plants better. Much of the plants' history is lost forever, due to the secrecy of early growers and lack of interest by later ones. Certain characters will emerge as pioneers, who saw the pelargonium as something special, with an almost infinite potential for development. It is their story as much as the pelargonium's. For whatever reasons, they used the plants for their own purposes and their own pleasure. They developed a passion for one of the most versatile and extraordinary plants we as gardeners will ever know.

A Note on Terminology

For the general reader who is not a botanist, it should be explained that botanical names consist of two words in Latin form, the genus (i.e. *Pelargonium*, usually written in italics and with a capital letter) and the species (e.g. *inquinans*, also italicised, but starting with a lower case letter). The species name either describes the plant (e.g. *inquinans* means 'staining' because of the sap causing a stain) or sometimes comes from a proper name, which may be that of the discoverer of the plant or someone else significant (e.g. *fothergillii*, after Dr Fothergill who raised the plant). If the plant is a hybrid (i.e. its parents are different species) its name is written with an × before the specific name (e.g. *Pelargonium* × *fragrans*). A cultivated variety of a plant is known as a cultivar, and its name is written in quotation marks after the botanical name (e.g. *Pelargonium* × *hortorum* 'Paul Crampel'). In this book, to avoid repetition, most Pelargonium species and hybrids will simply be written using the specific name in italics. Cultivar names will usually appear with capital letters but without quotation marks.

1

Splendid Curiosities

The Sad Geranium

There is of late brought into this kingdome, and to our knowledge, by the industry of Mr John Tradescant, another more rare and no less beautiful than any of the former; and he had it by the name of Geranium Indicum noctu odoratum: this hath not as yet beene written of by any that I know; therefore I will give you the description therof but cannot as yet give you the figure, because I omitted the taking therof the last yeare and it is not as yet come to its perfection.[1]

The plant being described is then said to have tansy-like divided leaves and tufts of yellow flowers with a black-purple spot in the middle, 'as if it were painted', and is named the Sweet or Painted Crane's-bill. Such was the earliest pelargonium to be identified in Britain. It was a strange plant, quite unlike any modern pelargonium, but although it could be said to be a distant cousin of many other pelargonium species, it is unlikely to be an important ancestor of modern hybrids, although some influence cannot be ruled out. Yellow-flowered and night-scented, it disappears below ground for a large part of the year. However, it has a curious charm, and its story must be told because it always appears at the beginning of accounts of the history of pelargoniums and needs to be put into context. It is now called *Pelargonium triste*, but in the tradition of botanists before the time of Linnaeus it had several earlier names.

The plant was seen in the garden of John Tradescant (*c*. 1570–1638) in Lambeth, south London, in 1632, and was described in the 1633 edition of John Gerard's *Herball*. A herbal was a reference book for herbalists and apothecaries, who in the seventeenth century performed many of the functions of modern-day doctors and pharmacists. John Gerard (1545–1612) had been gardener to Lord Burghley and also had his own garden in Holborn, London. Gerard's *Herball* was published in 1597 and claimed to list all the plants known in Britain at the time. By 1630 it was out of date, particularly as many of the illustrations were already old when they were first used. Gerard had died in 1612 and the revision was entrusted to Thomas Johnson (*c.* 1600–44), an apothecary practising at Snow Hill, London. He had already made detailed studies of plants in Kent and on Hampstead Heath, and was an enterprising businessman who attracted people to his shop with curiosities, such as exhibiting the first bananas to be seen in Britain. The bananas had come from Bermuda and stayed in his shop for two months before they were eaten.[2]

P. triste

(The sad or dull pelargonium, after the colour of its foliage)

A tuberous-rooted, night-scented, feathery-leaved plant with flowers of yellow, green or black. Its foliage periodically dies down and it has not been widely used for hybridising. Its interest lies in its being the first pelargonium to be recorded as growing in Britain, in 1632.

Pelargonium triste from Jacques Cornut's *Canadensensium plantarum, Historia*, of 1635. *(RHS Lindley Library)*

4. John Tradescant's house in Lambeth, the site of the first pelargonium recorded as being grown in Britain. *(Print from a drawing by John Thomas Smith (1766–1833)/Museum of Garden History)*

Johnson was required to produce the new edition of the *Herball* in one year, which was extraordinary considering its size. The work he did can be seen because the amendments and additions are marked in his edition to distinguish them from the original entries. Johnson was about 30 years old and his work would have guaranteed him a good future as both a herbalist and a writer, but he was wounded during the English Civil War in 1643, fighting for the Royalists at Basing House in Hampshire, and later died of fever brought on by the injury.

Johnson had visited John Tradescant at his house, The Ark, to review his new plant acquisitions for the book. In 1632 Tradescant was in his fifties and had a reputation as a plant collector, as well as being gardener to Charles I. His connections with the royal family gave him the opportunity to travel, first to

Russia and then to north Africa, and he brought back new plants to study and grow. He had good business relations with many plant collectors and nurserymen in France, Holland and Germany. His son, also called John (1608–62), carried on his work as royal gardener and made a speciality of collecting plants from America, which he visited three times. The Ark was so named because it contained many curiosities as well as plants, and both house and garden were often open to the public for viewing. The whole collection later became the basis of the Ashmolean Museum in Oxford.

The pelargonium appeared in the *Herball* at the end of the section on geraniums, or cranesbills as they were commonly known, because, in Johnson's words, 'The seed [was] set together like the head and bil of a bird; whereupon it was called Cranes-bill, or Storkes-bill.'[3] Johnson's description of the plant as 'sweet', meaning sweet-scented, accords with the name Tradescant knew it by, *noctu odoratum*, meaning 'night-scented', but the anomaly is in the description of the plant as Indian. Tradescant knew it as Indian because he believed it had come from India, although Johnson does not mention this. We now know, of course, that it came from South Africa, but anything coming from India in the seventeenth century would come via South Africa, as the only sea route was round the Cape of Good Hope, and the only reason to sail round the Cape in those days was to go to India or what was known as the East Indies. Therefore it was logical to suppose that a plant received from an East Indiaman (as ships on this route were called) had come from India. What confused later writers were the words, 'brought into this kingdome . . . by the industry of Mr John Tradescant'. Shirley Hibberd (1825–90), the Victorian garden writer, speaking to the Royal Horticultural Society in 1880,[4] fantasised about Tradescant's plant that:

It was in all probability among the treasures acquired in his voyage to Barbary, in the fleet sent out against the Algerines in 1620. . . . As the Cape was discovered in 1497, the plant had 123 years to complete the journey to the Mediterranean, and no doubt had the help of Portuguese traders in so doing.[5]

This is quite an extraordinary leap of ideas. He is saying that the plant had somehow found its way from the Cape, via Portuguese traders, to the Algerian coast, whereupon Tradescant spotted it and snapped it up, carefully bringing it home and keeping it for twelve years before it was recorded as growing in his garden. Even if all that were true, why would it be described as Indian? It is an absurd story, but we must allow for the fact that at the time no one else had given a better explanation.

The nature of this curious plant is what allowed it to survive the voyage from the Cape to Europe in the days before Wardian cases,[6] and may also explain why Johnson could not 'give the figure' when he saw it. *Pelargonium triste* is a geophyte,[7] which means it spends a large part of its life dormant as an underground tuber, only producing leaves and flowers when the conditions are suitable. In its dormant form it looks dried up and dead, and would be easy to transport on a sea voyage. Possibly, although Johnson saw it on his first visit and could describe it, it was not available for drawing on his second as it was in its dormant phase. Who knows why this plant was taken on to the ship at the Cape? Perhaps it was sold to sailors as a curiosity, or perhaps it was included by mistake with vegetables or herbs.

The true explanation of how Tradescant acquired the plant appeared after Shirley Hibberd's time.[8] Tradescant kept records of his plants, showing when and how he had acquired them, in his copy of John Parkinson's book, *Paradisi in Sole*, published in 1629. The name of the book is a pun on the author's name, as it translates from the Latin as 'park-in-sun'. It is the first book to describe plants for their decorative value, rather than as herbs. Tradescant had used the blank pages at the end to write down records of his new plants. At the end of a list of six geraniums he put, 'Reseved in the yeare 1631 from Mr Rene Morin . . . Geranium noctu odoratu'. Johnson had gone on in his description to say, 'I did see it floure about the end of July, 1632, being the first time that it floured with the owner therof.' So the story fits together, and nothing more mysterious had happened than that Tradescant had bought the plant from Morin and had kept it about a year. He did not, however, record that the plant had come from India, although Morin himself says so elsewhere.

René Morin (d. 1657–8) was the elder of two brothers, who were Parisian nurserymen, specialising in bulbs, particularly tulips. He produced a catalogue of his plants in 1621, in which is listed *Geranium Indicum nocto odorato*. Many of the bulbs he sold were from Holland, and the Dutch were the principal traders round the Cape to the East Indies. Therefore, the pelargonium probably found its way to Holland on a Dutch ship, and was then sent to Britain by Morin, possibly in mistake for a tulip or other bulb. If he had had the plant for over ten years he had probably distributed it to other collectors, if any others wanted a dried up specimen that was not a tulip and looked more like a carrot when it did produce foliage. It seems that someone who did was Jacques Cornut, another Frenchman, who described the plant in his *Canadensium Plantarum, Historia*, of 1635.[9] He stated that it had come from Morin, who, he said, was a very honest man and had told him that it had come from India. This, therefore, was the corroborative evidence. Cornut's description emphasises the night-scented properties of the plant, and he was the first to call it 'Geranium triste', meaning sad, dejected or gloomy. It would seem to be a description of the appearance of the plant, in particular its drab colour, rather than any inherent nature. Cornut does, however, dwell on the fact that the plant does not like the sun, but only responds to the moon, and he really does seem to be implying something about the feelings of the plant. This could be connected to the idea, prevalent at the time, that medicinal plants affect the balance of the 'humours' in the body and thereby control a person's health.[10] Cornut also provided 'the figure', so at least we can see what they were all talking about.

Five years later the sad geranium appeared in John Parkinson's herbal, *Theatrum Plantarum* or Theatre of Plants, subtitled 'a herbal of large extent'. There had been a race between Parkinson (1567–1650) and Johnson to see who could finish his book first. As Johnson had won, Parkinson had to show that his book had something extra, claiming that it was 'showing withal the many errors, differences and oversights of sundry authors that have formerly written of them'. He lists the plants in seventeen classes, or tribes. In Tribe 5, Vulnerary or Wound Herbes, appears a group he describes as 'Cranesbills with Jagged Leaves' which included what he calls 'Geranium triste sine Indicum nocte olens, or Sweet Indian Cranesbill', and he thereby summarised all the names so far used for the plant by other herbalists. The illustration is clearly a simplified copy of Cornut's, but at least he was able to come up with something. It may be doubted, however, that he actually saw the plant, because he simply gives a literal translation of Cornut's Latin, with his own embellishments. It barely sounds like a real plant at all:

The roots of this Cranesbill are tuberous or Asphodil like, from whence rise foure or five long and large sad greene leaves, diversely cut into many parts, each part jagged on both sides somewhat resembling the leaves of filipendula but softer, the middle ribbe being reddish and the reste sad greene: the stalke is jointed or kneede with the like leaves rising with it, and at the toppe a tuft of many flowers, like for forme unto those of other Cranesbills, but of a box like yellow colour, each leafe having two purple spots on them, which being fallen there come such like long beakes as in the former with reddish seede on them, the flowers smell very sweete like Muske in the night onely, and not at all in the day time, as refusing the Sunnes influence, but delighteth in the Moones appearance; it tasteth somewhat sower, and both rootes and leaves are lettice for the Indians lippes.

Perhaps it was thought to be a vegetable after all, but how did he know what it tasted like? We can assume that if he did see it, he may have tasted it: apparently some years earlier he had cooked and eaten a tulip bulb to see what it was like.

The sad geranium continued to appear in plant lists and illustrated books during the next hundred years. It was in the seed list of William Lucas of The Strand in 1677 (called *geranium noctu olens*),[11] and in 1678 an engraving of it appeared in Jacob Breyne's *Exoticarum Aliarumque Minus Cognitarum Plantarum Centuria Prima*, published in Danzig. It was in the catalogue of the nurseryman George Ricketts in 1688 and was listed by Thomas Fairchild in 1722–3, but even by that time no other tuberous pelargoniums appear to have joined it. The sad geranium continued as a curiosity in splendid isolation. Unfortunately, the fact that it is so well known as the first pelargonium to appear in Europe has led some writers to imply that it was a direct, near ancestor of our modern plants. This is far from the truth. Its geophytic nature makes it unsuited to providing a plant for general garden use: even the most enterprising nurseryman would find it hard to sell to the average gardener who wants 'colour all the year round' as they wouldn't even have a plant all the year round. Sadly, no one yet seems to have been able to use the night-scented quality to create a good garden plant, but perhaps one day they will.

As far as the story of the modern pelargonium is concerned, the sad geranium is something of a red herring. It was used

P. cucullatum

*(The cup-shaped pelargonium,
after the shape of its leaves)*

Large purplish-pink flowered shrubby plant introduced into Britain from Holland in the late seventeenth century. Widely used for hybridising to produce Victorian Show and Fancy pelargoniums, leading to the creation of Regal pelargoniums at the end of the nineteenth century.

Pelargonium cucullatum. (Bill Pottinger)

occasionally in hybridising during the time of experimentation in the late eighteenth and early nineteenth centuries, and as such it is impossible to completely rule out its having some influence. Nevertheless, it remains an interesting plant to grow for those who appreciate botanical and historical curiosities and want a 'complete set' of pelargoniums. For the general grower, and the early hybridisers, there were much more enticing and useful plants to come, and again they arrived from Holland.

The Faithful Dutchman

The Dutch had been the principal plant traders in Europe since the peak of tulipomania in 1634, and nurserymen there took in plants from all over the world to pass on to horticulturalists in the rest of Europe. A Dutch settlement was established at the Cape in 1652, and in 1672 the Dutch botanist Paul Hermann (1646–95) visited the colony on his way to Sri Lanka and collected plants. He found what became known as *Pelargonium cucullatum* growing on

Pelargonium zonale. (Author's Collection)

P. zonale

(The zoned pelargonium, from dark markings on the foliage)

Typically, a pink-flowered, narrow-petalled shrubby plant, with a horseshoe mark on its leaves. Thought to be one of the many ancestors of the Zonal pelargoniums which became popular in the mid-nineteenth century for bedding out and for use as pot plants.

Table Mountain in the south-west Cape, and sent specimens and possibly seeds to Leiden Botanic Garden. He became professor of botany at Leiden in 1680 and his 1687 list of plants included *cucullatum* and eight other pelargoniums.[12] *Cucullatum* is a large-flowered shrubby plant, which can grow up to 2m high. This gives an indication of the true scale of many species pelargoniums when grown in favourable conditions. Anyone who only knows the modern hybrids may be surprised when they see 'the real thing'. In British gardens, pelargoniums must be kept inside in the winter, and many amateurs can never achieve the true potential of the plants because they simply do not have the space in which to let them grow. However, a visit to some of the many restored or re-created greenhouses and conservatories in great country houses or botanic gardens, such as Kew, will give the pelargonium fancier a true idea of what can be done with the right facilities. *Cucullatum* usually has purple flowers with darker veining on the upper petals. It can easily be recognised as one of the ancestors of the modern Regal pelargoniums.

Two other important ancestors of the modern plants appeared in Europe at about the same time. *Pelargonium zonale* was illustrated by Jan Moninckx in *Hortus Botanicus Amsterdans* in about 1690. His illustrations also appeared in the catalogue of the Amsterdam Physic Garden,[13] which was under the direction of Jan Commelin (1629–92).[14] *Zonale* is so-called because of the marked zone on its leaves and it is an ancestor of the modern Zonal pelargoniums. It is also a tall, rangy plant, coming from the southern Cape, where it grows on rocky hillsides and in scrub vegetation. The other ancestor was *Pelargonium peltatum*, from which were produced the Ivy-leaved, or trailing, pelargoniums. It was described by Caspar Commelin (*c.* 1667–1731) (nephew of Jan) in his *Praeludia Botanica* in 1703. It grows in a similar area and habitat to *zonale*, but is a prostrate scrambler, needing support from the surrounding plants. Commelin's plant was grown in Holland from seeds sent from the Cape by the governor,

P. peltatum

(The shield-shaped pelargonium, from the shape of its leaves)

A scrambling, trailing plant with pink or white flowers, large in relation to the size of the foliage. One of the earliest pelargoniums known in Europe, but not widely hybridised until the nineteenth century, when the cultivars became known as Ivy-leaved pelargoniums, used for pot and balcony work.

Pelargonium peltatum. (Shirley Hibberd, Familiar Garden Flowers/*Author's Collection)*

Willem Adriaan van der Stel, in 1700. Altogether eight pelargoniums[15] were described by the Commelins, the most important of which, as far as later hybridising is concerned, was *P. lobatum*. This is a tuberous, night-scented plant, which the early botanists sometimes confused with *triste*, although its foliage is completely different.

Before 1700, therefore, at least three of the ancestors of the main groups of modern pelargoniums, the Regals, the Zonals and the Ivy-leaved, were known in Holland. At the same date some of them had also appeared in Britain, where important private collections were being built up. Their introduction can almost certainly be traced back to the succession to the throne of William of Orange as William III in 1688. As part of his entourage, William brought with him Hans Willem (William) Bentinck (1649–1709), a childhood friend and his chief statesman. It is said in most books on garden history simply that William III appointed Bentinck as Superintendent of the Royal Gardens, and it would appear to be a reflection of the importance of gardening to William as a Dutchman that he felt the need to have a super-intendent for his gardens. Bentinck is credited with introducing many plants to Britain and a new style of gardening, but as usual when the details behind the story are examined, a slightly different picture emerges.[16]

Bentinck was from an aristocratic Dutch family and was sent to the Dutch royal court as a child to be a companion to William, who was almost the same age. William's father (William II) had died of smallpox a week before William was born and he was brought up in an atmosphere of rivalry between his mother and his paternal grandmother, always knowing that he would eventually have to take on the responsibilities of sovereign. Bentinck became a trusted friend and confidant among the turmoil and stress of life in the royal household.[17] William eventually ascended to the throne, not just of his own country, but of Britain as well. There were close links between the royal families of both countries. William's mother, Mary Stuart, was the sister of Charles II and James II, and William eventually married his cousin Mary, daughter of James II. In 1670 Prince William and Bentinck travelled together to England and visited both Cambridge and Oxford, where Jacob Bobart (1641–1719), the botanist, received them at the Oxford Physic Garden. Afterwards, at a service at Christ Church, the prince was assisted in following the English church service by Dr Henry Compton (1632–1713), youngest son of the Earl of Northampton and religious instructor to younger members of the royal family. He will reappear later in the pelargonium story.

Bentinck nursed William through smallpox in 1675, and in 1677 returned to England on a mission to meet Mary, William's future wife. A year later Bentinck himself married an English woman, Anne Villiers, granddaughter of the Earl of Suffolk and daughter of Lady Frances Villiers, who had been Princess Mary's governess. The Bentincks had seven children in the course of ten years. However, in the year that William succeeded to the throne of England, Anne died and Bentinck accompanied William as his chief companion and minister, leaving his family behind in Holland. Bentinck was not popular in England as it was felt he was too close to the king and not to be trusted. He certainly lived close to the king, mostly in the royal palace rather than in his own house, and he never felt the need to learn English, preferring to speak French at court. Part of his role was to redesign the king's apartments and gardens to the Dutch taste, and thus he was appointed Superintendent of the Gardens, rather than because William was particularly interested in gardening as a pastime. The king's main interest was actually hunting, while Bentinck, when he had a moment to himself, preferred building up an art collection as his form of relaxation. Queen Mary, however, was fond of gardening.

In creating the royal gardens, Bentinck brought over from Holland all that William was used to and loved, and that included the plants. Bentinck's own home was an estate at Sorgvliet, near The Hague, where he had inherited a garden from the previous owner, the poet Jacob Cats, and he had continued to build up a huge collection of exotic plants, particularly those from the Cape.[18] Part of the reason for growing exotic plants was to emphasise the royal family's power over the parts of the world where they had imposed their rule. The plants would be grown in large tubs outside in the summer, and taken into orangeries in the winter. At Hampton Court huge 'glass cases' were built to house the plants, and seeds were germinated in the melon ground. Throughout William and Mary's reign, the love of plants and gardens began to infiltrate palace life and became part of the accepted artistic background that became ingrained in British culture.

P. capitatum

(Named after the word for 'head', describing its compact flower)

A soft-leaved, slightly aromatic plant with small lilac flowers, brought to Britain in the 1690s. It produces an oil used for perfume and has been hybridised to produce many Scented-leaved cultivars such as Attar of Roses and Atomic Snowflake.

Pelargonium capitatum.
(Bill Pottinger)

In 1690 *Pelargoniums cucullatum* and *capitatum* were listed as being present in the royal garden. *Capitatum*, although less exuberant than *cucullatum* and more prostrate, has pretty pale lilac flowers and soft, greyish rose-scented leaves, and the plant is one of those used for oil of geranium. It grows along the southern coast of the Cape, and is an easy plant to grow in garden conditions, being one of the most hardy and robust of all the pelargoniums. Some writers on pelargoniums have referred to two species of pelargonium being grown at Kew in 1690, because it was assumed that that was the royal garden, but at that date Kew gardens had yet to be established. William did spend some time at Richmond Lodge, near Kew, and it is possible that the plants were in both gardens, being moved between the two, like the royal furniture.

Bentinck, although designated 'Superintendent' of the gardens, would not have spent much, or any, time actually planning them, let alone doing the practical work; that was left to his deputy, the gardener George London (d. 1714). He had been trained by another royal gardener, John Rose (1619–77), and had travelled in France and Holland as part of his education; he later went with Bentinck to Versailles and was shown round the French royal gardens. He married two or three times, and had five children with his first wife, one of whom, Henrietta, became a botanical artist. London spent most of his time travelling the country supervising work in all the great gardens. No doubt other wealthy landowners wanted to try to emulate the royal gardens, and hence he played a large part in distributing plants among those gardens. As he was one of the founders, in 1681, of the Brompton Park Nursery, an establishment of over 100 acres situated in west London where the Victoria and Albert Museum now stands, he could have arranged for any plants to be sent to interested customers. He probably helped to distribute pelargoniums to those who were interested in growing them.

5. Hans Willem (William) Bentinck, 1st Earl of Portland (1649–1709), painted by Hyacinthe Rigaud (1659–1743). Bentinck was influential in bringing Dutch plants, including pelargoniums, to Britain. *(Private Collection)*

London died after an illness of two weeks, caused by catching a fever after having been exposed to bad weather while travelling the country on horseback.

Bentinck was given several different country estates by William in recognition of his work, but the one that he retired to in 1700, after the death of the king, was Bulstrode in Buckinghamshire. He had been created Earl of Portland in 1688 and by the time of his retirement had married a second wife, Jane Temple, a widow said to be worth £20,000 in her own right. They went on to have another six children, the eldest son of that marriage taking over the estates in Holland as Count Bentinck, while Lord Woodstock, the only surviving son of the first marriage, inherited Bulstrode and was later given the title Duke of Portland. Bentinck was commemorated in the pelargonium world by *P. bentinckianum*, probably an early Zonal hybrid.[19]

George London was also gardener to Henry Compton, the clergyman who had attended William in Oxford in 1670. By the 1690s Compton was Bishop of London and developing the garden

Pelargonium inquinans. (Author's Collection)

P. inquinans

(The staining pelargonium, from the stain produced by its sap)

One of the most recognisable species from its bright red flowers and upright growth. Known in Britain in the early eighteenth century, it is thought to be one of the main parents of the Zonal or 'scarlet' pelargoniums, used in Victorian times for bedding and pot culture.

of Fulham Palace into a botanical collection. As part of his job, the bishop was responsible for the population of America, and as such he managed to acquire many plants from that continent. When he died in 1713 his collection was sold off when the new bishop showed no interest in gardening. One of those listed was *Pelargonium inquinans*, the bright red-flowered pelargonium, which, like *Zonale*, is an easy plant to grow and looks very similar to many of the modern varieties which are its descendants. It is found in a limited region in the eastern Cape and Transkei, and like many of the shrubby pelargoniums can grow up to 2 metres high. The plants from Compton's garden were sold to prosperous nurseries of the time, including that of Christopher Gray in Fulham and Robert Furber in Kensington Gore. In this way, pelargoniums began to infiltrate the collections of many more people.

Another of George London's aristocratic customers was Mary Capel Somerset, Duchess of Beaufort (1630–1714), who had collections of plants at both her country home at Badminton, Gloucestershire, and her London home in Beaufort Street, Chelsea. In 1699 she produced a catalogue of her plant collection and in 1700 she commissioned a series of paintings, known as a Florilegium, by a Dutch artist called Everard Kik (sometimes spelt Kick and Latinised as Kikius, with various spellings). He worked at Badminton between 1703 and 1705 and was assisted by Henrietta London, daughter of George London, and also by Daniel Frankom, an under-footman who showed talent as an artist and whom Kik trained. The paintings include both *Pelargonium peltatum* and *Zonale*. The Duchess was keen to describe her collection in as much detail as possible, and employed John Ray (1627–1705), a scientist and author of *Historia Plantarum*, to examine her collection and identify plants that she had grown from seeds sent to her from abroad. This was one of the fascinations of plant collecting at the time, as one never knew what would come up from the collections of imported seeds. They may have been mixed up on the journey, and may not even have been identified when they were collected. The gardeners had first to attempt to germinate them, then nurture them and discover how to cultivate them, and finally try to identify them by comparison to other known plants. The Duchess was keen to pass on her knowledge and love of botany to other members of her family. She employed as tutor to her grandson William Sherard (*c.* 1658–1728), who had studied botany in Paris and Holland, and had worked with Paul Hermann at Leiden from 1688 to 1689.

The Duchess was the forerunner of many aristocratic plant collectors of the eighteenth century who provided the raw material for the scientists, who then took upon themselves the task of ordering and classifying all living things. This new occupation provided a living, not just for naturalists, but for gardeners, nurserymen, artists, engravers, bookbinders and, on a wider scale, those who were brave enough to go out and collect the plants from their natural habitats.

2

Delights for Aristocrats

The first botanic gardens, known as physic gardens, were created and maintained by herbalists and apothecaries primarily to provide and study plants for medicinal use. Collectors such as the Tradescants, who seemed to grow anything they could get their hands on as curiosities, had been in a minority, which is why their collections were all the more important to historians. As the eighteenth century progressed, the herbalists' gardens became less important in providing evidence of new plants than those being built up by interested amateurs, driven by the enlightened curiosity of the time, and fuelled by private wealth. It made botany into what could almost be described as a competitive sport.

When Philip Miller (1691–1771), curator of the Chelsea Physic Garden, produced his *Gardeners and Florists Dictionary, or a Complete System of Horticulture*, in 1724, his was one of the richest collections in the world and therefore gives a good idea of the best that was available to British gardeners at the time. Miller had become curator in 1722 after the garden had been revived by Sir Hans Sloane (1660–1753), a physician who had worked in the West Indies and built up a collection of Caribbean plants and a fortune from popularising drinking chocolate. He is the first of several people featured in this book who spent all their money on indulging their love of gardening. Miller included several 'cranes-bills' in his book, described according to their appearance but without illustrations. He mentions three so-called African

P. gibbosum

(The gouty pelargonium, from the swollen appearance of its joints)

An unusual-looking plant, with yellowish-green flowers and bluish-green, lobed leaves. It periodically dies down as if dead, but has strong night-scented flowers. It was hybridised in the early nineteenth century, but rarely since.

Pelargonium gibbosum. (Geraniaceae Group Slide Library)

geraniums, one of which appears to be *zonale*, with pink, dark-streaked flowers and a horseshoe mark on its leaf; another must be *peltatum*, and a third he calls 'the sea-green cranesbill' or *Geranium Africanum frutescens folio crasso et glauco, acetosae sapore*. This he describes as having thick juicy leaves, with something of the taste of sorrel (another pioneer who ate his plants); it has weak branches and pale flesh-coloured flowers, variegated with crimson. It seems to be the plant later identified by William Curtis as *P. acetosum*.

Miller added two further 'dwarf cranesbills', which he called the anemone-leaved and the fennel-leaved, both of which are tuberous-rooted and night-scented. The fennel-leaved could be *triste* and the anemone-leaved perhaps *lobatum*. One plant that does not appear to be in Miller's list is *P. gibbosum*, although some writers say it was in England in 1714[1] and was grown at the Chelsea Physic Garden. Known as the 'gouty' pelargonium because of the knobbly joints where the leaves meet the stem, it is another night-scented plant, and people may be surprised to learn it is a pelargonium, with its pale green lobed leaves and its yellow flowers. It comes from the west coast of the Cape and the False Bay area and is a straggly upright plant, but its foliage sometimes dies off completely after flowering, giving the appearance of a dead twig, so it can be rather disappointing in a greenhouse setting. However, it is worth growing in a collection because when it *is* in flower, it is remarkable.

The next significant date pelargoniums were recorded in British gardens was 1732, when John Jacob Dillenius's *Hortus Elthamensis* was published. Dillenius (*c.* 1684–1747) was a German naturalist who had worked with William Sherard (who later worked for the Duchess of Beaufort) when he was at Leiden Botanic Garden. Sherard encouraged Dillenius to go to Britain to list the plants of Sherard's brother, Dr James Sherard (1666–1737), an apothecary in London, who kept a garden at Eltham in Kent. Like many botanic gardens of its type, it was claimed to hold all plants known in the country at the time, many of which had been collected by William Sherard when he had been consul at Smyrna

Pelargonium papilionaceum.
(Geraniaceae Group Slide Library)

P. papilionaceum

(The butterfly-like pelargonium, from the shape of its flowers)

A strongly scented plant with heart-shaped leaves and striking pink flowers looking similar to butterflies. It was traditionally used as a tobacco substitute in its native South Africa, and was introduced into Britain from Holland in the 1690s.

P. odoratissimum

(The very sweetly scented pelargonium)

A tufty, soft-stemmed plant with sprigs of tiny white flowers and very pungently scented foliage, said to smell like green apples. It was cultivated from the early eighteenth century for its natural scent and has been used for Victorian and modern cultivars. Easy to grow and propagate from cuttings or seed.

Pelargonium odoratissimum. (Sweet, Geraniaceae, plate 299/Author's Collection)

between 1703 and 1715 and had travelled in Turkey and Greece. *Hortus Elthamensis* was well illustrated and included seven 'African geraniums', which Dillenius recognised as being different from the European geraniums. He suggested that the name pelargonium, or storksbill, could be used for them, following the idea that although the seedpods of both groups of plants were similarly shaped, like the birds' similar beaks, the plants had other differing characteristics.

The pelargoniums described at Eltham were *cucullatum*, *inquinans*, *papilionaceum*, *odoratissimum*, *vitifolium*, *carnosum*, and *fulgidum*, a very important newcomer. *Papilionaceum* is so-called because its flowers have two large top petals that stand up like butterflies' wings. They are pale pink, with darker, well-defined markings. The leaves are strongly scented, but not very pleasantly – some people think they are reminiscent of billy-goat. In South Africa the leaves have been smoked as a tobacco substitute.

Odoratissimum couldn't be more different; its name means 'very scented or strongly scented' and it is thought to smell like fresh green apples. A small, tufty plant with rounded, smooth, crinkly-edged leaves and tiny white flowers which appear on sprigs, it is from the south and east Cape, but is also found in the Transvaal and Natal. *Vitifolium* is similar to *capitatum*, but has smoother leaves and a more lemony scent. *Carnosum* is another succulent shrub, with feathery foliage and knobbly stems, which varies in size and foliage depending on the conditions in which it grows. The really interesting one is *fulgidum*. Like *inquinans*, it has vivid brilliant red flowers (the name means shining or bright), but they are small and held in clusters at the end of a group of stems. The foliage is lobed, as in *gibbosum*, and is strangely scented with a chemical smell, slightly like turpentine. It comes from the western coast of the Cape, growing in rocky, windswept areas. This strange plant, totally unassuming when it is not flowering, and to many quite repellent with its acrid scent, was to become one of the most important of all pelargoniums when the hybridisers started to work with it.

Pelargonium fulgidum. (Geraniaceae Group Slide Library)

P. fulgidum

(The brightly coloured pelargonium, from its red flowers)

A strangely scented, lobed-leaved plant with woody stems and piercing, bright red flowers. It was used in the eighteenth century for hybridising several striking cultivars and probably for the Uniques, and is likely to be the origin of the red colour in Regals.

37

6. Lady Margaret Cavendish Holles Hartley, Duchess of Portland (1715–85), by Thomas Hudson (1701–95). The Duchess continued the botanical collection at Bulstrode. *(Private Collection)*

Beauty not Utility

From the mid-eighteenth century the trickle of new plants arriving in Britain turned into a raging torrent, as explorers brought back their finds and more people began to become interested in all sorts of 'naturalia'. Those with the money and time to indulge in hobbies began, almost obsessively, to collect plants, animals, shells and minerals (although the mania for fossils would not arrive for some time), as well as ancient works of art from classical times, which were brought back from 'the grand tour'. The interest in the natural world was partly brought about as a contrast to the increasing urbanisation and industrialisation of the age, but it was also to do with the yearning for knowledge and the desire to find order in nature. Although the theory of evolution and the discovery of genetics were still far into the future, it was at this time that the learned societies were being formed to study astrology, and biologists were theorising about the classification of plants and animals into natural orders. As soon as one theory had been put forward, more new organisms would be found and they had to be fitted in to the classification previously promulgated. Often they did not, and new theories had to be produced to make sense of the latest discoveries. The wealthy collectors who amassed exhibits and curiosities did it for different reasons and may or may not have developed into scientists themselves, but whatever their own interests, at least their collections provided specimens for the more academic to plunder and study.

One of the keenest collectors at this time, and one of the richest, was Margaret, Dowager Duchess of Portland (1715–85). She had been brought up at Wimpole Hall, Cambridgeshire, the daughter of the 2nd Duke of Oxford and Henrietta Cavendish Holles, heiress to the future Duke of Newcastle.[2] At the age of 19 she had married the 2nd Duke of Portland, grandson of William Bentinck, Earl of Portland, and she continued to live at Bulstrode even after the Duke's death twenty-seven years later. She had been interested in natural history from an early age and dedicated the latter part of her life to a study of plants and natural history generally, and was therefore a worthy successor to the gardens and hothouses founded by Bentinck. She had the Portland rose named after her, a late eighteenth-century hybrid rose of unknown origin, which was an important parent of the later hybrid perpetuals. She also bought what became known as the Portland Vase in 1784, from William Hamilton, husband of the later famous Emma Hamilton. The vase, intricately carved in glass and believed to be Roman, is still one of the treasures of the British Museum.[3]

One of the Duchess of Portland's main interests was shells, most of which she had obtained from George Humphrey (c. 1745– 1830), a dealer in natural curiosities. He bought complete collections from seamen returning from voyages around the world. Although the specimens gathered by the official botanists or naturalists would go into the collections of those who had sponsored the voyages, many crew members would also bring back whatever they could find or buy personally to sell on their return as an extra perk. Dealers like Humphrey would be well aware of which ships were due home and would try to be the first down to the docks to bargain for the pick of the trophies. It was Humphrey who bought most of the collections from Captain Cook's second voyage round the world.

The Duchess of Portland's constant companion, and a woman with interests complementary to her own, was Mrs Mary Delany (1700–88), also a widow, and said by Edmund Burke to be 'the highest bred woman in the world'.[4] While the Duchess studied molluscs for their scientific merit, Mrs Delany used the shells to make dramatic decorations of fireplaces and cornices. While the Duchess corresponded with botanists all over the world, Mrs Delany used specimens of the plants grown at, or sent to, Bulstrode for her 'paper mosaics'. This was a new form of artistic endeavour which we now call collage, but in Mrs Delany's hands it could be comparable to botanic painting as providing evidence of the plants known at the time. In the ten years from 1772 she made nearly 1,000 different pictures of flowers. She had previously used her artistic skills in needlework and silhouette-cutting, but one day, while at Bulstrode, she noticed the similarity between a piece of red paper on her table and a 'scarlet geranium' that was there with it.[5] She immediately cut the paper into the shape of the petals. When the Duchess entered the room she mistook the paper version for the real thing.[6] It would be convenient to think that the 'scarlet geranium' was a descendant of one of the plants Bentinck brought from Holland, but actually the reality may be more interesting. There appears to be just one reference to 'geraniums' in the six volumes of Mary Delany's autobiography and correspondence.[7] She wrote to her nephew, the Revd John Dewes, in May 1775, 'I am just returned with the Dss of P. from the kitchen garden and have seen Mr Granville's scarlet geranium in high beauty.' Mr Granville was probably her brother, who seems to have given the plant to the Duchess or Mrs Delany, and it may have been in the kitchen garden because there would have been glasshouses there for the more tender fruit and early vegetables. It was clearly thought interesting enough to comment on in a letter.

The first collage, with most of the others, is in the British Museum and is labelled simply 'Scarlet Geranium', although most specimens have a botanical name as well. Perhaps because it was her first attempt, it does not seem to be finished and is mounted on the same piece of paper as a later work, *Lobelia cardinalis*.[8] The pelargonium is dated 1773 and depicts a head of bright red flowers with quite narrow petals. They are not rounded like those of *Pelargonium inquinans*, and as there is no foliage it is difficult to be sure exactly what it is meant to be. It could even be *fulgidum*. Mrs Delany became more precise with her later works. Like a botanical painter, she liked to have two specimens with her as she worked: one to dissect to examine all the separate parts, and one to use as a pattern when putting the parts together. She referred to her work as her Herbal or her *Hortus Siccus*, the name used for dried flower collections. It must be said that some pieces are more successful than others. The best show extraordinary detail and deftness in technique, and as they are all mounted on black paper, the colours of the flowers stand out vividly. All her pelargoniums, except the first, are in volume IV of the British Museum collection and all are named as geraniums. They include familiar plants, such as *odoratissimum, papilionaceum, peltatum, inquinans, zonale, cucullatum, capitatum, alchemilloides, fulgidum, triste* and *gibbosum*, as well as *acetosum*, with its red-edged leaves and thin-petalled, pink flowers.

Most of the important naturalists of the day visited Bulstrode or the Duchess's London home, including Sir Joseph Banks (1743–1820) and Daniel Solander (1733–82), the botanist who had accompanied Banks on the first voyage round the world with Captain Cook. Banks told Mrs Delany and the Duchess about the plan to publish his account of the voyage and he invited them to visit his house in London and see the specimens and drawings for themselves.[9] Many of Mrs Delany's collages are labelled with the name of the place from where her specimens came, and several are shown as coming from Kew, which would have been at Banks's direction. Others came from James Lee (1715–95), the nurseryman, one from the Chelsea Physic Garden, and some from Sir George Howard.[10]

Another collector who was known to the Duchess and Mrs Delany was Dr John Fothergill (1712–80), a Quaker physician in London, who kept a botanic garden at Upton in Essex. They visited his garden in 1779 and some of Fothergill's plants were used for the collages. It became a common practice for gentlemen of a scientific bent, particularly physicians, to make such botanic gardens, sometimes many miles from where they lived.

7. Dr John Fothergill (1712–80) from a painting by Gilbert Stuart. Fothergill kept one of the best gardens of the eighteenth century at Upton in Essex. He grew a pelargonium named *P. × fothergillii*, later used extensively for hybridising. *(H. Hingston Fox*, Dr Fothergill and his Friends, 1919/*RHS Lindley Library)*

Dr Fothergill's aim when starting his garden was 'the cultivation of plants and trees which were beautiful, remarkable for their figure or their fragrance, curious to the scientific mind, or useful in the arts, and especially the introduction of new species which might be to the advantage of medicine or serve as articles of food'.[11] He bought the original estate of 30 acres at Upton in 1762 and later enlarged it. One glasshouse was 260 feet long, opening out from a sitting room. However, he was so busy at his practice in London that usually he could only visit his garden on Sundays, and sometimes he had to inspect the plants by lamplight. He employed fifteen men and kept three or four artists busy painting the plants to make a permanent record. The paintings, numbering 2,000, were bought by the Empress of Russia after his death. Fothergill, like a typical collector, took every opportunity he could to obtain more plants. He joined forces with another medical man, Dr William Pitcairn, who had a botanical garden in Islington (near where the Almeida Theatre now stands), to send a collector to the Alps. He once attended a sailor in the London docks who was ill with yellow fever, and instead of requesting payment in money, asked the captain to bring back two barrels of earth from Borneo, so that he could take it back to his garden and germinate the seeds it contained. Quite a novel lucky dip!

Sir Joseph Banks said that Fothergill's plant collection was 'equalled by nothing but royal munificence' at Kew. He also collected shells and corals, and his shell collection was second only to that of the Duchess of Portland. Many of his shells were obtained from Sydney Parkinson (c. 1745–71), the naturalist on Cook's voyage with Banks, who died before they reached home. There was a long dispute about what should happen to his drawings and specimens, and Fothergill acted as mediator in the quarrel that arose when Sydney's brother Stanfield tried to get the journal of the voyage published before Banks's official account.

Fothergill's plants were sold off after his death and many were bought by another city physician, Dr John Coakley Lettsom, who had been apprenticed to one of Fothergill's relatives. The site of Fothergill's garden was never built on and is now West Ham Park, and his name is commemorated in Fothergill Close, West Ham. Dr Lettsom's story is a strange one. He and his twin brother were born in Tortola in the West Indies in 1744. They were the sole survivors of seven pairs of male twins. Their father had been a plantation owner and Lettsom was sent to England for his education. When his father died he returned to Tortola and freed all the slaves, then set up a medical practice and made £2,000, whereupon he returned to London. He set up a garden in Grove Hill, Camberwell, and collected minerals, ores and crystals, as well as plants. He studied the use of mangel-wurzels as a food crop and maize as a substitute for wheat, as well as writing a paper on the effects of 'hard drinking'.[12] Lettsom was a philanthropist, and although he retired to his garden in his old age, he had lost most of his money through his gifts to the less fortunate.

The most important act of Dr Lettsom in relation to pelargoniums was that after he bought Dr Fothergill's plant collection, he had an inventory made, known as the *Hortus Uptonensis*, and it included a plant called *Pelargonium fothergillii*.[13] The plant was later described as 'the largest flowered zone-leaved . . . to be met with in every garden', but unfortunately no description or illustration of Fothergill's plant ever appeared and there were no details as to its ancestry. Later writers always refer back to it as being grown in 1780, but of course this is because that was the date of Fothergill's death, when the inventory was made. It may well have been grown for many years and may have been hybridised by Fothergill or his gardener, or it may have been a 'sport', a spontaneous mutant that arises on a plant and that can be removed and grown on as a separate plant. Many new varieties of pelargonium are produced in this way. No other pelargoniums were listed as being grown in Fothergill's garden, but this may be because the others were not considered unusual enough to bother with, which implies that *fothergillii* was an interesting new plant. On the other hand, it may have been brought from someone else's garden, but why then name it after Fothergill? The importance of the plant comes much later, in the mid-nineteenth century, when it is referred to as a parent to a group of hybrids called Nosegay pelargoniums. These were a type of Zonal with large heads of flower and narrow petals, and they also appeared in a wider range of colours than the ordinary Zonals. By then Zonals had not been greatly hybridised, and *fothergillii* seems to have been commonly grown alongside the other Zonals, and by the time people started to try to find out where it had come from it was far too late to get any information. The origins of the plant will never be known, but its later importance ensures Dr Fothergill's name is retained in the pelargonium story.

By the later part of the eighteenth century, therefore, there was a network of wealthy, educated people who were spending a large part of their disposable incomes on plants. They were receiving them from friends, from business associates abroad and were buying them directly from seafarers. The next step for those who really had money to spend was to finance expeditions themselves, paying people to search out new plants from other parts of the world.

Insatiable Collectors

The first official professional plant collector to be sent out from Britain was Francis Masson (1741–1806), who went to the Cape region of South Africa at the direction of Sir Joseph Banks in 1772 to bring back plants for Kew. The Royal Botanic Garden began like the other botanic gardens of its time, as the whim of a wealthy collector. In this case it was Augusta, the Dowager

Princess of Wales. She had been married to Frederick, Prince of Wales, who was expected to succeed his father, George II, as king. However, he died young, in 1751, and his brother succeeded instead, becoming George III. Augusta had taken advice from Lord Bute on building up her botanic garden. The 3rd Earl of Bute (1713–92) married Lady Mary Wortley Montagu in 1736 and they spent the early years of their marriage on the Isle of Bute in Scotland, where the Earl studied botany and agriculture and corresponded with other enthusiasts. Lady Mary was the daughter of the more famous Lady Mary Wortley Montagu (1689–1762), the traveller and writer. In 1745 Bute joined the royal court of the Prince of Wales. He had a brief political career, being Prime Minister in 1762, but retired early when he was criticised for being too close to George III. In 1763, with his wife's inheritance, he bought Luton Hoo in Bedfordshire, a 4,000-acre estate, for which he commissioned the best designers of the time: Robert Adam to build the house and Capability Brown to lay out the gardens. He also had a home at Kenwood, now part of north London. In 1784 he published *Botanical Tables*, a nine-volume study of British plants, of which only twelve copies were made. He favoured those who were in the elite circle: one was presented to Queen Charlotte, one to the Dowager Duchess of Portland and one to Sir Joseph Banks.

Bute's place as adviser to Kew was taken over by Joseph Banks after George III acceded to the throne, and Banks was responsible for founding the Royal Botanic Gardens as we know them today. Banks was a Lincolnshire landowner and wealthy in his own right, but dedicated his life to the furtherance of science, particularly botany, using the royal collection and his own almost indiscriminately. He established a herbarium and library at his own home in Soho Square, which functioned like a private university and gentlemen's club combined, where botanists from all over the world could study plants and produce publications.

Francis Masson was not sent out to collect pelargoniums, but he did return with over fifty varieties. Banks had briefly stopped at the Cape of Good Hope on the way back from his voyage round the world, but the ship was almost home and they had little time to spare. The crew had succumbed to illness on the last stages of the voyage and the ship was loaded down with specimens. Banks could see that there was great potential for a botanist and made it one of his first tasks on returning to Britain to send out a collector. Masson was a Scottish gardener who had been at Kew for some time. He was promised £100 a year, to be paid on his return, plus £200 for expenses. He left on the *Resolution*, again commanded by Cook, and arrived at the Cape in December 1772. In September 1773 he started the first of two trips with the Swedish explorer Carl Pehr Thunberg (1743–1828). They travelled on horseback, with covered ox wagons for supplies and equipment, and were away for four months. Thunberg had studied with Linnaeus in Sweden and was also trained as a doctor. He had already travelled about 400 miles from the Cape and had found the famous *Strelitzia*, or Bird of Paradise flower. By the time Masson arrived Thunberg had run out of money, so he took the opportunity to accompany Masson, who could pay their joint expenses.

Masson wrote the account of his journeys when he returned home in 1775. He mentions few of the plants he found, as these were classified separately, but he vividly describes the terrain, the animals and the people he met. At last we get a glimpse of the home of the plants that were being collected so avidly by those who could afford them. This would ultimately help the gardeners back home who had to learn how to cultivate them in their glass-houses. Masson and Thunberg waded through rivers, crossed barren stony deserts, and frequently ran out of water. The cattle became ill and the horses went lame. Some of the Europeans they met lived in small huts, crowded in with their animals and servants, with a poor diet and a wretched existence. Others he came across had plenty of food and provided good hospitality. Some sights of the terrain were spectacular, and Masson describes the 'whole country . . . enamelled with flowers'.[14] Having lived in Britain all his life, Masson must have been amazed when he saw the indigenous people for the first time. They wore oxen hides with

no other covering for their private parts, than a muzzle of leather exactly covering the extremity of the penis, and suspended by a leathern thong from their girdle, which was commonly ornamented with brass rings. Some had the skin of a steenbock hung over their breast, with the skin of its forelegs and hoofs behind, which they look upon as a great ornament; others had a buffalo's tail, fastened to a girdle which was tied round the thigh; others a porcupine's quill stuck through each ear; others had plates of brass of six inches square fastened to their hair, hanging on either side of their head; others large ivory rings round their arms . . . The women were dressed almost in the same taste, except that a great number of small thongs of leather, suspended from their girdle, reached down to their knees, and in some measure concealed their nakedness.[15]

On his third journey Masson provided this picture of the abundant game and vegetation:

They have two kinds of partridges, which are exceedingly plentiful and easy to shoot; and a person cannot walk ten paces without raising a brace of quails. Their hares are of an extraordinary size, but differ little otherwise in character from those of Europe. We hunted every day, and by the assistance of the peasant's son, who was an excellent marksman, never failed to come home loaden. The sterile appearance of this country exceeds all imagination: wherever one casts his eyes he sees nothing but naked hills, without a blade of grass, only small succulent plants. We expressed great surprise at seeing such large flocks of sheep as . . . subsist in such a desart; on which [a local person] observed, that their sheep never ate any grass, only succulent plants, and all sorts of shrubs; many of which were aromatic, and gave their flesh an excellent flavour.[16]

The only account of a specific pelargonium appears near the end of Masson's second journey at the Great Thorney River in the Karoo:

We passed the night with little comfort, having eaten nothing all that day; but to our great satisfaction we heard the murmuring of a stream, which we went in search of, and found good water: our concern, however, was still great for our poor horses that had nothing to eat. We spent the night in gathering wood and keeping our fire up till day-light, when I climbed up a high precipice, and viewed the country. Here I collected several curious plants, *Geranium spinosum* . . .[17]

Spinosum is a woody pelargonium that develops thorns from its older stipules.

Masson returned to Britain in 1775. Although his pelargoniums were not all newly discovered, the further specimens would allow botanists to examine them in more detail. Before the days of the Wardian case the specimens would have been mainly dried plants, drawings and seeds, which it was hoped would germinate later at Kew. Two that were newly discovered were *betulinum* and *denticulatum*. *Betulinum* has birch-shaped leaves and delicate purple or pink flowers. It grows in the coastal areas of the Cape, often with *cucullatum*. The plants look similar but *betulinum* is smaller. The two plants hybridise naturally and this made it particularly appropriate for later growers to use both species in

Pelargonium betulinum. (Author's Collection)

P. betulinum

(The birch-leaved pelargonium, from the shape of its leaves)

A shrubby plant with small oval leaves and deep pink flowers, this plant naturally hybridises with *P. cucullatum* and therefore was probably used for early hybrids. It is almost certainly an ancestor of some of the Uniques as well as the early Show and Fancy pelargoniums, from which evolved the Regals.

cultivation. *Denticulatum* is another widely different plant from that thought by many to be a typical pelargonium. It has very finely divided, tough-textured leaves with a pungent scent. The flowers are similar to the closely packed heads of *capitatum*. It comes from a very small area of the Cape, near Herbertsdale.

Later collectors at the Cape were sent out by private sponsors. In 1798 James Niven (1774–1827) arrived in Cape Town on behalf of the Duke of Northumberland, who owned Sion House in southwest London, on the other side of the Thames from Kew Gardens. Afterwards he collected on behalf of the nurserymen Lee and Kennedy, who formed a syndicate with the Empress Josephine, who is best known for her collection of roses. Niven collected at the Cape for over fourteen years, mainly looking for proteas and heaths. Other collectors who found pelargoniums were Franz Boos and George Scholl, sent out by Emperor Joseph II of Austria to find plants for his garden at Schönbrunn, near Vienna. They had arrived in 1786 and Scholl stayed for over ten years, sending back bulbs and seeds, as well as living plants.

Sometimes collectors accompanied expeditions for other purposes. Antoni Pantaleo Hove was born in Poland but trained in horticulture at Kew. He visited Africa in 1785, sailing on the *Nautilus*, which was searching for a site for a new penal colony in West Africa. After the American War of Independence the British could no longer send convicts there, and needed to find new settlements for the purpose. West Africa eventually proved to be unsuitable, and Botany Bay in Australia was later used, but while Hove was exploring, he found a specimen of *Pelargonium crassicaule* in the Bay of Angra Peguena (now in Namibia), on the south-west coast of Africa. It was discovered

> in the chasms of a white marble rock, apparently without any earth; for, on pulling up the plant, the roots were several yards in length, naked, and hard as wire, and evidently appeared to have received their nourishment solely from the moistness lodged there during the rainy season, assisted by a little sand drifted by the wind into the cavities. The heat was so intense on these rocks, as to blister the soles of the feet.[18]

Crassicaule is a succulent plant, well suited to dry conditions as it can store water when it is available. It has tufts of heart-shaped leaves growing from a woody stem, and pale lilac flowers. Hove said he had collected seventeen different 'geraniums' in the bay, but only three survived the journey home, the others being *cortusifolium* and *ceratophyllum*. These are also succulents, the second later described as the 'horn-leaved cranesbill' in William Curtis's *Botanical Magazine*.[19]

Another traveller to South Africa was William James Burchell (1781–1863), who arrived there in 1810. He was born in Fulham, south London, in 1781, the son of Matthew Burchell, who inherited the Fulham Nursery. Although he worked at Kew, he had trained as a teacher. In 1805 he had travelled to St Helena and planned to marry when his fiancée came out to join him. However, he was disappointed when she changed her mind and married the captain of the ship that brought her out. Perhaps this prompted him to go further into unknown regions. He travelled around the Cape until his men refused to carry on, discovering animals as well as plants, including the white rhinoceros. He stayed on until 1815 and when he returned to London he published two volumes of his journeys,[20] as well as a book of helpful hints for emigrants. Later, he explored Brazil. Whether being jilted by his fiancée had a lasting effect, or whether she rejected him due to his character, he seems to have been a difficult, solitary person. He lived in Fulham until the age of 82, but became eccentrically obsessed with classifying and arranging his collections. He committed suicide when he seemed to have nothing more to live for.

Burchell gathered *P. grossularioides*, the gooseberry-leaved pelargonium 'on the edge of the warm rill' at Zwarteberg.[21] This plant grows over a wide area and is now naturalised in California. In the pass of the Roggeveld Mountains Burchell said he collected a plant up to 2 feet tall called *P. renifolium*.[22] Along the Yoke river,

8. A page from the Record Book held in the Royal Botanic Gardens, Kew, showing *P. echinatum* being sent to Lady Bute in 1796. *(Reproduced by kind permission of the Trustees of the Royal Botanic Gardens, Kew)*

P. echinatum

(The spiny pelargonium, from the spines on its stem)

This is a succulent-stemmed plant which sometimes goes into dormancy, and then revives. It has clusters of long, narrow leaves and long-stemmed white or purple, beautifully marked flowers. The hybrid, Spotted Gem, was produced in Victorian times, and it is still used for creating new plants.

Pelargonium echinatum. (Curtis's Botanical Magazine, plate 309/ Author's Collection)

in the Karoo, he also found *P. spinosum* 'with a fleshy stem and large white flowers was more abundant and well deserved its name; and a succulent species of pelargonium was so defended by the old panicles, grown to hard woody thorns, that no cattle would browse upon it'.[23] Burchell also named a rocky outcrop Geranium Rocks, because a 'pleasantly-scented shrubby species' of pelargonium grew there, nowhere near any others he had found.[24]

Plants coming to Britain from the early explorers sent out by Banks would be kept and cultivated at Kew Gardens, and some would then be shared with favoured members of the aristocracy or nurseries. It became fashionable to collect 'Cape plants', which included ericas and proteas as well as pelargoniums, and they could be kept in temperate houses, rather than the 'stoves' that were needed for the more tropical specimens. The Kew record books are written in a haphazard longhand, apparently at random, with no attempt to keep any sort of official records. It is obvious that patronage and favour played a large part in deciding who got specimens and who did not. One extract reads: 'Sent to Lady Bute at Chelsea 23 Nov. 1796 for which the Royal Gardens have received a collection of Spanish Chili seeds . . . no. 12 . . . *Pelargonium echinatum*.' This is another succulent pelargonium, very easy and rewarding to grow. It has knobbly spines on its stem and periodically dies down completely. Then it will suddenly spring back into life and produce sprays of attractive white flowers with deep pinkish-purple markings and grey-green leaves. It became a favourite with the Victorians and they produced a number of hybrids from it.

Another extract reads: '1797 sent foll. Plants to Lady neale by Command of HRH Princess Augusta by Brookman's Lymington Waggon, dec17 . . . *P. echinatum, P. tricolor, P. bicolor*.' *Tricolor* and *bicolor* sound as if they may be similar, but are widely differing plants. *Tricolor* refers to the flowers which are three-coloured: white lower petals, red uppers and black in the centre. It has been used to produce interesting hybrids, which look more like pansies or violas than pelargoniums. *Bicolor* is a synonym for a variety of *lobatum*, so named because of its two-coloured flowers.

P. tricolor

(The three-coloured pelargonium, from the three-coloured flower)

A small plant with grey-green leaves and flowers that resemble pansies with white lower petals and black and red upper petals. The cultivar Splendide was hybridised in the 1950s and Renate Parsley was produced in the 1990s hybridised with *P. ovale*. Islington Peppermint is *P. tricolor* × *P. tomentosum*.

Pelargonium tricolor. (Sweet, Geraniaceae, plate 43/Author's Collection)

One final example from Kew:

> 1798 Sent the following cuttings to Her Grace the Duchess of Dorset, instead of plants, which Her Grace would have wished for, but as they were not to be spared cuttings were sent to Knowlet in a large tin box. The box has been, never returned . . . 22 *pelargonium tricolor* . . . 31 *Geranium odoratissimum* . . . 43 *pelargonium variegatum.*

Again, *variegatum* is not a valid modern name, and it was probably a hybrid with a two-coloured flower. By the 1790s there were so many pelargoniums being grown together that hybrids were being produced through cross-pollination, and unless they were very familiar with the plants, the gardeners would not necessarily be able to tell a species from a hybrid. The time had come for serious work to be done in identifying and classifying them, and the task was not going to be easy.

3

The Impudent Frenchman

By the late eighteenth century, parallel interests in horticulture and botany began to merge and attempts were made to regularise ideas and consolidate learning. The wealthy collectors may have been interested in the science of botany and seen their vast numbers of plants as a contribution to learning, but on the other hand they may simply have wanted to outdo their neighbours. Anyone who built up a collection, however, must have wanted some guidance as to the plants he or she had, and others that might be available, as well as on the best way to look after them. It was against this background that different theories of classification evolved and people with similar interests came together to share knowledge and publish their findings. Learned societies such as the Linnean and the Royal Society were formed and the concept of the botanical magazine was realised. Commercial interests eventually had their effect and the nursery trade developed from a simple branch of market gardening into huge enterprises on a scale never seen before.

First, classification. The pelargoniums known in Europe as far back as the 1600s were a widely differing selection, some proving to be more useful in hybridising than others. All had originally been accepted as different sorts of geranium, or cranesbill, but as more plants came into Europe and could be examined in greater detail, it became clear to some botanists that they were consistently different from geraniums, but not everyone thought they were different enough to invent a new group of plants to put them in. Botanists continued to use Latin or Latinised words to describe plants, distinguishing their features using as many words as necessary. So a plant would be described as a previously known one, but with extra words added to show the difference, thus the names 'sweetly-scented Indian cranesbill' and 'alchemilla-leaved, red-flowered cranesbill'. As time went on this became more and more unwieldy and was not really adding anything to the study of plants. One method, promulgated in 1753 by Carolus Linnaeus (1707–78), the Swedish botanist, seemed to solve the problem. In *Species Plantarum* he summarised his system, using only two words to describe any plant; this became known as binomial classification. He did this by splitting up plants into far more groups than had been used before, and distinguishing each group or genus with one word (such as pelargonium), and using one word to define each different member of the group, or species. He did not, however, always use a descriptive word for the species, but sometimes used the name of the person who first discovered or identified it. This was criticised by some later botanists. The main way Linnaeus distinguished plants was by identifying the differences in their reproductive parts. He did not, however, distinguish between geraniums and pelargoniums, keeping them all in the genus geranium.

Other botanists did make a distinction, however. In 1738 Johannes Burman, professor of botany at Amsterdam, had published *Rariorum Africanum Plantarum* (Of Rare African Plants), in which he described and illustrated six species of geraniums and eight pelargoniums, but he continued to describe them in the pre-Linnean way, using as many words as were needed. In 1787 the Spanish botanist, Antonio José Cavanilles (1745–1804) looked at the differences between geraniums and pelargoniums, and in his *Dissertation sur le Genre Geranium* classified the plants with actinomorphic (symmetrical) flowers as geraniums, and those with zygomorphic (asymmetrical) flowers as pelargoniums. This is a convenient way to separate the plants and the most obvious one for gardeners, but later botanists classified them more accurately by defining pelargoniums as those with a distinctive nectar tube at the base of the upper petals, and this is the classification accepted today. Cavanilles illustrated about seventy pelargoniums, then subdivided them into groups depending on their leaf shapes and whether they were zoned or not. In Austria, in 1794, another botanist, Nikolaus Joseph von Jacquin (1727–1817), described several species of pelargonium in *Icones Plantarum Rariorum*; then in 1797 he illustrated the collection of plants at Emperor Joseph II's Schönbrunn Palace. This included many pelargoniums, mostly brought back from the Cape by Francis Boos and George Scholl, whom the emperor had sent there to collect plants in 1785.

The first person to classify pelargoniums as a distinct genus *and* use the Linnean system to do so was the French botanist, Charles-Louis L'Heritier de Brutelle (1746–1800). L'Heritier's work on pelargoniums has never been published as a whole, and his text is locked away in the Conservatoire Botanique in Geneva and not readily accessible to the public. However, many of the illustrations of pelargoniums prepared at his direction were published in about 1792 in his *Geraniologia*,[1] and many more were used in the publication *Hortus Kewensis* from 1789 under the direction of William Aiton (1731–93), Director of Kew Gardens. In looking at L'Heritier's work and its importance, it is necessary first to examine the way botanical works were produced in the eighteenth century and also the background to L'Heritier's time in London.

One of the best-known works on botany dating back to the second half of the eighteenth century is William Curtis's *Botanical Magazine*, which was started in 1787. Curtis (1746–99) originally trained as an apothecary in Alton, Hampshire, where he was born.[2] He was sent to London to continue his training because his father felt he was spending too much time on his own study of natural history instead of dedicating himself to his career.

However, his enthusiasm and talent were recognised by the senior physician at St Thomas's Hospital, who encouraged him to become a 'demonstrator' there, which meant he led groups of students on botanising expeditions, identifying and explaining the medicinal properties of wild plants. At about the same time, the apothecary he was then working for died and left him his practice, which he soon persuaded his partner to buy, leaving him the opportunity to make botany his career. With some financial help from Thomas and Benjamin White, brothers of Gilbert White of Selbourne, Curtis established a botanic garden in Lambeth in which to grow a collection of British native plants, and he began planning a publication, *Flora Londinensis*, in which to describe them. His first book, however, was *Instructions for Collecting and Preserving Insects, particularly Moths and Butterflies*, which appeared in 1771. This was so well received that it brought him to the attention of, among others, Sir Joseph Banks and the Duchess of Portland, and he began corresponding with botanists and naturalists from all over Britain and Europe, often receiving new plants from them. Curtis then became demonstrator at the Society of Apothecaries at their Chelsea Physic Garden and in 1783 began publishing *Flora Londinensis*. It was a serial publication, appearing in parts, known as fascicles, consisting of six plates and six pages of text.

Producing a botanical work in the eighteenth century was a complicated and expensive undertaking. First it was necessary to obtain the specimens, either by growing them or collecting them yourself, or by obtaining them from someone else who could be relied upon. They had to be at their perfection of growth, and several specimens would be needed. One would be dissected and the separate parts drawn, another would be drawn whole, and most artists would try to depict both the flower and the seed-head, which meant plants at different stages of growth. Often the roots would be drawn too, if available. The drawing would be painted,

9. William Curtis (1746–99), founder of the *Botanical Magazine*, from a painting by Joseph Wright. *(RHS Lindley Library)*

in colours as lifelike as possible, then the painting would be handed over to an engraver to make a plate for printing. Once printed, on good quality, expensive paper, the illustrations (also called plates) would be sold either 'plain', like a line drawing, or 'coloured', which meant hand painting each individual piece of paper, which was naturally more expensive. The colourists were yet another part of the workforce. These hand-coloured plates still retain their vivid colours today, and seeing and handling the originals makes one realise how expensive they must have been to buy. A good botanical work would also contain a description of the plant, details of its origin and some cultivation advice, so a literate botanist or nurseryman had to be employed as well to write it. At a later stage an index might be compiled and provided to subscribers, who would then pay a bookbinder to put the whole collection together.

All the workers in the process of creating a botanical magazine would expect to be paid as they went along, so to finance the work the publisher would usually have to borrow money, and would sometimes ask for subscriptions in advance from those interested in buying the publication. In Curtis's case, he borrowed lump sums from Dr Lettsom, the physician and botanist who was a friend of Dr Fothergill, and Lord Bute, the politician who was the earliest adviser to Kew Gardens. Organising the finances and marketing the finished product called for skill and diplomacy in cultivating both patrons and customers, not to mention accounting skills, while the work of supervising the painting and engraving called for expertise in botany and meticulous care to ensure that the plates accurately depicted the original plants.

Not all publishers had the necessary skills for botanical publication in equal amounts, and Curtis's main failing was in not being able to keep production of *Flora Londinensis* to a regular timetable. He received criticism as well as favourable comments from many customers, one advising him to include more information on the soil conditions for the plants, another suggesting a pronunciation guide for those who were not acquainted with Latin. Many people asked for coloured sets to replace the plain ones they had originally purchased, while some complained that the colour on theirs was not as good as some others they had seen. However, by 1787 he was sufficiently encouraged by his readers to consider another publication and he started production of the *Botanical Magazine*. This was potentially more lucrative because it was only the wealthy who could afford the exotic plants it described, unlike the wild flowers of London that could be picked by anyone. Consumers were crying out for more information on foreign plants. Linnaeus's binomial classification was gaining popularity with some botanists, while others still relied on the work of Philip Miller of the Chelsea Physic Garden, so Curtis made a point of mentioning that he included references to both their works. By this time, he had opened a larger botanic garden to which he admitted 'subscribers', who paid a yearly fee of a guinea to visit the garden and use the library, so he had become known and respected as an authority on plants. The *Botanical Magazine* was imitated by many other publications produced in the same way, but none survived as long.[3]

It was into the thriving botanical atmosphere of London that L'Heritier arrived in 1786. He was a French amateur botanist from a wealthy family, who had built up his own collection of plants in Paris, and in 1784 and 1785 had started to record it in a work entitled *Stirpes, novae, aut minus cognitae*. Being well connected in the highest level of society, he was able to use plants from many other gardens, including the royal garden in Paris. One of the artists who provided drawings from which the engravings were made was Pierre Joseph Redouté (1759–1840). Redouté trained as an artist, following his family tradition of interior design, but he gravitated towards botanical illustration, in which L'Heritier gave him instruction. He taught him to dissect the plants and depict the characteristics that botanists needed for classification. In 1783 L'Heritier received an introduction to Sir Joseph Banks, as a correspondent, from the botanist Pierre M.A. Broussonet (1761–1807). Broussonet had studied in England with Banks, and all three men were followers of the Linnean system. Banks was then President of the Royal Society and had established his reputation as a botanist and naturalist. His London home at 32 Soho Square became a favourite meeting place and workplace for botanists in London, where they could share and study specimens and knowledge, and where publications were produced. The house backed on to another in Dean Street, forming a courtyard from which outhouses and stables led. Banks and his family lived in the main house, with his study at the back on the ground floor. From next to this room, a passage led to the Dean Street building. Here, in the attic, his herbarium from the round-the-world voyage was held, sometimes under lock and key, depending on who was working in the house at the time. Beneath it was a large library, and on the ground floor an engraving room. Specimens from all over the world were delivered there and made available for study.[4]

Banks and L'Heritier corresponded over the early parts of *Stirpes, Novae* and L'Heritier was probably planning to visit London in due course. However, his visit was precipitated in 1786 as a result of a collection of plants brought back from Peru and Chile by Joseph Dombey (1742–94), a French botanist who had been travelling in those countries on behalf of the Spanish govern-ment.[5] Because of his agreement with the Spanish he was not allowed to publish details of the specimens himself and instead donated them to the royal garden in Paris, in return for some monetary compensation for his trouble. L'Heritier saw a chance to further his own interests and he offered to publish details of the plants in his *Stirpes, Novae*. Buffon, the director of the royal garden, handed the specimens over to him, but this upset the

Spanish government and Buffon was ordered to ask for them back. L'Heritier was tipped off over what was happening and before he received the order he immediately packed up the plants, with Redouté's help, and sent them off to Boulogne for the ferry to England. He left Paris himself, laying a false trail to his country house in Picardy, and arrived in London ten days later. Where he misjudged the English temperament was in addressing the plants to Sir Joseph Banks. This in itself may not have been a problem, as plants were constantly being sent around the countryside in boxes addressed to famous botanists. However, in order to get the plants into the country, they would have to go through customs, and when L'Heritier used Banks's authority for this, he sparked off a lot of bad feeling and suspicion.

It was unfortunate for L'Heritier that at the time he arrived in London Banks was just recovering from two disputes that had shaken his authority over the Royal Society and made him more careful about who he allowed free access to the research materials in his library. One involved James Price, an Oxford man who claimed he could change quicksilver into gold. Banks had supported his election to the Royal Society, but inevitably he was exposed as a fraud, whereupon he committed suicide.[6] Banks had never supported him personally, but to some extent he had turned a blind eye to what had been going on, and realised that he should have been taking more interest in the day-to-day running of the society. The second problem concerned Banks's intention to reorganise the administration of the society, and in particular the procedure for electing fellows. Some members thought that he acted in an overbearing manner and he particularly incurred the opposition of the astronomers and scientists, who considered that their learning and knowledge was superior to that of the botanists and zoologists.[7] He learned from this that he had enemies and he should not trust everyone who asked him for favours. Some writers also commented that he was too possessive about the Kew collection and as it was really held on behalf of the nation it should be more freely available.

We may think that in the modern world with mobile telephones and the internet we have more sophisticated methods of communication than existed in the past. However, in the eighteenth century all educated people seemed to spend half their day scribbling letters and notes to each other, and there was little delay in getting news backwards and forwards by the mail coaches plying their trade across the country, or indeed by human messengers within towns. Servants were constantly being sent out with missives. Banks's librarian, Jonas Dryander (1748–1810), acted as his secretary when Banks was away from London. He kept him informed of L'Heritier's actions, and at first Banks encouraged L'Heritier to bring in the plants because he was keen to be the first to see them and publish anything new, so upholding the reputation of Britain as leader in the botanical world. However, once he heard about the Spanish objections and the fact that L'Heritier had used his name to get the plants through customs, he changed his mind and was angry that L'Heritier had presumed on his good faith and was being underhanded about presenting Banks with the plants. When L'Heritier asked Banks if he could study Banks's *Geraniaceae* herbarium and publish details of it himself, Banks told Dryander to get the specimens back and send them to him at his Lincolnshire home, where he was spending the summer. He told Dryander to first check they were all there because, 'if a man does one thing not quite in the square of sight we have a right to suspect the rest of his conduct'. Banks had already described L'Heritier as 'of all the impudent Frenchmen in the whole world he is the most impertinent and dangerous'.

Banks eventually came round to letting L'Heritier have full use of the library and the herbarium, if only to retain some sort of supervision over his work, and he stayed on in London for over a year. Correspondence with William Curtis shows that L'Heritier lived at 13 Broad Street, Carnaby Market, just a short walk from Soho Square, and that he entered into the small world of botanists and wealthy aristocrats who exchanged information and specimens. L'Heritier's reputation rests not on his accomplishments as an editor or publisher, but as a botanist. His life was so chaotic that he was unable to organise or sustain a regular publishing output, and the plates that have been attributed to him are only part of his complete work. *Geraniologia* consists of forty-four plates, produced by a total of sixteen illustrators and engravers from original specimens. The plates are black and white engravings, and the original artist for the majority was Pierre Joseph Redouté. Other artists included James Sowerby (1757–1822), who also worked for Curtis, and Redouté's younger brother Henri Joseph. The chief engraver was Fr Hubert, but seven others were also employed.

Originally L'Heritier's work was supposed to encompass the genera Erodium, Pelargonium, Geranium, Monsonia and Grielum. However, he quickly realised that Grielum was unrelated and so it was not included. Of the finished work, six plates were classified by L'Heritier as erodiums, five as geraniums, two as monsonias and thirty-one as pelargoniums. In modern classification it is accepted that thirty-two are actually pelargoniums. Out of all forty-four, L'Heritier is considered to have established twelve as species, and nine more had been established by him in *Hortus Kewensis*. The others are now considered as cultivars or misdescriptions. However, to establish twenty-one out of forty-four over 200 years ago, simply by observation, proves L'Heritier's reputation. He had planned further work, in particular a study of succulent plants, on which Redouté was already working, but his finances suffered during the course of the French Revolution and when he returned to Paris in 1800 he was imprisoned for debt. Later that year he was attacked in the street and killed. None of

P. panduriforme

(The curved pelargonium, from the shape of its foliage)

A shrubby species with dark, soft, pungent leaves and strikingly marked large flowers. This is more truly the 'oak-leaved' pelargonium, and should therefore be called '*quercifolium*', but there is much confusion between the species and the cultivars produced from them.

Pelargonium panduriforme. (Author's Collection)

L'Heritier's works was ever finished. His herbarium of 8,000 plants was sold to the Swiss botanist Augustin Pyramus de Candolle (1778–1841) and still remains in Geneva. L'Heritier was an excellent botanist, but he did not have the infrastructure and contacts for creating a botanical work that Curtis had built up over many years, so that his name tends to be forgotten. However, in relation to pelargoniums, his work took classification and nomenclature one step further.

Many of the pelargoniums identified by L'Heritier are well known and widely grown today. *P. crispum* is the upright-growing, lemon-scented pelargonium with tiny lilac flowers, which is known in a *minor* and *major* variety, as well as a variegated one, and has been used extensively for hybridising. Another that is easy to grow and available from specialist nurseries is *exstipulatum*. It has small greyish leaves which are slightly sticky and aromatic, and small lilac-coloured flowers. *Ovale* is a clump-forming grey-leaved plant that has been hybridised with *tricolor*, while *cotyledonis* is much more unusual; uniquely it is the only species of pelargonium to come from the island of St Helena. Some of L'Heritier's plants have led to later confusion. The name *graveolens*, which identifies a rose-scented plant in *Hortus Kewensis*, is often used by nurseries for a coarser lemon-scented plant,[8] while *glutinosum* is often indistinguishable from a hybrid called *filicifolium*. Most confusion relates to *quercifolium*, which means 'oak-leaved'. L'Heritier was probably at fault this time, by describing the wrong plant, but later botanists and horti-culturalists have used the name for *panduriforme*, for *graveolens* and for various other hybrids.[9]

Before progressing the pelargonium story further, it is interesting to note that the 'geranium' may have had another connotation in the late eighteenth century. In the British Library is a poem called 'The Geranium' written by, of all people, the human rights lawyer, Thomas Erskine (1750–1823). It begins:

> In the close covert of a grove,
> By nature form'd for scenes of love,
> Said Susan in a lucky hour,
> Observe yon sweet geranium's flower:
> How straight upon its stalk it stands,
> And tempts our violating hands,
> While the soft bud as yet unspread,
> Hangs down its pale declining head,
> Yet soon as it is ripe to blow,
> The stem shall rise – the head shall glow.
>
> Nature said I my lovely Sue,
> To all her followers lends a clue . . .[10]

Thus it continues in a similar vein and, suffice it to say, by the end 'lovely Sue lay softly panting, while the geranium was planting'.

By the beginning of the nineteenth century a popular interest in the pelargonium had begun to take hold. L'Heritier's nomenclature was not accepted by all, but William Curtis acknowledged there was some worth in it. He began to describe pelargoniums in detail in the *Botanical Magazine*, although the terminology was still confused. He featured eighteen between 1787 and 1801, and although circulation figures for his work may not be known, the fact that it continued so long shows its popularity, so that during those years the pelargonium became familiar to many botanical collectors and an object of interest. The first three, *peltatum* (plate 20), *lanceolatum* (plate 56) and *radula* (plate 95) are named geraniums, with their English name also given as a type of geranium, such as 'ivy-leaved'. However, from plate 103 onwards the plants are called pelargoniums but, strangely, their English names are given as cranesbills.[11] Curtis provides information about where and how the plants were originally found, or whether they were first grown from seeds in Britain. He says that some originally came from Masson, such as *tetragonum*, the square-stalked 'geranium', and *cordifolium*, the heart-leaved 'geranium', while *acetosum*, 'the sorrel cranesbill', was first cultivated in Chelsea in 1724 and therefore must be the one described by Philip Miller in his *Gardeners Dictionary*. He becomes a bit exasperated by the numbers of new pelargoniums by then being hybridised in British nurseries and private collections. In his commentary to plate 95, '*Geranium radula*, the rasp-leaved geranium',[12] he says:

> As a botanist, desirous of seeing plants distinct in their characters, we could almost wish it were impossible to raise these foreign geraniums from seed; for without pretending to any extraordinary discernment we may venture to prophesy, that in a few years, from the multiplication of seminal varieties, springing from seeds casually or perhaps purposely impregnated with the pollen of

different sorts, such a crop will be produced as will baffle all our attempts to reduce to species, or even regular varieties.

If he were to read present-day comments from people trying to classify cultivars he would feel entirely vindicated!

Curtis does not usually say specifically where his specimens came from, but he refers to the collections at Kew, to Colvill's nursery, the garden of George Hibbert in Clapham and that of Charles Greville in Paddington. Colvill's was to become one of the most important nurseries for pelargoniums in the next century, eventually having up to 40,000 square feet under glass, with up to 500 varieties of pelargoniums. George Hibbert (1757–1837) was an alderman of the City of London and a West Indies merchant. He was MP for Sleaford, Lincolnshire, from 1806 to 1812, in which context he possibly had some dealings with Banks at his country home at Revesby. Hibbert sent James Niven to the Cape as a collector and employed Joseph Knight (c. 1777–1855) as his head gardener. On Hibbert's death Knight obtained the collection and set up the Exotic Nursery, Chelsea, which was later taken over by Veitch's and became the foremost nursery for exotic plants in England. The Hon. Charles Greville (1749–1809) was the second son of the Earl of Warwick and one of the founders of the Horticultural Society. He collected rare minerals and works of art as well as plants, and his love of the beautiful may have been what instigated his love affair with Emma Hart, whom he later relinquished to his uncle, William Hamilton, from whom she obtained her later famous name.[13]

We know less about some of the other growers mentioned by Curtis. Edward Woodford, mentioned under *P. quinatum* (plate 547), lived at Belmont House, Vauxhall, and later at Rickmansworth. The Countess de Vandes, whose exotic plants and pelargoniums were used as specimens in many botanical magazines, had a 'magnificent collection of curious exotica'[14] at her home in

Bayswater. Her gardener was a Mr Fordyce and although her garden was described by John Claudius Loudon in his *Gardener's Magazine* in 1832,[15] after her death, he gives no further details about the woman herself. Most of Curtis's specimens were painted by Sydenham Teast Edwards (*c.* 1769–1819), who worked closely with Curtis for many years, but in 1815 he left to join James Ridgway on the *Botanical Register*. One of the plants Curtis claims to have 'figured' for the first time is the beautiful *Pelargonium reniforme*, the 'kidney-leaved cranesbill'. It stands out in a collection because it has erect greyish leaves and the most vivid magenta flowers. Curtis says it was first raised in Britain from seeds sent to Kew. Another plant raised in the same way was the subject of plate 240, *P. tricolor*, the 'three-coloured cranesbill'. Of this he says: 'In point of beauty [it] is thought to eclipse all that have hitherto been introduced into this country; its blossoms are certainly the most shewy, in a collection of plants they are the first to attract the eye.'

Some plants seem to have been raised almost by accident. The seeds of *lanceolatum* were apparently found only when James Lee, the nurseryman, was sorting through some dried specimens in Banks's collection and was struck by the unusual shape of the leaves, whereupon he managed to find some seeds and took them home to raise. Another well-known plant described by Curtis was *P. tomentosum*, which he calls the 'penny-royal cranesbill', although he says it is also known as *piperitum* (meaning pepper-like). 'Pennyroyal' was used because it is peppermint-scented, but anything less like pennyroyal is hard to imagine, as pennyroyal is one of the smallest sorts of mint, whereas this pelargonium has huge, soft, downy leaves, and is one of the quickest and easiest to grow.

Curtis soon had many rivals in producing plates of exotic plants and one of the most successful was Henry C. Andrews (1794–1830), who brought out his *Botanist's Repository* from

P. tomentosum

(The hairy pelargonium, referring to the downy leaves)

This plant is better known as the peppermint-scented pelargonium, from its strong smell. It is a greyish, soft-leaved, large plant, very easy to grow, and with small white or lilac flowers. It has been used to create many plants with a peppermint scent, such as Chocolate Peppermint.

Pelargonium tomentosum. (Author's Collection)

1797 to 1811. Very little is known about Andrews; he does not seem to have been a botanist, but he was married to the daughter of John Kennedy (1759–1842), who ran the Vineyard Nursery at Hammersmith in partnership with James Lee. Andrews did also run a small nursery, but it seems to have been a sideline to his publishing business, probably originating as a convenient way of selling off surplus plants once they had been used for illustration. Andrews therefore acted as a publisher, and Kennedy may have written the botanical descriptions of plants, although because they do not conform to the usual botanical terminology, it may be that he simply acted as an adviser and probably provided some of the specimens. Andrews's descriptions use words like 'chives' instead of stamens.[16]

Andrews did not agree with L'Heritier's division between geraniums and pelargoniums and took every chance he could to pick out any plant that he did not feel fitted neatly into one genus or the other. He stated that if he were to make all the divisions that had been suggested, 'The approach to botanical science would be so choked up with ill-shaped, useless lumber, that, like a castle in a fairy tale, guarded by hideous dwarfs, none but a Botanic Quixotte would attempt investigation.'[17] He went on to say that he did not favour one system of nomenclature or the other and 'at present walks alone'. He also referred to having the assistance of a botanist in the last volume of the *Repository* (who is not named) whose opinions were diametrically opposite to other gardeners and cultivators who had helped in other volumes. He therefore resolved to try by his own strength, 'not to totter between the support of two unequal crutches'. Under *G. laciniatum*, or the 'ragged-leaved geranium', Andrews comments:

> A continual harping on the same subject may perhaps appear rather tiresome; but, as almost every real new species of geranium, which falls under our observation, seems to add a fresh proof of the futility of the new arrangement, we cannot forbear noticing it. This species has every other essential generic character of Mons L'Heritier's Pelargonium, but unfortunately the most essential.[18]

The Botanists' Repository was said to be 'for New, and Rare Plants, containing coloured figures of such plants, as have not hitherto appeared in any similar publication; with all their essential characters, botanically arranged, after the sexual system of the celebrated Linnaeus'. The pelargoniums appeared in volume III and forty-two are listed. Each is given a botanical name and an English name, but all the pelargoniums are called geraniums. It begins to seem as if he will soon run out of names when he has to resort to, for instance, 'the Macedonian parsley-leaved geranium', unless Macedonian parsley was a particularly well-known plant in 1800. For each plant details are given of who brought it to England and when, how to cultivate it, and where the example drawn came from. The last pelargoniums appeared in 1804, but

Andrews realised that there was demand for a publication dedicated to 'geraniums' alone and some plates originally made for the *Repository* were eventually used later.

In Andrews's *Geraniums* another sixty plants were described, many from private collections as well as nurseries, and the series continued until 1829. It does not seem to have been planned logically from the beginning, as he issued the parts haphazardly and suddenly produced an index halfway through, splitting the collection into two volumes, not in alphabetical order.[19] The fact that Andrews described over 100 plants in the course of about thirty years shows that the plants were becoming extremely popular and new hybrids were continually being produced. It may be that Andrews panicked halfway through because he was afraid of the competition. Many of his plants came from George Hibbert's collection, which was described in 1801 as 'now we presume, the first in Europe', and that of the Countess de Vandes. Another collection he used was that of the Marquess of Blandford at White Knights, near Reading, described as 'the most elegant emporium of the vegetable kingdom at present known'. The Marquess compulsively bought all the exotic trees, shrubs and plants he could get hold of, many of which were supplied by Lee's Hammersmith Nursery, to which he owed £15,000 by 1804.[20] He also constructed hothouses, ornamental buildings and all kinds of garden features. By 1816 he had to mortgage the house to pay his debts, but the following year he succeeded to the Dukedom of Marlborough and then began another collection. *P. blandfordianum* is named after him. Andrews said he received the plant in about 1807 from White Knights and that it is a hybrid of *quinquevulnereum* and *radula*. A large shrubby plant with the *radula*-type leaf, it is quite scented, and is still grown today.[21] *Pelargonium quinquevulnereum* seems to have been a hybrid raised by a Mr Armstrong of Hampshire, with a *graveolens*-type appearance.[22]

P. × ardens

(The glowing pelargonium, from its brightly coloured flowers)

An acclaimed hybrid produced at Lee's Nursery, Hammersmith, in the early 1800s. It is a cross between *fulgidum* and *lobatum*, with a deeper crimson, more marked flower than the former, but the large rounded leaves of the latter. It is easy to grow, but periodically goes into dormancy.

Pelargonium × ardens. (Sweet, Geraniaceae, plate 45/Author's Collection)

Two other great collections being built up in the early years of the nineteenth century were those of the Earl of Liverpool at Combe Wood, near Chislehurst in Kent, and Robert Jenkinson of Sandy's End, Fulham. The Earl of Liverpool's gardener was a Mr Smith and he seems to have carried on the collection even after the death of the Earl in about 1828. Over thirty plants from the garden were used in Andrews's publications and the later one produced by Robert Sweet. One of the most important was *P. involucratum*, probably a cross from *P. cucullatum*, raised between 1817 and 1820. It had white flowers, veined mauve, and many different varieties were produced, one known as 'Commander-in-Chief', and others 'High Admiral' and 'Coronation' (the first two with pink flowers). At this date hybrids were sometimes given 'common' or varietal names, but often continued to be named in Latin as well.

Robert Jenkinson's collection was used even more extensively, about fifty plants being cited as coming from his gardens. His gardener was Mr Avron, and one of their specialities were hybrids from *P. gibbosum*, such as *glaucifolium*, which is *gibbosum* crossed with *lobatum*. Again, it is still grown today and has black flowers with a green edge, scented at night. Another hybrid he made using *lobatum* was *lawranceanum*, probably crossed with × *ardens*, the hybrid between *lobatum* and *fulgidum* produced by James Lee of the Hammersmith nursery. *Pelargonium× apiifolium* was a further hybrid from *gibbosum* provided from Jenkinson's garden, although not originally raised by him.

Some other notable plants described by Andrews were *grandiflorum* and *crenatum*. *Grandiflorum* is so called because it has large flowers in relation to its foliage, in particular large upper petals, which are pinkish-purple and beautifully marked with darker veining and feathering. The leaves are also unusual in that they are bluish-green and very smooth, almost shiny. In Europe the name 'grandiflorum' is used for what are known in Britain as Regal pelargoniums, and this has led to the belief that the species was used in hybridising those plants. However, there is little evidence of this in historical records. The species is a beautiful plant to grow in itself. *Crenatum* is important because of its probable later connection with the Nosegay pelargoniums. It was probably a hybrid from *zonale*, and was known by Sweet as 'Bath Scarlet'. Andrews's works on pelargoniums were a revelation, but seem to fade into insignificance when his great rival's publication started to appear in 1820.

4

'The First Practical Botanist in Europe'

Robert Sweet's *Geraniaceae, the Natural Order of Gerania*, produced between 1820 and 1830, was to become the best-known work on pelargoniums, and remained the definitive reference work on the genus until the twentieth century. There was a natural rivalry between Sweet and Andrews, and sometimes their descriptions of the same plant cite different putative parents and origins. Because Sweet was a gardener and a botanist there is an inclination to believe his opinion over that of Andrews, but often Sweet seems to put in different ideas simply to show he knows more than Andrews. Sweet's work encapsulates the genus pelargonium at the beginning of the nineteenth century, containing descriptions of about 500 plants. The earlier volumes feature species almost exclusively, although under the modern classification some are now defined as erodiums. As the work progressed hybrids began to predominate, and it is clear from looking at the works of both Sweet and Andrews that between 1805 and 1830 there was an astonishing growth of new varieties among the greenhouses of the wealthy. Sweet rather endearingly describes how some plants, known to be hybrids, might have been thought species if they had been brought directly from the Cape. Of *Pelargonium jonquillinum* he says, 'we cannot possibly conceive how it can be otherwise in the tropical countries, where the insects and humming-birds are continuously flitting from flower to flower, and fertilizing one with the pollen of the other'. (No matter that the Cape is not actually in the tropics, nor does it contain humming-birds.)

Robert Sweet (1782–1835) was a nurseryman from Devon, who had trained in the West Country before working at Woodlands, Blackheath, the garden of John Julius Angerstein.[1] There he worked under David Stewart, to whom, as he states in the *Geraniaceae*, he was

> indebted for the first rudiments of education on the cultivation and propagation of plants, having been for some time one of his pupils, and by his permission [was] allowed to try different experiments, which has afterwards enabled [me] to establish quite a different system in the cultivation and propagation of plants, than any hitherto used.

In 1810 Sweet became a partner in the Stockwell nursery until it closed in 1815, and he then moved to Whitley, Brames and Milne in Fulham, where he was foreman for four years. At that time he published his first book, *Hortus Suburbanus Londinensis*, a survey of plants grown in the London area. In 1819 Sweet became foreman at Colvill's nursery, Chelsea. James Colvill the Younger (*c.* 1778–1832) had been in partnership with his father, James Colvill (*c.* 1746–1822), who had been a leading nurseryman since 1786 and was in business with his son until his death.[2] By 1824 Sweet seemed to have the prospect of a prosperous and successful career in front of him as both a writer and nurseryman but, as has been seen before, there was an underlying atmosphere of rivalry and resentment in the horticultural world, and an attempt was made to damage his reputation by an accusation of receiving stolen property, culminating in a trial at the Old Bailey.

The charge was made that Sweet had received a box of seven exotic plants, valued at £7, contained in seven pots, valued at 6*d*, from the Royal Botanic Gardens at Kew. The story reported in *The Times*[3] was that the plants had been taken by a gardener called Hogan, who handed them over the wall to a man named Noyce,

10. *P.* × *striatum*, the Streak-flowered Stork's-bill, from Sweet, *Geraniaceae*, plate 1 (1820). Sweet chose this very decorative hybrid to start his great work on pelargoniums in 1820. *(Author's Collection)*

who was instructed to deliver them to Mr Sweet. Hogan then disappeared without collecting his wages. When an assistant gardener, Mr Smith, found the plants were missing, he called the police and accompanied a senior officer to Colvill's nursery to investigate. Sweet denied all knowledge of the plants, but when the nursery was searched, the plants were identified in one of the hothouses. Sweet was thereupon arrested and taken to the police station at Bow Street. Colvill was also questioned but charges against him were dropped.

At that date the penalty for theft of anything over a shilling, or for receiving stolen property, was death. The trial took place on 24 February 1824. Sweet received the support of many eminent gentlemen as character witnesses, including William Anderson of the Chelsea Apothecary's Garden, James Ridgway, the publisher, Joseph Knight of the Exotic Nursery, and George Loddiges of Loddiges' Nursery, Hackney. Mr Colvill, however, was not present, nor was William Townsend Aiton (1768–1843), the Superintendent of Kew Gardens. During the questioning of Mr Smith, it was discussed whether or not Mr Sweet was an author and whether Mr Aiton was also an author and had received some criticism from the pen of Mr Sweet. It was later explained that the criticism mentioned had been in the *Botanical Register*, which was nothing to do with Sweet, although published by Ridgway who also published Sweet's work. It seems that the matter may have been connected to some resentment by Aiton, who was the son of William Aiton and more of a landscape gardener than a botanist like his father. He had certainly been criticised by nurserymen and publishers, and Sweet had put some critical remarks in *Geraniaceae*, although he had not mentioned any names:

We understand we are very much envied in a certain quarter for raising so many beautiful hybrid plants, and more so for publishing them. But we mind not their envy as long as we are so ably supported by our numerous subscribers to whom we beg our most grateful acknowledgements.[4]

The closed world of experimental science was now being invaded by commerce. It was also mentioned in the report of the trial in *The Times* that it 'appeared from a mass of testimony adduced that for a considerable time past the Royal Botanic Gardens at Kew have been plundered of rare exotics and other plants'.[5] Sweet seems to have been chosen to be made an example of because of his remarks, although they may have quoted the wrong ones at the trial. Unfortunately it was only too easy to set him up because it was a perfectly normal practice for unsolicited plants to arrive at Colvill's or even Sweet's home, for him to examine. Sweet was said at the trial to be 'the first practical botanist in Europe' and that 'botanists were in the constant habit of receiving plants for experimental and other purposes without any intimation accompanying them as to the parties who had sent them'.[6]

Although Sweet was acquitted of any crime, his career and health were damaged. He left Colvill's in 1826 and concentrated on finishing *Geraniaceae*, as well as producing *Cistineae* (1825–30), *Flora Australasica* (1827–8), *The British Flower Garden* (1823–37) and *The Florist's Guide* (1823–37). The illustrator he worked most closely with was Edwin Dalton Smith, who had worked with him previously on a book about birds, *The British Warblers* (1823). In 1830 Sweet moved to Chelsea and rented some land at Cook's Ground where he grew plants for selected customers and friends. One of the correspondents to whom he sent plants was the Revd Henry Thomas Ellacombe (1790–1885) who gardened at Bitton, Gloucestershire, a garden that became better known under Ellacombe's son, Canon Henry Nicholson Ellacombe (1822–1916). Sweet suffered a deterioration in health in his final years and died in some poverty. His plants were taken over by William

Dennis (1785–1851), whose nursery in Grosvenor Row, Pimlico, specialised in dahlias before he took to pelargoniums.

Sweet's *Geraniaceae* is a definitive work because it is so comprehensive and consolidates the known pelargoniums over the decade between 1820 and 1830. The plates were produced regularly, almost one a week, but some of the illustrations are not as good as those of Andrews and there is uncertainty about some of the information given. Sweet used Colvill's plants extensively: over eighty of their plants were used in the publications of the 1820s. Sweet followed L'Heritier in distinguishing Pelargonium and Geranium, but he also invented new genera of his own when he thought the plants differed enough. Thus he created the names Campylia, Ciconium, Dimacria, Grenvillea, Hoarea, Isopetalum, Jenkinsonia, Otidia, Phymetanthus and Seymouria.

The best and most extensive collection that Sweet used was that of Sir Richard Colt Hoare (1758–1838) at Stourhead in Wiltshire. Colt Hoare inherited the magnificent landscaped garden from his grandfather, but spent much of his time away from it, travelling throughout Europe following the death of his wife after only two years of marriage. His interest in the arts and history cultivated throughout his long 'grand tour' provided a full-time occupation on his return. When the French Revolution prevented travel in Europe, he travelled round Britain and Ireland instead, and then set his mind on British antiquities. Perhaps it was fortunate that he had one of the most important British historic sites, Stonehenge, almost on his doorstep. He was one of the first people to see archaeology as a subject for study in itself, producing *Ancient History of North and South Wiltshire* between 1812 and 1821, and many more books on travel, art history and archaeology.

Colt Hoare began growing pelargoniums early in the nineteenth century and received specimens from Lee and Kennedy as well as from Colvill's.[7] In the 1820s he published a monograph on the Geraniaceae, which contains details on how he cultivated the

11. Sir Richard Colt Hoare and his son Henry, by Samuel Woodforde, The Hoare Collection, Stourhead. Colt Hoare had one of the largest collections of pelargoniums in the eighteenth century. *(The National Trust/© NTPL/John Hammond)*

plants himself.[8] He divided pelargoniums into five classes, which gives us an insight into how hybridisers of the time saw the plants and what they were trying to do in developing new varieties. Colt Hoare's classification was as follows:

(1) *Inquinans* or Scarlet,
(2) *Purpureum* or Purple,
(3) *Maculatum* or Spotted,
(4) *Striatum* or Streaked, and
(5) *Grandiflora* or Large-Flowered.

1. Scarlet

Colt Hoare states that, apart from *zonale*, no other scarlet 'geranium' was known (i.e. before hybridising began) other than *fulgidum*. By mentioning *zonale* only, which is generally pink, he seems to be implying that *zonale* and *inquinans* had already been hybridised into a 'Zonal' type. *Zonale* and *inquinans* do not seem to have been used in Colt Hoare's hybridising programme. His aim was to try to produce new, red plants using *fulgidum*. For many years he sowed the seeds but they only produced plants similar to the parents (implying that he sowed *fulgidum* seeds, not knowing how they were pollinated), until one season four different seedlings appeared. These were named *ignescens*, *scintillans* and two dwarf varieties. He calls this the 'grand epoch in the history of this plant from which the numerous varieties of scarlet, with its different shades have originated'. It is clear that *ignescens* was a great breakthrough, with its brilliant red and black flowers (*ignescens* means burning or fiery), and it appeared in many different varieties, raised by Colt Hoare himself, Colvill and Jenkinson, and was described by Sweet, Andrews and Loddiges in the *Botanical Cabinet*.[9] It was the parent of many known hybrids and as such is the ancestor of an unknown number of modern varieties. Colt Hoare mentions examples of the next generation:

P. × ignescens

(The fiery pelargonium, from its burning red flowers)

A hybrid from *P. fulgidum* grown by Richard Colt Hoare at Stourhead and used for later hybridising. It is bright red with black markings. However, many similar hybrids are described by Sweet and Andrews, and the plant may be the same as Unique Aurora or Aurora's Unique.

Pelargonium × ignescens. (Sweet, Geraniaceae, plate 2/Author's Collection)

'Daveyana', 'Defiance' and 'More's Victory'.[10] Daveyana is also known as *davyanum*, named after the Camberwell nurseryman Thomas Davey (1758–1833). He later moved near to Colvill's in King's Road, Chelsea, and also specialised in florists' flowers, tulips and camellias. Daveyana was likely to have been a hybrid of *ignescens* and *barringtonii*, a plant of unknown parentage but probably produced from *cucullatum*. Daveyana was shrubby, with cordate leaves and large flowers, having pinkish lower petals and darker crimson upper petals with black veins.[11] So already the *fulgidum–cucullatum* cross was being used. Defiance appears to be a plant raised by Jenkinson, called *cuneiflorum*, which Sweet suggests was produced from a *quercifolium* hybrid.[12] More's Victory, also known as *moreanum*, was produced by More's nursery, also in King's Road, Chelsea (which was carried on by Mrs More after the founder's death). This plant is believed to be a hybrid of *ignescens* with 'Dianthiflorum', or 'Fair Helen (or Ellen)', itself a descendant of the same *quercifolium* hybrid producing Defiance.[13] It is believed to survive today under the name of Scarlet Pet.

2. Purple

These are likely to be mainly hybrids from *cucullatum*. Under this heading Colt Hoare lists *yeatmanianum, concinnum, coruscans, humei, exornatum, calamistratum* and 'the New Oxford'. *Yeatmanianum* was produced by a Miss Jane Yeatman of Dorchester from Davey's 'Maria Isabella', whose parents are not recorded. According to Sweet, *concinnum* was also named by Colt Hoare as *purpureum* 'Superbum' or the Comely Storksbill,[14] but no parentage is given. *Coruscans* is said by Sweet to be derived from *concinnum*, and was named 'Lady Clinton' by Davey.[15] *Humei*, or 'Sir Abraham Hume's Storksbill', was raised by the nurseryman Mr Paul of Cheshunt, and was a hybrid of Daveyanum and another hybrid of unknown parentage, 'Generalissimum'. *Exornatum* was raised by the Earl of Liverpool's gardener, Mr Smith, from unknown parents, and *calamistratum* came from Mr Dennis, another Chelsea nurseryman, and was believed to have been produced from More's Victory and 'Congestum' (also from Dennis and possibly *fulgidum* × *ignescens*). As to 'the New Oxford', Colt Hoare says it is 'an old inhabitant of our conservatories, very dwarf and gay, especially when a cluster of them are placed together'. This is the first of the very unhelpful and frustrating descriptions frequently met with when reading about pelargoniums in the nineteenth century. It seems that many pelargoniums were so popular and grown so commonly by everyone (as many are now) that writers did not bother to describe them or illustrate them. The term 'New Oxford' implies that there may have been an 'Old Oxford' plant, probably originally from the Oxford Botanic Garden. Andrews depicted two varieties of *oxoniense*, which had an oak-shaped leaf and pink flowers with purple markings, and Sweet produced a similar plant called *cynosbatifolium*, which had been raised at Oxford Botanic Garden in about 1759, which perhaps makes it the 'Old Oxford'.

3. Spotted

Colt Hoare described these as being distinguished by 'a dark stain on the upper petals'. He went on to say that the tribe was 'very numerous, and possesses great beauty and variety in the distribution of its colours'. He gave examples of *nubilum*, *tinctum* and *instratum*, as well as his own 'Fair Rosamund' or *hoareanum*, said by Sweet to be the handsomest plant in his collection. It had white lower petals and purple upper petals with a white edge. *Nubilum* was one of Jenkinson's hybrids, produced from *jenkinsonii* (of unknown parents) and named 'Rob Roy' by nurserymen. *Tinctum* was from Dennis, and also known as 'Rival'; it was said by Sweet to be something between *jenkinsonii* and *youngii* (a hybrid from Charles and James Young of Epsom). It was pink and maroon with crimson edges on the top petals. *Instratum* was produced by another nursery, Messrs Chandler of Vauxhall, of unknown parentage, and was white with purple blotches.

4. Streaked

For this group Colt Hoare only gave one example, *striatum*, from Sweet. This was Sweet's first plant in his *Geraniaceae* and was a hybrid from Davey's nursery, named 'Fairy Queen'. It had white *cucullatum*-type flowers, very strongly veined in purple.

5. Grandiflorum

This section was an afterthought by Colt Hoare, and he says the varieties are numerous, the best example being *macranthon*, but he comments that there is still no rich scarlet or purple in the 'genus'. *Macranthon* had been raised by Jenkinson from 'Crenaeflorum' and *involucratum* 'Incarnatum' (known as 'Commander-in-Chief' and previously mentioned under Andrews's work). 'Crenaeflorum' had

P. × *fragrans*

(The fragrant pelargonium, from its spicily scented leaves)

Known in the eighteenth century and thought to be a species, this plant is now believed to be a naturally occurring hybrid between *odoratissimum* and *exstipulatum*. It has bluish-green pine-scented leaves, is small and shrubby with tiny lilac flowers, and there are variegated versions and many hybrids.

Pelargonium × *fragrans.*
(Author's Collection)

been derived from *P. grandiflorum. Macranthon* was used extensively for further hybridising.[16]

Some of the other most striking pelargoniums featured by Sweet were *fragrans, nodosum* and *schizopetalum. Fragrans* was something of a mystery in Sweet's day, as it was thought by many to be a species and by others to be a hybrid, naturally occurring. Sweet speculated that it was produced from *exstipulatum* and *odoratissimum*, which has now been proved correct. It is unlikely to have been produced in the wild in South Africa, however, as the plants do not come from the same habitat, and it must therefore have been first produced when the plants were grown together in Europe.[17] It has small, greyish-green leaves and tiny lilac flowers, is more upright than *odoratissimum* but more bushy than *exstipulatum*, and has strong pine- or nutmeg-scented leaves. It is easy to grow and propagate and has been used over the centuries to produce many more scented-leaved hybrids which are grown today. *Nodosum* was described as a hybrid raised at Colvill's from *multiradiatum* and 'Flexuosum' (itself a hybrid of *reniforme* and *echinatum*). *Multiradiatum* is a tuberous geophyte with filigree-like leaves and radiating, many-branched flowers, yellow with deep maroon central markings. It can be imagined, therefore, that the hybridisers must have been expecting something fairly spectacular from this parentage, considering that *reniforme* had deep magenta flowers and *echinatum* white ones with purple markings, as well as the succulent stems. Of course it did not really work this way: the parentage is simply supposed by Sweet, working backwards from the appearance of *nodosum*, and may not have been accurate. *Nodosum* is actually spectacular though: it is tuberous, with greyish, carroty leaves and red-edged black flowers. Finally, in this selection, *schizopetalum*: a tuberous species introduced by Colvill, of the same group as *caffrum* and *bowkeri*. They are remarkable-looking tuberous plants, with fringed pink and green flowers.

Sweet also used Robert Jenkinson's collection. He is mentioned as having received *P. abrotanifolium* from Burchell. Sweet says of *glaucifolium*, 'the flowers are exquisitely fragrant, their fragrance beginning about 5 or 6 o'clock in the evening, and continuing until about nine the next day'. Another *gibbosum* hybrid, from Colvill's, was *rutaceum*, crossed with the extraordinary *multiradiatum*. This produced a plant with black flowers, marked with green or yellow, with a pungent rue-like scent, that Sweet said was not very pleasant to be near to.

By the late 1820s and 1830s there were many more nurserymen taking an interest in pelargoniums, and some of their names were given to hybrids. *Pelargonium rollissonii* is described as 'a very desirable plant, as it makes a compact little bush and produces an abundance of flowers all the summer'. It was named after William Rollisson of Tooting, south London, who also gave his name to another plant which was to become much better known later in the century. There is also a *Pelargonium dennisianum*, a cross between *cucullatum* and *barringtonii* named after William Dennis, the nurseryman who took over Sweet's plants. By 1834 it was said in Loudon's *Gardener's Magazine* that Dennis was growing over 700 varieties. Then there was *Pelargonium veitchianum*, a large-flowered hybrid named after James Veitch (1792–1863) of the family that originated in Exeter, Devon, but who took over the Exotic Nursery in Chelsea. James Veitch did part of his training with Rollisson, from whom he bought the orchids that formed the basis of a collection for which he later became famous.

Other nurseries selling pelargoniums were Weltje of Hammersmith, Allen's Union Nursery in King's Road and Bailey of Clapton. Charles and James Young of Epsom, Surrey, listed seventeen varieties in their catalogue, called *Hortus Epsomensis*, in 1828, including *triste* and *lobatum*. The *Hortus Addlestonensis*, or catalogue of John Cree of Chertsey, Surrey, of 1829, listed old favourites like Defiance, Commander-in-Chief, Daveyanum, *ignescens*, *moreanum*, *ardens* and Citriodorum. Reginald Whitely of Old Brompton, west London, listed nine pelargoniums in the 1830s, including *carnosum*, *fulgidum* and *cotyledonis*. There was therefore nothing to stop a keen gardener trying to hybridise new plants him or herself; the raw material was freely available.

It was not only nurserymen who were becoming addicted to pelargoniums. Mention has already been made of Miss Yeatman of Dorchester producing a new variety. There was also a Miss Burnett of Crayford who produced about half a dozen hybrids mentioned in the great works, Captain Francis of Norfolk, the Marchioness of Northampton and the Duke of Bedford. In Mary Russell Mitford's diaries, written in the first half of the nineteenth century, there are frequent mentions of her seedling 'geraniums' being distributed to friends, and even a story of her gardener stealing plants to give to a neighbour and then stealing them back when he was found out.[18]

Botanists also continued to take an interest in classifying pelargoniums as part of larger works on the plant kingdom. In 1800 Carl Ludwig Willdenow (1765–1812), later director of the

Berlin Botanic Garden, identified further pelargonium species in his revision of the Geraniaceae for the third edition of *Species Plantarum*. In 1821 Ernst Gottlieb Steudel (1783–1856) in *Nomenclatur*, asserted correct names for pelargoniums but did not provide illustrations. In 1824 Augustin Pyramus de Candolle, professor of botany at Geneva, who it will be remembered had acquired L'Heritier's herbarium, divided pelargoniums into twelve sections in volume I of *Prodromus Systematis Naturalis Regni Vegetabilis*. He described 369 species and hybrids but did not provide illustrations. He reduced Sweet's ten genera to sections within the genus Pelargonium.

There were also some European rivals to Curtis, Andrews and Sweet, providing detailed illustrated botanical works in German and French for the wealthy European collectors. A four-volume work by the Austrian botanist Leopold Trattinick (1764–1849) came out between 1825 and 1834, describing about 400 hybrids, all of which were named or renamed in Latin. In 1835 two German botanists, Christian Friedrich Ecklon (1795–1868) and Karl Ludwig Zeyher (1799–1858) published *Enumeratio Plantarum Africae Australis*, which reviewed the Geraniaceae in volume I. Zeyher was at the Cape for about twenty-five years from 1822, while Ecklon had visited in 1823. They changed the sections of pelargonium back to genera and included some new species, although many were synonyms for existing species. They did, however, describe the habitat of the plants, which provided vital information for gardeners.

The horticultural world in Britain was changing with the change of the monarch in 1837. Both Sweet and Colt Hoare had died by 1838, and with their deaths there passed away the first great age of the pelargonium. The plants were by no means the 'perfect' specimens we expect today; many were shrubby and rangy and were not necessarily easy to grow. But Andrews and Sweet loved them for the brilliancy of colour, which can barely be reproduced in print, and the excitement of producing new plants, wondering what they would be like. Many pelargonium flowers seem to glow in the sun, which is hard to reproduce, even in photographs. The plants were still so close to the species that they had the variety of colours that grow in nature – the blacks and yellows, the magenta, and the cream buds opening to pale pink. The foliage was varied too – not only was it scented, but it could be a soft grey-green or almost silver, or there could be dark streaks and red tips to the leaves. The Georgian pelargonium growers had concentrated on the *cucullatum* and *fulgidum* hybrids, and they had introduced many species into hybridisation to enrich the colours of the flowers and the scents of the foliage, but they had barely touched *Zonale, inquinans* and *peltatum*, which they seemed to consider unworthy of consideration. They must have felt that there was so much scope yet to come, but it is doubtful whether they could have imagined how their beloved pelargoniums would soon be manipulated by the rampant commercialisation of the Victorian age.

5

The Quest for the Perfect Pelargonium

The Victorian age was one of novelties, and a time when life changed for the whole population as people began to move to urban living. The consumer society gradually developed as the nation continued to prosper and many more people could afford luxuries. The railways meant that it was easier to move about and trends began to sweep the whole country, rather than just one district. Cheap newspapers and books, with an increased literacy rate, meant that ideas spread quickly and fashions could be followed wherever one lived. One of the leisure activities that developed with the new urban middle class was gardening.[1] Plants became cheaply available and gardening appealed to the Victorians' liking for useful and educational pursuits. Leisure gardening was nothing new, of course, but it was in the middle of the nineteenth century that different classes of gardeners started to come together as equals and became interested in the same plants, rather than growing different plants depending on their status in society.

Traditionally, working people had grown fruit and vegetables as food, and 'florists' flowers' for pleasure. Floriculture, as it was known, has nothing to do with floristry as we know it today, meaning flower selling or flower arranging. Someone who sold decorative flowers for a living in the nineteenth century would be known as a market florist; their importance with regard to pelargoniums comes later. The florists who grew flowers competitively as a hobby formed Florists' Societies, which had existed as early as the seventeenth century. The societies were usually centred round a market town or one district of a larger city. Members were typically tradesmen or craftsmen and they would meet several times a year in a public house, hold a 'Florists' Feast' and then an exhibition of their plants. The early florists' flowers were the anemone, the ranunculus, the carnation, the pink, the hyacinth, the tulip, the polyanthus and the auricula. These were all plants that could be grown outside, could be grown from seed and could also be propagated vegetatively. It was therefore not expensive to grow them, and working people were the main growers. New varieties could be hybridised by cross-pollination, and then good plants could be divided or have cuttings taken to make new ones. The florists' aim was to produce a new variety, more perfect than any other, but within the strict rules of the society. A good plant would win prizes, which could be money or sometimes a piece of silver or copper. The florist would then be able to make money by propagating his plant and selling it on.

It is not known how florists' societies started; they may have begun when professional gardeners grew plants in their spare time and competed informally with each other.[2] There were similar societies in the Low Countries and France, and when the Huguenot refugees came to Britain in the seventeenth century they brought many new plants and ideas with them. Most plants were exhibited as cut flowers in glass jars, but tulips were usually grown in specially constructed beds, and the judges would go round the neighbourhood viewing them all before awarding prizes. It is obvious that florists were expert horticulturalists, able to breed plants long before the science of genetics had been developed, and they were skilled at caring for their plants and transporting them to shows so as to keep them in top condition. It is not surprising, therefore, that when more plants became readily available they would want to try their skills on them. The only reason they had been restricted from doing so before was because they had to rely on plants that they could easily afford. By the nineteenth century the categories of florists' flowers started to expand as soon as new plants could be bought cheaply enough and there was a steady supply in urban areas. The dahlia was a popular choice, and the pelargonium soon followed, with its huge variety of flowers and foliage to titillate the florists' ingenuity.

By the early nineteenth century many nurserymen were specialising in the expanded categories of florists' flowers and were beginning to dominate the shows. Professional gardeners started to grow them for decorating conservatories and greenhouses, and they would be put outside in pots in the summer. Some professional gardeners took pride in growing them competitively and they liked to develop new varieties. From reading the gardening magazines of the nineteenth century it is difficult to know whether there were many working people left among amateur growers as most florists seemed to be retired military men, businessmen, clergymen and doctors. The character of the old florists' societies changed and eventually new societies were formed for individual plants. It was therefore a profitable business for nurserymen to grow these flowers and produce as many new varieties as they could to sell on to those who were becoming interested in them.

Unfortunately, although the magazines of the nineteenth century are filled with details of pelargoniums, very few are illustrated. By the 1840s the botanical magazines were fading in popularity and the much cheaper weekly horticultural magazines, in a newspaper format, were becoming the usual medium for topical gardening news. They included very few illustrations and no colour. There were monthly magazines in a smaller, book-like format, which usually included one colour plate per issue, but they were not of the same quality as the plates in the botanical works, and the demand to produce illustrations of a great number of different plants meant that those of pelargoniums were few and far between. The more common the plant, the less likely it was to be illustrated, as the editors assumed everyone would know it. They were far more likely to depict a new plant, and more often than not it was some novelty that did not last.

The other problem when trying to trace the ancestry of plants is the lack of detail given on their parentage. Obviously, plant breeding was becoming a good commercial enterprise and no nurseryman was going to give away his trade secrets. Therefore, although many new plants are described, it is rarely possible to discover exactly how they were produced. This has led to almost total speculation among writers who have tried to trace the ancestry of the plants. There are exceptions, however. It seems that once a plant had become a legend, the proud raiser would be only too pleased to reveal its secrets, because by then he had produced something better to take its place.

Between the 1830s and the 1850s florists and nurserymen concentrated on hybrids created from the varieties known to Sweet and Andrews. They did not look at the Zonal, Zonate or horseshoe pelargoniums, generally referred to as 'scarlet geraniums'. These varieties carried on quietly in the background, used as decorative garden plants in urns and pots, but were not considered exciting enough for the florists. Nor did anyone give much attention to the ivy-leaved pelargonium, *peltatum*; its day was yet to come. As to the so-called 'Cape varieties', the random selection of all other species and early hybrids known in the preceding century, they were left languishing in the glasshouses of those who had collected them, and were mentioned occasionally as curiosities. However, the fact that many of them were still there means that some of the unknown seedlings that appeared from time to time were probably their descendants. We will never know.

The links between Sweet's plants of the 1820s and the 'florists' pelargoniums' of the 1830s and 1840s cannot be definitely explained, but in his lecture to the Royal Horticultural Society in 1880 Shirley Hibberd attempted to provide some ideas.[3] He surmised that the 'large-flowering' florists' pelargoniums were the offspring of *P. speciosum*, although he has some difficulty in ascertaining which plant that was, concluding that it was actually Sweet's *involucratum* (a hybrid raised by the Earl of Liverpool, which Sweet thought was *cucullatum* × 'Superbum', a pure white flower with purple veining, different from the *involucratum* 'Incarnatum' described by Andrews). He also names *spectabile* (a *cucullatum* × *ignescens* hybrid) as the other likely parent, but he does say that 'the blood of a score or so of species is mingled in them'. He then goes on to say that the first florists' flower 'to be figured' was 'Grandissimum', raised by Mr Widnall of Grant-chester, and featured in the *Floricultural Cabinet* in 1834[4] (where it is actually called Grandissima). It had rich dark purple upper petals and blushed pink lower ones, but was said by Hibberd to be small and feeble in comparison with later hybrids.

In June 1835 a list of the 'most handsome flowering pelar-goniums' was given in the *Floricultural Cabinet*, all obtainable from Dennis's nursery.[5] The price, per plant, varied from 1*s* 6*d* (7.5p) to over 40*s* (£2)! One variety, Duchess of Sutherland, was even priced at 5 guineas,[6] although it was remarked that the price would soon lower once the plant had 'got into the trade', perhaps to even a quarter. It was still a high price for the best plants. Over 100 varieties were given, divided into colours, including different shades of red, purple, lilac and orange, with stripes, spots, shading and other markings. Several were also described as 'oak-leaved' with different coloured flowers. Some familiar names were in-cluded, although sometimes with variations, such as 'Rollissonia', 'Dennis's Yeatmanianum grandiflora', and 'Humei grandiflora'. This brings up another difficulty with identifying pelargoniums throughout their history. The same names were used by different nurseries for what were probably different varieties of the same plant, but may have been completely different plants, and as there is often a limited description and no illustration, it is impossible to know what the name refers to. Also, because new seedlings were being produced every year, and many did not survive long, the same names were recycled fairly quickly.

Florists did not use many of the Cape varieties for hybridising as they were considered too difficult to grow. In the *Floricultural Cabinet* in 1837 Thomas Appleby, a professional gardener near Sheffield, divided pelargoniums into three groups: (1) species with tuberous roots; (2) species that had not been hybridised; and (3) those that had been hybridised. He advised readers to steer clear of (1) and (2) as being harder to cultivate and more difficult to obtain. He included in group (2) *bicolor*,[7] *tricolor* and *fulgidum*. He said of group (3), however, that the varieties were almost endless and new ones were produced annually, chiefly in or near London. He recommended in particular 'Daveyanum' which had been mentioned in Colt Hoare's Scarlet section. Appleby explained that it had not been released by Mr Davey until he had grown 200 plants and then it had been sold at 5 guineas a plant. Davey is also mentioned in the *Floricultural Cabinet* of November 1840,[8] where he is said to have been the raiser of 'Prince Regent' and 'Commander-in-Chief', which Colt Hoare had given as a parent for *macranthon*. These plants were both described by Sweet and are both *cucullatum* types.[9] Appleby also mentioned 'Yeatmanianum grandiflorum', and says that his recommended varieties could be bought for 6*d* or 1*s* each from 'any respectable nurseryman'.[10]

Results of shows were often quoted to give a plant credibility, and it never did any harm to mention the name of an aristocratic-sounding or clerical gentleman as the raiser. 'The Efulgence', raised by the Revd T. Jarvis, was announced in 1838. It cost £2 10*s* per plant and 'its unrivalled beauty was universally admitted' at the Jersey Horticultural Show in May 1838. It had upper petals of bright carmine, with a dark spot distinctly marked, and under petals of crimson with a white eye and blended with a purple hue.[11]

12. The Victorian large-flowered
pelargoniums were developed by florists from
the early hybrids of Sweet and Andrews.
(Shirley Hibberd, Familiar Garden Flowers,
c. 1880/Author's collection)

By 1841 the pelargonium appears to have been accepted as a fully fledged florists' flower. The *Gardeners' Chronicle* gave a short history of the plant and approved of the way new plants were being developed:

> From a wild flower hardly superior to the Geraniums of the road-side, [it] has passed through various stages of improvement, the flowers becoming enlarged in their size, rounded in their petals, changed in their colour, and invigorated in their growth, till at last the oak-leaved, and ivy-leaved, and horse-shoe geraniums, which were the favourites of our childhood, are no longer to be recognised under the comparatively matchless forms of the Pelargoniums called Nymph and Jesse.[12]

This passage is interesting in several ways. It implies that certain plants, namely the 'oak-leaved', the 'ivy-leaved' and 'horse-shoe geraniums' had been enthusiastically grown by many people and were so well known they did not need description. It also implies that the new-style florists' pelargoniums had evolved from those plants, which of course they had not.[13] On that point, it shows that the *Chronicle*, as usual, was not very well informed about, or interested in, florists' flowers, mainly because they considered them and their growers inferior to more refined flowers and properly trained professional gardeners. This was the founding year of the *Chronicle* but in years to come it became apparent that the magazine, and the Horticultural Society, for which to a large extent it was a mouthpiece, were not prepared to give florists much space, or allow them to participate in the society's shows.

The florists were hybridising with specific aims in mind, rather than simply hoping to get a better or prettier flower, as the eighteenth-century growers had done. [The] Nymph was described in a different issue of the *Chronicle* in 1842.[14] It was said to represent a 'near approach' to roundness, with fine broad, stiff petals. It was bright rose pink with a dark spot, the under petals terminating in white. The article in 1841 goes on to refer to some of the later plants described by Sweet, such as 'Daedelum', 'Drakae' and *cordiforme*, which it cites as examples of how new varieties were losing the 'narrow and feeble petals universal in the wild species, and were acquiring the roundness and firmness so requisite to constitute true floral beauty'. 'Daedelum' was pink and had been raised by Mr Dennis by 1829. Sweet suggested the parents were 'Solubile' and a hybrid from 'Beaufortianum'. Solubile was a new name for 'Duchess of Gloucester', which had been illustrated by Sweet in 1820, so called because water dissolved the purple of the petals. Sweet thought the ancestry included *cucullatum* and/or *angulosum* and/or *cochleatum*. Beaufortianum had appeared in Andrews in 1806 and he suggested the parentage was *ovale × speciosum*. Sweet, on the other hand, had thought *acerifolium × lanceolatum*. Drakae had originally been called Mrs Drake and had been raised by Mr Weltje of Hammersmith before 1829; it supposedly had a red flower and a maple-like leaf. *Cordiforme* had been raised by Joseph Robinson, who was Mr Dennis's gardener, and was believed to have been produced from *P. platypetalon*, which had come from Colt Hoare before 1822. The writer in the *Gardeners' Chronicle* in 1841 also stated that Sweet's plants called 'Weltje's Isabella' and 'Dennis's Rival' were equal to some sorts then (1841) being cultivated, and the latter was the best variety known in 1830. Isabella was also known as *suffusum*, and was pale pink with feathering. Rival was described in the previous chapter under Colt Hoare's 'Spotted' section.

In the same issue of the *Gardeners' Chronicle* in 1841 the criteria for the pelargonium as a florists' flower were set out. The ideal was 'beautiful compact flowers . . . with broad stout petals so entirely overlaying each other as to leave scarcely an indentation in the outline of the flower', rather than 'the long, narrow, flimsy

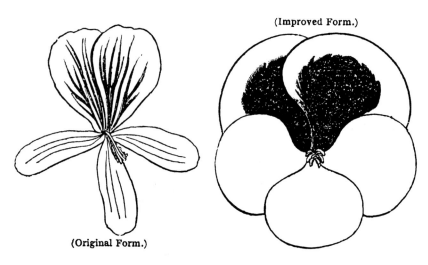

13. Diagram showing the florists' aspiration in manipulating the pelargonium. *(Gardeners' Chronicle, 1841/Museum of Garden History)*

petals of the old varieties, moved by every breath of wind, and separated to their very base by broad open spaces'. So already the trend is towards the stiff, upright round flower we know in modern times, rather than the more delicate plant known in the eighteenth century. Further, the broad petals should be free of 'crumple or unevenness of any kind' so that they should form a flat circle. The colour should be clear and the under petals free from veins. The upper petals should have a dark spot running to the bottom with no suspicion of a white feather. Finally, the leaves should be large. The notable characteristic at this time is the blotch on the top petals only, and the aim to extend it so as to leave just a narrow even margin round the edges. A diagram was given to show the difference between the original form and the 'improved' form, and one can safely say that they bear almost no resemblance to each other.[15]

In 1841 the best raisers of these new plants were said to be Edmund Foster Esq and the Revd Mr Garth, and a warning was

14. Captain Thurtell's 'Pluto', an early florists' flower, which seems to conform to the ideal. *(Floricultural Cabinet, 1843/Museum of Garden History)*

given that because of their success there were now many competitors. Purchasers were told to be discriminating in choosing from the new plants. The nurserymen–florists produced their seedlings as quickly as they could and there was little in the way of protection against fraudulent advertising and selling. Any grower could make fantastic claims that his was the perfect plant everyone was looking for. The correspondence columns of the gardening magazines abounded with disappointed customers stating that their supposed perfect plant turned out to be a 'leggy weakling' once they grew it on. The Revd Garth was the breeder of what was regarded as a novelty in the new flowers of 1841, called 'Queen of the Fairies'. It was remarkable for its continuous and well-defined rim of pure white surrounding its upper petals. The spot on the top petals was deep maroon, while the under petals were pure white.[16]

People clearly wanted pelargoniums, but many were confused by the number of varieties becoming available and needed guidance on how to choose. A correspondent to the *Floricultural Cabinet* asked:

> You or some correspondent would much oblige me by a list of modern geraniums, arranged in something the following way, say twelve of each: the most fragrant (a most important and much neglected quality); whitest; deepest coloured; strongest blotches; most veined in the blossom; boldest flowering; longest flowering; earliest; latest; those peculiar for anything (such as unique). The number of magnificent varieties is now so great that some arrangement of them, according to colour and quality, seems necessary to enable people to suit themselves: selection among so many perfect and beautiful flowers is now almost impossible. If you have only to go into Covent Garden market, you become bewildered. What can be expected when you go to Mr Catleugh's, Gaines, Groom's etc., and twenty other excellent establishments?[17]

The editor simply answered that he hoped another reader would supply the necessary information: it was clearly beyond him!

The main topic dealt with in articles on pelargoniums at the time was colour. There was a notable absence of red, which was not surprising if the plants were mainly derived from *cucullatum* and similar species; the *fulgidum/ignescens* blood must have been running a little thin by then. The *Gardeners' Chronicle* in 1843 visited Henderson's Pine Apple Place nursery in north London and described two new varieties. 'Unique' was said to be 'altogether wanting in form, but of the most novel colour, this being a dark sanguine purple'. The other was 'Shepherd's Queen Victoria', which had a dwarf habit but abundant blossoms, a mixture of white and crimson. The *Chronicle* commented that they both differed strikingly from the ordinary kinds, and would be likely, with hybridisation, to introduce a 'fresh race, and thus maintain the novelty of character, without which all florists' flowers must pass into oblivion'.[18]

The florists also wanted to improve the markings on the top petals to provide a solid colour without any feathering. This seems to be sacrilege when one remembers the descriptions in Sweet, where the markings were valued in themselves. However, they did want the lower petals to retain markings. These rules seem arbitrary, but are based on the rules of all florists' societies, which laid down strict standards for the plants that would win prizes. Florists did not try to do anything different: their sole aim was to produce something as near as possible to the standard. It was certainly a manipulation of nature and it is interesting to wonder why they did it. Was it something to do with the spirit of the age, which had changed so much since the eighteenth century? Then they wanted something different and beautiful in itself, and were happy to enjoy random results if they turned out to be good plants. Now, all that florists wanted was to change the natural inclination of flowers into a pre-set ideal, which had nothing to do with natural beauty. The idea of trying to flatten the flower into a disc was so that the colour could be better seen and admired.

The *Floricultural Cabinet* of 1843 described the methods of Captain Charles Thurtell of Devonport in raising seedling pelargoniums.[19] He vehemently asserted that 'none but first rate kinds should be cultivated' and they should be secured from bees to prevent pollen being brought from 'ill-shaped rejected flowers'. The Captain purchased all the best sorts at 'enormous expense', and selected thirty-three plants for raising seedlings, rejecting seventy others, though they had been purchased 'at a cost of about as many pounds value'. He had succeeded in producing several seedlings 'of the very first order; viz., roundness in outline, proportionate equality in size of petals, firmness in substance, and a due expansion of the face of the bloom'. One of his successes, Pluto, was depicted, with almost black upper petals and deep crimson pink lower ones.[20]

There was also some advice in the magazine on cultivation. Captain Thurtell agreed with other growers that pelargoniums really needed a house to themselves, but if that were impossible, then pit frames should be used. Canvas shading would be necessary at the hottest time of the year. Potted-up young plants could go out in summer, on boards or slates in a warm position, but again shading should be afforded, and mats should be kept at the ready for frosty nights in autumn. Instructions had been given in a previous issue for making a canvas covering:

Take two parts by weight of resin, one part of hog's lard. Melt them well together, and when thoroughly incorporated, spread it over the surface of your canvas (previously stretched horizontally), by means of a very hot iron, <u>but not so warm as to burn the fabric</u>.[21]

Turfy-loam, mixed with leaf mould and sandy peat, made the best compost, with a small portion of bone dust. Another writer suggested putting pelargoniums in melon pits to overwinter.[22] References were made occasionally to 'Cape varieties'. It was said that many of them, especially *zonale*, were good for healing wounds.[23] *Echinatum* still seemed to be popular. One correspondent to the *Gardeners' Chronicle* described a specimen he had with fourteen trusses of flowers, looking like 'a cloud of white butterflies, with pink spots on their wings'.[24]

With all the accusations about sub-standard plants being produced, steps were taken to try to improve the reputation of the florist–nurseryman. In 1846 a correspondent to the *Gardeners' Chronicle* called 'Philo' reported how the rules at shows had been tightened up to ensure that seedlings were tested at one and two years to prevent inferior plants being sent out.[25] It was also remarked that Mr Foster and the Revd Garth were not now producing as many plants as before, implying that theirs had not been of the top quality. Mr Edward Beck, however, was praised for still sending out good ones.[26]

Edward Beck (1804–61) lived at Worton Cottage, Isleworth. He had been named in an advertisement in 1843 in the *Floricultural Cabinet*[27] as already having won the Gold Banksian medal twice at Chiswick (the Horticultural Society's show) and awards at the Regent's Park exhibition. Beck was not a professional nurseryman by training, but seems to have taken up florists' flowers in retirement. He had been a very successful businessman in Isleworth, maintaining his own wharf on the Thames to where his sailing barges brought timber, slate, stone and bricks from the Medway. He employed a huge workforce to dress the stone and saw the timber, while teams of horses and wagons stood ready to transport the end products to the building trade. He was a Quaker philanthropist, the father of eight children, several of whom carried on the business. His ships were named *Faith*, *Felicity*, *Hope*, *Concord* and *Charity*.[28] He was just the right man to try to improve and uphold the standards of the nursery trade. In the *Gardeners'*

Chronicle of 4 October 1845 he set out the terms by which he sent out his plants:

> First . . . I require pre-payment; and secondly . . . I make no allowance for the trade . . . experience has taught me that, as a certain amount of bad debts must be incurred when credit is given, it is necessary as a principle of business to take this into consideration when estimating the charge at which such business can be done; in other words those that do pay must pay more, because there are those who do not pay at all, or very badly.

He went on to say that he would not reserve plants, as those who asked for them first often paid last. He did not give an allowance for the trade because to do so would mean having to ask those he did not know whether they were tradesmen or not, and then demanding plants back if they did not tell the truth.

Edward Beck's establishment was described by the *Chronicle* in 1848:

> This neat little villa is now brought within an easy distance of town, as far as time is concerned, compared with a two or two and a half hours ride by omnibus. Half an hour's ride by rail and twenty minutes walk brings the visitor to the finest collection of pelargonium plants, whether stock, two year old seedlings or seedlings of the present season, we have ever yet seen.[29]

Beck's gardener was a Mr Dobson, and they used the 'tank' system for heating the glasshouses, which seems to have consisted of an open tank of hot water placed below the growing benches. The tank was made of slate, which was no doubt a good advertisement for Beck's slate business. The glasshouses also contained a collection of orchids. Mr Dobson and his son, John Dobson (*c.* 1832–78), set up the Woodlands Nursery in Isleworth,

15. Edward Beck (1804–61) of Isleworth, the amateur florist who made it his mission to improve the plants and the reputations of pelargonium growers. *(*Carte de Visite/*RHS Lindley Library)*

which carried on pelargonium growing into the later part of the century.

In January 1847 'Philo', in conjunction with the Horticultural Society of London, offered a prize of £7 for the best six seedlings not less than 2 years old and not having been sent out, with the most novel and distinct colour and of first-rate quality, to be judged in June.[30] Mr Beck endorsed the idea, although he asked for clarification of the rules, as it seemed it was not a requirement that all six seedlings had to be raised by the person showing them.[31] When June came, it was not surprising that Mr Beck carried away the prize. However, he promised to return the prize the following year on condition that a further £7 be provided by other growers, and that the prize money be divided among the best plants according to their worth.[32] The *Chronicle* did point out, though, that only two people had competed for the prize. It warned breeders of pelargoniums that they would lose public favour if they did not vary the sorts of plants produced: 'When the novelty is gone, the pelargonium . . . will be cast off and doomed to neglect . . . The World will have variety.' The writer also mentioned that the 'fancy' varieties were becoming more sought after, as 'their masculine beauty contrasts well with the highly refined "show" pelargoniums, unfavourably to the latter'. He advised the breeders to turn their attention to the wild species of the Cape for more variety.[33]

Edward Beck became the most respected pelargonium grower because he refused to send out his seedlings until they were two or three years old and therefore could be relied on. In September 1847 he produced *A Treatise on the Culture of the Pelargonium*, explaining his growing methods. This was partly in response to requests from pelargonium fanciers, but also to the remarks in the *Chronicle* on the lack of development of pelargoniums, already set out above:

That the eminent Botanist who edits the Horticultural part of that excellent periodical really believed this to be the case when he penned the articles in question, no one that has the pleasure of knowing him will for a moment doubt; but that it is at variance with the facts, every one must know that has even a superficial acquaintance with the subject. When any production imported into this country begins, under the skill and cultivation of the florist, to assume greater beauty in size, colour, texture or form . . . a rage for the flower commences; and any thing and every thing goes forth to the public, is bought, and welcomed. Presently the advance becomes more slow, the difference smaller; those who run with the crowd drop off as buyers, and join those who cry, 'There is no advance.' But apart from this crowd are the thorough-going enthusiastic florists, always aiming at perfection with attainable beauties in their eye: we say attainable beauties, because they see them dispersed among a number of flowers, and their aim is to obtain them in combination. Who does not remember the rage for Dahlias? And now that is over, ninety out of a hundred will tell you it is because 'there is no advance.' Is it so? Let the following facts speak. A nurseryman of our acquaintance has this year given £100 cash for the stock of one flower, and £70 for another. This gentleman has to obtain these sums again, with a profit; and he does not fear it . . . A few years back, the Horticultural Society provided a tent specially for florists' seedling productions; and no part of the exhibition was more disagreeably crowded the whole day. Since then they have been coldly received; placed here and there, as room could be found to squeeze them in; and now they are banished altogether.

In his *Treatise* Beck illustrated eight of his seedlings of 1846, in full colour as in the manner of a botanical magazine, stating that they had been painted from 'average-sized flowers and with their faults prominently displayed', so that if cultivators did not get similar results 'they must consider themselves unsuccessful'. He said that success was purely due to management and that he possessed no secrets; all he knew was set out in those pages. The eight flowers depicted were Centurion, Cruenta, Cavalier, Cassandra, Gulielma, Gustavus, Honora and Rosamund. No details on their parentage were given. The predominant feature of these flowers is that the two upper petals are dark, with a blotch or spot sometimes spreading almost to the margins, but with a lighter edging, while the lower petals are lighter and sometimes veined. The deep colours and velvety texture of the top petals are emphasised, and several have white eyes in the centre.

Beck was not the first to criticise the *Chronicle*'s and the Horticultural Society's lack of interest in florists' flowers. It had been done much more vehemently by George Glenny (1793–1874), who even set up his own society to promote florists' flowers,[34] and had an ongoing feud with John Lindley (1799–1865), 'the eminent Botanist' referred to by Beck. Beck was more reasonable, but felt strongly enough about the lack of attention received by florists and their flowers to set up his own magazine, *The Florist*, to promote their interests.

By November 1847 the *Chronicle*[35] decided to go into more detail on pelargoniums and their advance, although still rather grudgingly. It said it was surprising that considering the developments in the years between 1827 and 1841, little had changed since. This was felt to be because growers had continued to use the same varieties for hybridisation and had reached the limit of what was possible, although some were trying new lines of breeding to produce another type, known as 'Fancies'. Mr Beck was cited as being the chief grower of the best varieties known at the time. The *Chronicle* then went on to reproduce the advice of George Gordon,[36] a grower who was familiar with the work of Robert Sweet. He suggested that rather than going back to the species to try new hybridisation, it would be better to use the old hybrids and cross them again with the species. Gordon thought varieties known as Queen Victoria[37] and Anais (described as fancy kinds) could be crossed with *fulgidum, ignescens* and *sanguineum*,[38] and he went on to suggest that the best new sorts to try and create might be yellow flowers, based on the Cape species grown at Colvill's in Sweet's time. He then trawls through many of Sweet's crosses, suggesting further hybridisation, and adding that there is no reason why double flowers should not eventually be produced. Gordon suggests some crosses that might be attempted with the 'common scarlet', which could be taken to refer exclusively to *inquinans*, but generally by then was considered to be a hybrid between *inquinans* and *zonale*.

Despite Beck's criticism of John Lindley, Lindley gave Beck's *Treatise* a good reception. He called it 'a beautiful and very useful pamphlet', informing the readers that it was 'the forerunner of a monthly floricultural work, also under the superintendence of Mr Beck'. He added:

Although we find that our humble remarks and gentle admonition have been in some measure misunderstood, we cannot regret that circumstance if the result should really be the establishment of a florists' periodical in which intelligence and fair dealing shall take the place of that 'prejudice, jealousy, and envy which once marked the delightful pursuit in question', as Mr Beck gently intimates, but which we, who care little for mincing matters, say rendered it disreputable, if not disgusting. Mr Beck is the very man to give floriculture a good tone, and to make it a pursuit for gentlemen; and we wish him all possible success. The undertaking could not be in better hands.[39]

This gives some insight into the reason why florists were excluded from the Horticultural Society's shows. It was considered that they had become too commercially minded and were simply there to make money.

Edward Beck's *Florist* was a great success. Its backers were other florists and nurserymen, among them Charles Turner (1818–85) of the Royal Nurseries, Slough, who was also an expert florist and keen pelargonium grower. Beck used the magazine to expand his views on pelargoniums and lay down rules for new seedlings. He illustrated what *not* to look for as well, showing a plant called Harlequin with ragged narrow ruffled petals.[40] He said it had no merit as a florists' flower, yet had won a medal at the Regent's Park exhibition and attracted the attention of the Queen. He thought its appearance was the result of too much inbreeding, and was conducting more experiments to see what further results he would get. Perhaps this was an opportunity for him to veer away from the strict guidelines of the florists and try something new. Interestingly, Harlequin resembles a much later type of pelargonium, known as the Stellar, which was introduced from Australia in the 1960s. Beck was further ahead of his time than he realised.

In the *Florist* Beck set out his own criteria for the pelargonium as a florists' flower.[41] It should have broad petals, be a compact, bushy plant, and the stalk should have a truss of at least four flowers, preferably five. The flowers should be 2 inches in diameter and be composed of five petals, two upper ones and three lower, all forming a circle. The flowers should be free from curl or crumple, should be stout and velvety in texture, with the appearance of being 'stamped out' (an interesting industrial metaphor for an industrial age), and with the whole green calyx showing. The colour should be pure and clear, free of veins, with a spot at the base, extending upwards and terminating in a margined flower with a distinct edge. In the upper petals the shading should be of great delicacy, with no watery margin. Beck commented that illustrations did not do the flowers justice, as they could not show the velvety texture or the glowing colours. He thought novelty of colour was one of the most important features,

16. Edward Beck's 'Harlequin' and two other similar pelargoniums, which appear to be early 'Stellar' types. *(Florist, 1848/RHS Lindley Library)*

17. George W. Hoyle (*c.* 1801–72) of Reading, an early hybridiser of the pelargonium as a florists' flower. *(Carte de Visite/RHS Lindley Library)*

whereas another influential grower, George W. Hoyle (*c.* 1801–72) of Reading, felt abundance of flower was more important. Hoyle was, however, remembered in later years especially for working towards the scarlet Show pelargonium.[42] Beck was so keen to improve the reputation of seedling raisers that he proposed a society especially for them, possibly in Exeter, as the journey was easy by train.

In the late 1840s, although the florists were keenly developing their flowers, and the nurserymen were also developing the new 'Fancy' pelargoniums, some people, probably a minority, were still growing the Cape varieties. A correspondent to the *Florist* from East Anglia, in 1849, suggested that florists should turn their attention to improving *echinatum*, as he remembered once seeing a purple one, which seemed to have disappeared. At the Horticultural Society exhibition that year there was even a class for Cape varieties, in which several species and early hybrids were shown, namely *echinatum*, *ardens*, *flexuosum* (a *fulgidum* cross), *quinquevulnera* (properly known as *quinquevulnereum*, probably a *bicolor* hybrid) and *bipinnatifidum* (a derivative of *quinquevulnereum*).

The 'Fancy' pelargoniums had been described by the *Gardeners' Chronicle* as being more 'masculine', by which they seemed to mean that they were plainer and less 'frilled'. It did not tie up with anyone else's description. In 1849 the *Florist* described them as being 'dwarf and delicate in habit and most profuse bloomers, they form, when well grown, perfect nosegays in themselves'. The best raisers were Mr Ambrose and Mr Gaines of Battersea. The *Florist* was happy for the two types of pelargonium (the older florists' flower was by now being termed the 'Show' pelargonium) to exist side by side.

Beck's determination to improve seedlings led to a seedling exhibition held at Upton Park in June 1849.[43] There were nine competitors and each voted on the others' plants. Although Beck won fourth prize (of £1 10s[44]) with 'Aurora's Beam', he was not happy as he said it was 'a large stout flower, calling for no particular notice' and there had not been as much 'interchange of opinion' as he had hoped.[45] There was more interchange as time went on, however. Comments in 1850 included suggestions that there should be independent judges and better prizes. A paper was read out by Mr Sowerby at the Royal Botanic Society, which gives some insight into what knowledge hybridisers had about genetics. Mr Sowerby said that pelargonium fanciers were trying to produce two top petals distinct from the three lower ones. However, sometimes a sport appeared with five equal petals and the same colour and he thought the nectar tube sometimes disappeared. He believed that cultivation might make one species run into another, or destroy a generic characteristic:

> But I do not think this is exactly the case; for although he may apparently reduce a Cape pelargonium to a European geranium in the eye of the botanist, or partly so, still he would have a more truly beautiful flower if he could obtain a full truss of large rose-coloured or pink flowers.

He seems to be introducing a revolutionary concept in the eyes of the florists, but is actually foretelling what will become the ideal in years to come. He recommended that a trial be made of the seed from such sporting flowers.

By the 1850s, therefore, there is a clear distinction between the original florists' or Show pelargonium, on the one hand, and the Fancy pelargonium on the other. An accurate explanation of the terminology does not appear until ten years later, in the *Floral Magazine* of 1862. This magazine had been started the previous year by Thomas Moore (1821–87) of the Chelsea Physic Garden, and the editorship was taken over in 1862 by the Revd H.H. D'Ombrain (1818–1905), who later became better known as a rose grower. D'Ombrain was commenting on the illustration of what he termed a 'hybrid greenhouse geranium', and began to reminisce about 'everybody's flower', which could be found in the cottage window, a lonely garret and even within prison walls:

> We can well remember the time when the Revd Mr Garth of Farnham, and Mr Foster of Clewer Manor, first started in the race for public favour and nothing was heard of but Garth's 'Sylph' and Foster's 'Joan of Arc'. Then there was only one class, florists' geraniums. Some years after, Fancies were introduced, at first ill-shaped and faint in colour, now perfectly symmetrical and of beautiful tints. A variety with spots on each petal was the *avant-courier* of what one now calls Spotted pelargoniums, while some years ago M. Chariviere of Rue de la Rochette, Paris, has led the way in bizarre and spotted varieties, known as French pelargoniums.[46]

The early florists' pelargoniums of the 1840s were based on the hybrids known to Sweet, and from these were eventually produced perfectly round flowers. This 'new' type became known as the Fancy pelargonium, while the early ones, which became more and more elaborate, continued to be known as Florists' or Show pelargoniums. The aim had been not only to broaden and flatten the petals into a circle, but also to eliminate veining or feathering to produce a solid colour. The markings on the top petals had gradually been enlarged so as to create a solid colour petal with a

18. A French, or 'Spotted' Pelargonium, 'La Belle Alliance', put out by Henderson's nursery in 1857. *(Shirley Hibberd,* The Floral World, *April 1858/Author's Collection)*

distinct edge. The lower petals, in comparison, were generally paler and plain-coloured, though a white eye was encouraged. The next step was to emphasise the markings on the lower petals to create a spot, so that later Fancy sorts appear with two large blotches on the top and smaller spots on the lower petals. From these emerged the spotted sorts with a spot or blotch on each petal. The so-called 'bizarre', spotted or French sorts were a further departure. Clearly, by the mid-1850s the magic of hybridising had only just begun to be exploited and the true scope of the pelargonium was starting to be realised at last.

By the middle of the century it seemed that the Geraniaceae were due for another review by botanists. William Henry Harvey (1811–66), an Irishman who was colonial treasurer at the Cape from 1835 to 1842, must have seen a study of the plants as a way of passing his leisure hours, and he produced *Flora Capensis* with O.W. Sonder in 1860. The pelargoniums were divided again into fifteen sections, based on both leaf and flower structure as well as the habit of the plant, and 163 species were listed.

6

The Age of Bedding

The best known pelargoniums in modern times are the bedding pelargoniums, often called geraniums, that are grown in pots, window boxes and bedding schemes throughout the summer, and with their predominantly red flowers and zoned leaves appear to be derived from *zonale* and *inquinans*. They have become such a fixture of modern parks and gardens, and seem to be most people's idea of a typical Victorian bedding plant, that it may come as a surprise to hear that they were not the Victorians' first choice of bedding pelargonium, and that their ultimate perfection came only right at the end of the nineteenth century. Indeed, it was their success as the very brightest and most reliable of all bedding plants, the result of fifty years of selective breeding, that was to lead to their eclipse from favour at the beginning of the twentieth century and their permanent removal from many 'purist' gardeners' lists of desirable plants.

Tender or half-hardy flowers in brilliant colours were used by the Victorians as components of carefully designed flower beds and borders, providing temporary displays for one season at a time. The idea, like most ideas in gardening, started in the country houses of the wealthy, but was imitated, often unsuccessfully, by the middle classes in their more modest gardens. It was much more successful in parks and public gardens and became the mainstay of all municipal gardening, even up to modern times. The first formal 'bedding schemes' appeared in the 1840s, and gradually became more sophisticated and complicated as more plants were discovered as suitable for the formal treatment. Designers and gardeners slowly learned to carry out the planting and maintain it throughout the season. Colour theories were used to find the best combinations, and gardeners discovered how to choose the right plants that would keep to the desired size and floriferousness to prevent the schemes deteriorating. The skill and experience that created 'traditional' bedding should not be despised as it often is by modern writers and designers. When the Crystal Palace was moved to its permanent site at Sydenham, south London, in 1856, Sir Joseph Paxton was able to present bedding schemes on such a large scale, and seen by so many people, that everyone wanted to try out the ideas in their own modest gardens.

The Mystery of the Unique

In the early days of bedding, gardeners tried whatever plants they could find, as long as they had the colours they needed. The *Floricultural Cabinet* in 1837 listed the best pelargoniums for bedding as the old faithful multipurpose plants, such as Macranthon (said to have pink stripes), Daveyanum, More's Victory, Flagrans (or Lord Yarborough's Storksbill), Humei, Yeatmanianum Grandiflorum and Grandissima,[1] most of which had been well known for at least ten years and must have been considered as reliable as anything available at the time. By the 1850s more plants had been developed and at Shrubland Park, the pioneer in bedding, the main ones used were Purple Unique and Golden Chain, a variegated kind, as well as many unnamed 'scarlet geraniums'.[2] Purple Unique was classed as a 'hybrid bedding pelargonium', a class probably produced from the early hybrids derived from *cucullatum* and other species, but which had not been as highly developed as the florists' flowers. As such, they provide a link back to the plants known to Sweet. They were not, however, particularly suited to bedding.

In 1860 the Royal Horticultural Society carried out a series of trials in their gardens at Chiswick to find the best pelargoniums for different purposes, but the trials failed because of bad weather and they repeated them the following year. The differences between the original list of proposed plants in early 1860 and the actual plants reported on in October 1861 show the development of pelargoniums during that time.[3] When the original list was drawn up the organisers had asked for plants in different categories, assuming that the 'hybrid bedding pelargoniums' would be the ones most suitable for bedding. In the final results, however, forty-one varieties were recommended in the categories of Plain-leaved, Zonate and Nosegays, listed in several different colours, and even three Ivy-leaved plants were included. The poor old 'hybrid bedding' section, however, had been demoted to a 'Miscellaneous' category consisting only of Rollisson's Purple Unique, Antler and Pheasant's Foot.[4] Antler, as a name, never seems to surface again, but Pheasant's Foot rather perplexingly does, as will be seen later.

The presence of Rollisson's Purple Unique in the list sparked off a lively correspondence in the *Gardeners' Chronicle*, as few people knew which plant was being described. Presumably they knew the name Purple Unique as a bedding plant, but did not know whether this was the same one. Rollisson has already been mentioned as a nurseryman from Tooting, south London, in Sweet's time, but the *P. rollissonii* described by Sweet as having pink flowers is not the same as Rollisson's Purple Unique, which the *Gardeners' Chronicle*, on 19 October 1861, described as having bold oak leaves and deep purple flowers. It does not describe, either, the plant called Unique which was grown in Henderson's Nursery in 1843, mentioned in the previous chapter. There are two noticeably different plants sold today by nurseries as Rollisson's Unique and Purple Unique. Rollisson's Unique has deep purple flowers with cerise veining and dark green oak-shaped leaves with a slight scent, and it tends to grow tall and upright, needing some support. Purple Unique is more branching and woody. Its flowers are a lilac-purple with a dark purple blotch and less veining. Its leaves are more rounded, lighter green and strongly cedar-scented. Where the difficulty comes is in their origin. The *Gardeners' Chronicle* stated that the plant they were referring to was believed to be a sport from 'the old Lilac Unique' grown at Chiswick. A sport is produced when a plant sends out a stem or flower that is markedly different from the parent plant. It can be removed and rooted as a separate plant, which will retain the new character-istics, and is one way of producing new pelargoniums. The problem with this information is that no one, even in 1861, could positively identify 'the old Lilac Unique'.

John Salter (1798–1874) of the Versailles Nursery, Hammer-smith, stated in the *Chronicle*[5] that he had always supposed that

Rollisson's Unique

(Unique pelargonium)

A beautifully marked magenta-purple flower, in the nineteenth century confused with Purple Unique. It was named after the nurseryman William Rollisson of Tooting, south London, who is believed to have produced it, although whether from a seedling or a sport has never been confirmed.

'Rollisson's Unique'. *(The Garden, 24 November 1877/RHS Lindley Library)*

Purple Unique (i.e. Rollisson's Purple Unique) was understood to be a cross obtained by Rollisson from *quercifolium* and 'another Cape variety'. He could 'bear testimony to its sportive character'. He went on to say that at Chiswick there were four sports from Rollisson's Unique: Lilac, *Conspicuum*, *Coccineum* and Rose d'Amour. This goes directly against what had previously been stated, as it implies that Rollisson's plant was a deliberately produced seedling and that Lilac Unique came from it, rather than being the original plant referred to as 'the old Lilac Unique'. Salter went on to say that in 1861 *coccineum* had produced flowers of rose, red and lilac on the same truss, and on other trusses were flowers half-red and half-lilac.

An 'old Purple Unique' had been referred to back in 1856 by Donald Beaton (1802–63) in the *Cottage Gardener* when talking about the White Unique.[6] He does not mention Rollisson, but refers to 'the old Purple Unique' as if it were a well-known plant.[7] It would seem that 'the old Lilac Unique' may be the same as Beaton's 'old Purple Unique', as the colours purple and lilac could conceivably be confused, and also there is no plant known today as Lilac Unique, which suggests that the name Purple Unique became more frequently used than Lilac Unique, and then Rollisson's Purple Unique simply became known as Rollisson's Unique. There is nothing in what Beaton says to imply that Purple or Lilac Unique could not have been a sport from Rollisson's Unique. The *Gardeners' Chronicle* description certainly sounds more like the plant known today as Rollisson's Unique. One other mention by Beaton, however, may help to clarify. In 1852 he had referred to new plants at the Horticultural Society's garden at Chiswick. There he saw 'a Lilac Unique', which he thought would be a good acquisition, but he said that there was not the slightest difference, except for the flower, between it and 'the old Unique'. What better proof than that the Lilac Unique was a sport from the old Unique, which was purple?

Some further information came from a correspondent to the *Chronicle* called PAW,[8] who stated that the Lilac Unique was first sent out from Ivery's nursery at Peckham, having been obtained as a sport from Rollisson's Unique growing at Peckham Rye. He surmised that one of the parents was Daveyanum, but he also asserted that there were two versions of Rollisson's Unique in existence, one stronger than the other, which partly compounds the problem but perhaps helps to explain the confusion. He then added that there were also two kinds of Scarlet Unique in existence, one an oak-leaved sort called Defiance and another of continental origin. This was replied to by the nurseryman William Paul (1822–1905).[9] He claimed that it was he who had brought Scarlet Unique back from M. Boucharlat's Nursery in Lyons, France, many years before, and had named it. However, he also said that Mr Gaines of Battersea had obtained or raised another plant himself, which he also named Scarlet Unique. This plant is completely different from another 'Unique' called Scarlet Pet, which some books give as a synonym for More's Victory or *moreanum*, thought by Sweet to have been raised in 1823.[10]

As to the other sports mentioned by Salter, *conspicuum* was rose crimson. The name appears in the 1880s in *Cannell's Floral Guide*, described as bright magenta. By 1910 the name had changed to Conspicua. *Coccineum* does not seem to appear again as a Unique, although the name had been used in the late eighteenth century for a Zonal hybrid with crimson flowers.[11] Coccinea was also used later for both an ivy-leaved plant and a scented-leaf plant, known also as Mrs Taylor.[12] Rose D'Amour, which was rose pink, was said to be a sport from *coccineum* and the name was used for a Zonal in 1862, but not a Unique. As time went by, more complications arose through inexact naming by nurseries. In the 1880s *Cannell's Floral Guide* listed eight varieties under the heading 'Hybrids from the Old Unique', including Rollisson's Unique (rich violet crimson) and Old Unique (deep lilac). This should not be taken too literally; it also included Crimson Unique and Scarlet Unique, which were never thought to be hybrids from 'the old Unique'. At that stage there were so many subdivisions in the pelargonium listings that it was just a convenient way of putting anything called a Unique into one category.

In 1877 an illustration of Rollisson's Unique actually appeared in *The Garden*,[13] along with the information that the plant arose as a seedling in Rollisson's nursery, probably from a plant known as Gloryanum. The apparently new information was probably based on a remark made the year before in the *Chronicle* by the correspondent FJH, who said that the lilac sport was known twenty-five years before as *glorianum*, or Lilac Unique.[14] FJH was Frances Jane Hope (d. 1880) of Wardie Lodge, Edinburgh, a frequent contributor to gardening magazines. However, her information was probably wrong. The *glorianum* described by Sweet had been raised at Dennis's nursery and was also known as the Queen of Portugal's Storksbill. Since it had red flowers it could not possibly have been Lilac Unique.

All this speculation about 'the old Unique' and its hybrids may seem rather pointless and something of a diversion from the story being told. However, the so-called 'Uniques' are one of the best links back to the plants of the eighteenth century and everything possible should be done to preserve them and to try to discover their origins. As a group, they hold together rather loosely: not all are called Uniques and some plants with Unique as part of their name are not part of the group. They are shrubby, often with scented leaves, although not always pleasantly scented, but it is their vivid flowers that help to explain what the eighteenth-century growers were so captivated by.

White Unique, which was mentioned above in connection with Donald Beaton, is another of uncertain origin. In 1856 Beaton said that 'the most scientific cross-breeder' of the time (unnamed) had succeeded in obtaining a cross between the White Unique and the old Purple Unique, which he had set his heart on many years before, when he had been the only gardener who possessed White Unique. He claimed to have received the plant from someone's cottage window and given it the name himself. When he could not get it to seed he sent it to Hendersons to see if they would have more success. He then referred to the suggestions he had had for breeding from Shrubland Pet, 'which is of the same strain'. If he had obtained White Unique from someone's window sill, how would he know Shrubland Pet was of the same strain, unless he knew the breeding of White Unique? Or did he simply assume so because of their similar appearance? Beaton was head gardener at Shrubland Park and had probably bred Shrubland Pet himself, or at least named it.

Another Unique mentioned in the 1860s was Judd's Rose Unique, grown by Earl Spencer's gardener, Daniel Judd (d. 1884), and said to be a hybrid between Unique (which one?) and 'an old cut-leaved sort' called Bagshot Park seedling.[15] This plant does not seem to have survived. Then there was Cerise Unique, from Fraser and Kinghorn, and Golden Cerise Unique, grown by several nurseries, and having a golden leaf with a red zone. These, however, are probably not part of the recognised 'Unique' class, which do not normally have zoned or coloured leaves. Scarlet Unique's origin is described above by William Paul. Unique Aurora, or

Aurora's Unique, is sometimes identified with *ignescens*. It has characteristic soft greyish leaves and red and black flowers. Although the Uniques turned out to be unsuitable for bedding, they play an important part in the pelargonium story, and continue to be grown and hybridised, forming a specialist group in the genus.

'Beauties Run Wild'

If the 'hybrid bedding pelargoniums' were no use for bedding, something else had to be found to do the job, and nurserymen turned to other members of the family which had previously been thought of as beyond consideration. An article in the *Floricultural Cabinet* in 1847[16] entitled 'Culture of Scarlet Pelargoniums', by 'a practitioner', furthered the prevailing view that there was 'a grossness of habit' in such varieties that rendered them 'unsuited for small collections' and he thought some method should be employed to check 'such exhuberence' and induce a more compact and bushy habit. This exuberance, however, was just what was needed to survive in the conditions that Uniques could not endure. There is never any explanation as to exactly which plants are being referred to as 'scarlet pelargoniums'. Because the plants themselves are generally referred to as being both scarlet and Zonate (or with a horseshoe), it must be presumed that the flower is red and the leaves are zoned. This would suggest that from an earlier date, probably the time of Sweet and Andrews, *inquinans* and *Zonale* had been crossed to create the familiar hybrid, but as usual with pelargoniums much is left unsaid because it is presumed to be common knowledge.[17]

'Scarlet geraniums' could be very spectacular. Mr Smith, a nurseryman from Dalston, east London, had exhibited a plant he called Emperor at the London Horticultural Meeting with 134 blooms on a single head, each blossom an inch across of a superb scarlet colour, resembling a 'moderate-sized hydrangea'. It was said to merit a place in every greenhouse, flower garden or flower room.[18] Generally though, the plant was not very loved. Shirley Hibberd described it as 'a somewhat ugly thing, with coarse leaves that are distinctly zoned, and flowers that are distinguished by the narrowness of their petals, so that they are properly, though perhaps disrespectfully, spoken of as "windmills"'.[19] He admits the plants should be called pelargoniums and that they can be divided into two classes, *P. speciosum*, which is what he calls the florists' flowers, and the 'Zonals' or 'scarlet geraniums'. Although he refers to narrowness of petals, he actually depicts a round-petalled *inquinans*-type flower.

One of the earliest 'scarlet geraniums' that was successfully used for bedding was 'General Tom Thumb', which eventually achieved legendary status. It was so well known in its day that the magazines did not think it necessary to illustrate it. However, its story was told in the *Gardeners' Chronicle* in 1866, long after its reign as the best bedding plant of its time was over. According to W.P. Ayres of Nottingham,[20] it was raised at the seat of R. Piggott Esq, Dullington House, near Newmarket, by the gardener Mr B. Willson in about 1842. It was one of a batch of seedlings raised from 'old Frogmore Scarlet' grown in a basket edged with a white Ivy-leaved variety. It seemed to take its prostrate character and smooth leaves from the edging plant. The plan was to put it in a rock garden, but the young son of the family begged for the plant to put in his nursery window and it was given to him, whereupon it was forgotten about and left to die. When it was thrown on to the dustheap the gardener caught sight of it, rescued it and nursed it back to health. It became the starting point of thousands, or perhaps millions, of plants raised later. When Mr Willson sent one to the nurseryman W.P. Ayres at Blackheath, the plant was introduced to London and it was shown at Chiswick and other London shows. A few hundred were passed on to the nurseryman Philip Conway, of the Earl's Court Nursery, Brompton

Road, who distributed it. The first time Mr Conway saw it was in August at Blackheath, where upwards of a thousand were planted out (they didn't do anything by halves with their bedding schemes) and it was 'a blaze of bloom never surpassed to the present day'.

Ayres had intended to call the plant something descriptive, like Lucidum, Prostratum or Pumilum, but when he bent down to look at it more closely a card fell out of his pocket, advertising the dwarf then exhibiting at the Egyptian Hall, Piccadilly, called General Tom Thumb. So it was named! The plant was so successful that many others were passed off under its name. The genuine plant was a green-leaved scarlet bedder with a smooth, yellowish papery leaf. In 1846 W.P. Ayres wrote to the *Gardeners' Chronicle* saying that an advertisement for 100 pelargonium seeds saved from General Tom Thumb for *2s 6d* could not be genuine as the variety was a hybrid and did not set seed, 'so I have very little faith in the seed offered by Mr Waite who no doubt has been made the dupe of some designing knave'.[21]

Tom Thumb was popular for bedding because of its bright red colour and its compact, prostrate nature. It must be remembered that the species *zonale* and *inquinans* were both tall, shrubby plants, possibly growing over a metre high in the wild. These were not conveniently sized garden plants but had to be tamed. Anything called a dwarf or a compact variety at the time was only dwarf or compact in relation to these primitive hybrids. They were by no means dwarf or compact by modern standards. Various methods were tried to keep them in check. In 1849 Mr A. Kendall, a florist of Queen Elizabeth's Walk, Stoke Newington, explained how to bed them out in pots to prevent them becoming 'beauties run wild'.[22] By the late 1850s more attention was being paid to bedding pelargoniums and it was recognised that they would have to be classified into different groups, and that there was merit in using colours other than red. In the commentary to an illustration of the Zonal Princess of Prussia, *Henderson's Illustrated Bouquet* said of the group generally, 'their easy culture and gorgeous effect, are properties which render them invaluable in modern gardens'. However, 'an increasingly cultivated taste in relation to the true harmony of colours has of late caused a demand for an accession of permanent intermediate or secondary colours to relieve the monotonous effect of the large masses of scarlet and red, which for a considerable period predominated almost to the exclusion of any relief tints.'[23] They said of Princess of Prussia itself, 'Its prolificacy of bloom, its brilliant colour, and the globular outline of its flower heads, distinguish it from all existing varieties.' Each truss had fifty or sixty blossoms. The division into groups was suggested to be:

(1) Zonale, or horseshoe-leaved, and plain-leaved. This included Cerise Unique, and so-called dwarf varieties such as Attraction and Tom Thumb;

(2) Compactum section of *P. zonale*, of which Princess of Prussia was the only example; and

(3) Nosegay section, or varieties from *P. fothergillii*. These were further divided into two groups, the Carmine-crimson and Lake varieties, and the White ones.

These Nosegay pelargoniums are not known today and modern writers and nurseries give little explanation of them. It seems from the descriptions in *Henderson's Bouquet* that they differed from the other Zonals because of their huge heads of flowers with long narrow petals. Remember, the florists had been trying to breed out the long narrow petals from their pelargoniums for twenty years, but here they were used to advantage. *Henderson's* gives the names of the best Nosegays as Stella, Ossian, Cybister and Nosegay Queen, saying that they were derived from *P. fothergillii* of Sweet and *P. crenatum* of Andrews. Sweet's *fothergillii* was described as having scarlet single flowers and was said to be 'an old inhabitant of our greenhouses'. This clearly relates back to Dr Fothergill's plant listed in 1780, which must have been spectacular to have been such a survivor, but seems unlikely ever to be identified more precisely. Andrews's *crenatum* was also known as 'Bath Scarlet', which implies its colour, and was a seedling either directly from *zonale* or an early *zonale* hybrid, known as *hybridum*.

But were the parents of the Nosegays really red? Donald Beaton referred to them definitively in 1856 in the *Cottage Gardener* when describing the plants at Shrubland Park:

Nosegay Geraniums are estimated at their true value by Lady Middleton, who prefers them to the compact-trussed kinds and circular flowers for brilliancy of tints when the plants are shaken by the wind. They have the old original *fothergillii*, or pink nosegay, alias Purple Nosegay; a plainer pink kind very near it, and not so good; a Lilac Nosegay;[24] Frewer's Nosegay, a strong red or dark red kind; Mrs Vernon ditto, best light red. These two Nosegays blend well in shading; and Red Nosegay, a dwarf, dark red kind, and some others which are going under proof. To be a Nosegay, or of the same section as *fothergillii*, the flower must be labiate, as it were, or gaping, the two back petals should stand up straight, and the three front ones hang down, leaving wide spaces on each side between the upper and lower sets of petals – the reverse of a florists' flower. As soon as, by crossing, the two sets of petals come close together, the character of the section is lost.[25]

Beaton was considered the expert on Nosegays and what he says must therefore be listened to, but he seems to be saying that the original *fothergillii* was pink. This would make sense because one of the advantages of Nosegays over Zonals was their greater range of colour, as well as their larger flowers. So were Sweet and Andrews mistaken in their identification?

Stella[26] appears to be to Nosegays what General Tom Thumb was to Zonals. It was grown by Donald Beaton himself. Beaton had been head gardener at Shrubland Park, but by the 1850s was editor of 'The Flower Garden' section of the *Cottage Gardener*. He had been born in Scotland, the son of a cattle dealer, and had originally intended to go into the Church. His mother tongue was Gaelic and he had had to learn English as a foreign language when in his teens. When his father faced financial ruin due to falling cattle prices after the Napoleonic Wars, he was sent to be a tutor at the house of Lord Lovat and eventually found his niche as an apprentice gardener. He then spent his spare time and holidays visiting as many gardens as he could, meeting Sweet and visiting Colt Hoare's collection, which may have influenced him in taking a special interest in pelargoniums. Beaton retired to Surbiton in Surrey and established an 'experimental garden' to try out new varieties. He suffered a burst blood vessel in his brain in 1863, which impaired his memory, and died later that year.[27]

H.H. D'Ombrain gave his views on Nosegays in the *Floral Magazine* of 1865, when describing a new variety, Duchess of Sutherland:[28]

We have for a long time maintained the superiority of the bedding pelargoniums known as Zonal, to those which have claimed the designation of Nosegay, but as the general taste of the horticultural public seems to be inclined towards this latter section, we have selected one of the most beautiful of the novelties that are coming out next season.

He describes the plants as having petals more pointed and narrow, with a habit of generally dying away at the centre of the truss, leaving a blackened space, which detracts greatly from the beauty of the bed when viewed closely; but there were colours that could not be found in Zonals. He referred to Cybister and Stella, and

20. *Ciconium crenatum*, the Scolloped-leaved Ciconium (later renamed Pelargonium), from Sweet, plate 345 (1827). This was one version of *P. fothergillii*, which was later used to hybridise Nosegay pelargoniums. *(Author's Collection)*

then said that Duchess of Sutherland had been raised by Mr Fleming for the Dowager Duchess of that name at Cliveden. It was crimson-cerise with a very large truss. It would appear from the illustration that the foliage was more like that of a *cucullatum* type than a Zonal, and if there had been some hybridising with *cucullatum*, that would explain the richer colours of Nosegays.

Henderson's Illustrated Bouquet in 1859–61 went on to explain the origins of the other types of bedding pelargoniums, saying that improvements had only been made in the last twenty years (i.e. since the early 1840s).[29] However, they did comment that this was said in the absence of any definitive data in respect of the sources from whence many of the first species derived. The dwarf varieties of the time, with thin or medium trusses of brilliant scarlet and white centres, could be traced back to *P. bentinckianum* of Sweet (said to be known as Cape Scarlet and Bath Scarlet[30]) and to *P. fulgens*[31] of Sweet (known as Basilisk). Examples of plants of the time were Wellington Hero and Adonis. Further, *Henderson's* asserted that from another hybrid, Sweet's *glabrifolium*, came the slender branching habit and glabrous stems that produced Brilliant.

The periodical then explained that 'exhuberant growing Scarlets with large compact hemispherical trusses (useful for conservatory work and pillar growth)' went back to *P. inquinans* and *P. crenatum mollifoliatum*, both of Andrews. The rose-coloured bedding varieties went back to *P. cerinum* of Sweet, examples of which were Princess Royal and Christine. Where all this information came from, who knows? It could have been pure speculation by Mr Henderson going through copies of Sweet and Andrews that happened to be about in the nursery and comparing the hybrids of the day with the illustrations, or it could have been hearsay handed down by nurserymen and gardeners, or more likely a mixture of the two. Shirley Hibberd gives the information that the pink-flowered, bluish-leaved Christine was raised by Francis

21. Francis Rodney Kinghorn (1813–87) of the Sheen Nursery, Richmond, who was the raiser of Flower of the Spring and many of the early coloured-leaved plants. *(Carte de Visite/RHS Lindley Library)*

Rodney Kinghorn (1813–87), of the Sheen Nursery, Richmond,[32] in 1852 from Ingram's Princess Royal and a pink Nosegay. It eventually outran Tom Thumb in popularity. Rose Queen, sent out by Kinghorn in 1855, was another seedling from the same batch as Christine.

The bedding system reigned over the greatest private gardens with vast staffs to plant beds and containers, and maintain them in perfect condition. By the late 1850s the wealthy were probably beginning to tire of dazzling primary colours assaulting their senses, although they had loved it when it was new. The middle classes found it difficult to imitate in their more modest gardens but it did not stop them trying, and nurseries were happy to send out pelargoniums by the thousand every summer until the end of the century. Nurseries had vast acres under glass, depicted in their catalogues to show their expertise. Books on amateur gardening gave diagrams that could be tried out at home by anyone, with suggestions of plants to use, although ordinary gardeners' skills could never match those of the professionals. Donald Beaton developed the art of 'shading', which meant not only using subtle shades of the same colour (for which the pelargonium was eminently suited now so many varieties were available), but grading the plants carefully so that the height of different sections gradually changed to provide more interest from various angles, while always maintaining symmetry over the complete display.

Some of the most dramatic effects of bedding with pelargoniums can be seen in the paintings of E. Adveno Brooke, collected in his book *The Gardens of England*. Several gardens, such as Shrubland Park, Bowood House and Harewood, show exactly the same bright scarlet, zone-leaved pelargonium being grown in stone vases and in beds. Unfortunately the accompanying descriptions do not give details of which variety it is. Perhaps Mr Brooke did not realise the significance of providing such details, or perhaps he could only paint one sort. The plants are noticeably tall, particularly the flower stems, compared with modern plants, with small flower heads compared with the larger trusses that were depicted in later nursery catalogues and magazines. There is a detailed description, however, of the bedding schemes laid out at Shrubland, which also appeared in the *Gardeners' Chronicle*[33] and the *Cottage Gardener*.[34] Some of the named pelargoniums were Tom Thumb, Punch, Cerise Unique, Purple Unique and Golden Chain.

22. Opposite: Diagram for a 'panel garden' creating a 'harmony in red' or a 'harmony in blue'.

Red option: 1. Stella (crimson), 2. blue Lobelia and Golden Banner (gold-leaved), 3. Attraction (dwarf scarlet), 4. same as 1, 5. Christine (rose pink), 6. Amaranthus, edged with Centaurea, 7. Coleus, edged with yellow Calceolaria, 8. same as 3, edged with blue Lobelia, 9. Rose Queen (pale pink), 10. Avalanche (white leaves and flowers). Blue option: 1. purple Petunia or blue Verbena, edged with Cerastium, 2. dwarf scarlet Pelargonium edged with blue Lobelia, 3. Sunset (tricolour-leaved) edged with blue Lobelia, 4. and 5. in centre of each a dot of Thomas Moore (brilliant scarlet), the rest filled with blue Lobelia and edged with Cerastium, 6. Flower of the Spring and blue Lobelia, edged with Elegant (Ivy-leaved), 7. dwarf scarlet Pelargonium edged with blue Lobelia, 8. Lobelia Indigo Blue, edged with Flower of the Spring, 9. Lilac Banner (lilac) or Amy Hogg (pink), 10. H.W. Longfellow (dwarf salmon) or Harkaway (orange-scarlet), edged with Cerastium. *(Shirley Hibberd,* The Amateur's Flower Garden, *1871/Author's Collection)*

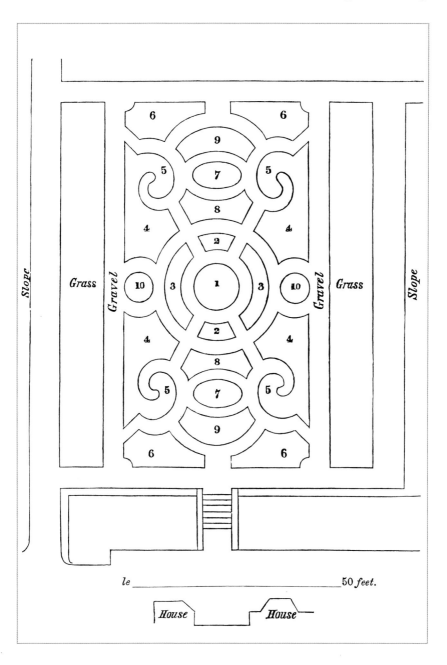

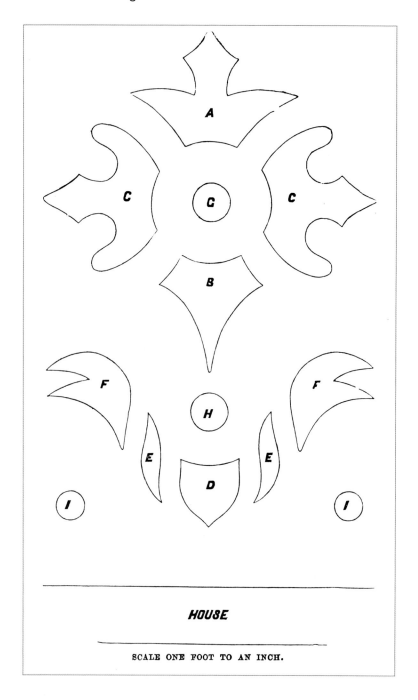

HOUSE

SCALE ONE FOOT TO AN INCH.

Above left: 1. Mary Delany's 'paper mosaic' of *Pelargonium fulgidum* made in 1775 at Bulstrode. *(Copyright © the Trustees of the British Museum)*
Below left: 2. *Pelargonium caffrum*, with its spectacular flowers and leaves. *(Geraniaceae Group Slide Library)*
Above right: 3. *Pelargonium oblongatum*, which was possibly used to try to create yellow-flowered hybrids. *(Geraniaceae Group Slide Library)*
Below right: 4. *Pelargonium triste*, once called the 'painted storksbill' for its striped flowers. *(Geraniaceae Group Slide Library)*

5. Bowood House by E. Adveno Brooke, from *The Gardens of England*, c. 1856. Scarlet-flowered Zonal pelargoniums are used in urns and as

Above left: 6. *P.* x *rubescens*, The Countess of Liverpool's Storksbill, from Sweet, *Geraniaceae*, plate 30 (1820), named after the wife of the Earl of Liverpool, owner of one of the most extensive collections of pelargoniums in the 1820s. *(Author's Collection)*

Above right: 7. *P. daveyanum*, Davey's Storksbill, from Sweet's *Geraniaceae*, plate 32 (1820). This was one of the most vibrant and beautiful of the early hybrids, named after the nurseryman Thomas Davey, and it was still recommended as a garden plant in the 1830s. *(Author's Collection)*

Right: 8. *P.* x *involucratum*, the Large-bracted Storksbill, raised by Mr Smith, gardener to the Earl of Liverpool, and used for further hybridising. *(Sweet, Geraniaceae, plate 33, 1820/ Author's Collection)*

9. Beaton's 'Indian Yellow' Pelargonium. Donald Beaton attempted to produce a yellow flower, but the plant was thought to be one of the best bedding varieties, even if the colour was not particularly out of the ordinary. *(Florist, 1865/RHS Lindley Library)*

10. Coloured-leaved Zonals (top to bottom): Aurora Borealis, Howarth Ashton, Peter Grieve, Miss Burdett Coutts. *(Shirley Hibberd,* The Amateur's Flower Garden*, 1877/Museum of Garden History)*

11. *Young Lady in a Conservatory* by Jane Maria Bowkett (1839–91). The collection of pelargoniums on the bench are typical of the varied hybrids of the mid-nineteenth century, with tall stems and delicate flowers. *(Roy Miles Fine Paintings/The Bridgeman Art Library)*

12. Duchess of Sutherland, a Nosegay pelargonium, with the characteristic upright top petals and rich pink colour. *(Floral Magazine, 1865/RHS Lindley Library)*

13. French or spotted pelargoniums of the mid-nineteenth century, two of which show an extra petal, a phenomenon that sometimes occurs in a hybrid, then disappears in the next generation. Top row, left to right: Hortense Parent, Comte de Hainaut, L. Nootens; bottom row, left to right: Madame Tasson, Garibaldi, Maria Massinon. (Unidentified French or Belgian publication) *(Author's Collection)*

14. *Pelargonium zonale* (centre) and hybrids, one with a silver-edged leaf, the other a bronze leaf. *(Nineteenth-century coloured plate/Author's Collection)*

15. Fancy, Show and Decorative pelargoniums, chromolithograph from John Wright's *Flower Grower's Guide*, *c.* 1890. Clockwise from the top: Queen of the Hellenes (Fancy), Lady Curzon (Fancy), Margherite (Show), Joe (Show), Edward Perkins (Decorative), Mr Coombes (Decorative). *(Author's Collection)*

The Geranium Grower's Guide
1954

THE CALEDONIAN NURSERIES
(*The Geranium Specialists*)

16. Front cover of the catalogue for Derek Clifford's Caledonian Nursery in 1954. The flowers featured are: 1. Audrey, 2. Capitan Jolivet, 3. Dagata, 4. Anais Segalas, 5. Charles Gounoud, 6. E. Herbert, 7. Lady Ilchester, 8. F.V. Raspail, 9. Double Henry Jacoby, 10. H.M. Stanley, 11. Brook's Purple, 12. Emperor Nicholas, 13. Baronne A. de Rothschild, 14. Mme Roseleur, 15. Flesh Pink, 16. Rainbow, 17. Captain Flayelle, 18. Lave, 19. Commines, 20. Countess. *(Museum of Garden History)*

23. Opposite: Design for a flower bed cut out of grass. A. white Verbena edged with purple Verbena; B. Mangles' Variegated edged with blue Lobelia; C. Lion Heart (scarlet) edged with Flower of the Day; D. Crimson Unique edged with Flower of the Spring; E. Tristram Shandy (cerise); F. blue Lobelia and Cerastium; G. Duchess; H. Louisa Smith; I. vases of Ivy-leaved Pelargoniums, Gazanias and Convolvulus. *(Shirley Hibberd,* The Amateur's Flower Garden, *1871/Author's Collection)*

24. Right: An example of a display used in the Liverpool Botanic Garden in the 1860s, about 135ft long, consisting mainly of early bedding pelargoniums.

Key

1. Purple trefoil with centre of *Chamae-puce diacantha* edged with *Saxifraga longifolia*
2. Queen of Queens
3. Christine
4. Little David
5. Stella
6. *Calceolaria canariensis* and scarlet Verbena
7. Bijou
8. Cottage Maid
9. Triomphe de Paris
10. Flower of the Day
11. Trentham Rose
12. Rubens Improved
13. Stella
14. Pink Nosegay
15. Bijou
16. Cybister
17. *Calceolaria aurea* and scarlet Verbena
18. Diadem
19. Alma
20. Sydonie

21. Duchess of Sutherland
22. Diadematum
23. Vitifolia
24. *Diadematum rubescens*
25. *Addisonii*
26. *Quercifolia coccinea*
27. Golden Fleece
28. [Missing]
29. Madame Vaucher
30. Cloth of Gold
31. Chancellor
32. White Perfection
33. Eve
34. Magenta
35. Alfred
36. Rose Queen
37. Beauty of Blackheath
38. Ribbon border of four rows, as follows: *Dactylis glomerata variegata,* Tropaeolum 'Sparkler', Christine, and Stella.

(Shirley Hibberd, The Amateur's Flower Garden, *1871/Author's Collection)*

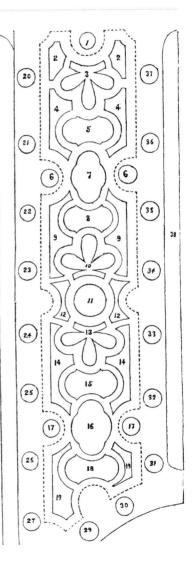

For ordinary gardeners Shirley Hibberd provided patterns to copy, with lists of plants to use. In *The Amateur's Flower Garden*[35] he first gives as an example a 'panel garden' about 50ft wide and 100ft long with flower beds divided by gravel. There were two colour schemes to choose from, first 'a harmony in red', made up with Stella (crimson), Golden Banner (golden-leaved), Attraction (dwarf scarlet), Christine (rose-pink), Rose Queen (pale pink) and Avalanche (white flowers and leaves), intertwined with blue lobelia, amaranthus, centaurea and coleus or calceolaria. The alternative was a 'harmony in blue', which although it used petunias and verbenas, as well as lobelia and cerastium, included even more varied pelargoniums, such as dwarf scarlets, coloured-leaved and variegated sorts, as well as Ivy-leaveds.

The next scheme consisted of beds cut out of lawn, which Hibberd said 'makes a poor appearance on paper, but in the fine large old-fashioned garden, where it embellishes the forefront of a lawn, it is a most effective arrangement'. The carefully cut swirls and crescents included verbenas and lobelias with many sorts of pelargoniums, several of which happened to be Hibberd's own varieties. He then reproduced some schemes from the Liverpool Botanic Gardens under the direction of Mr Tyerman. Hibberd said it showed the value of the zonate pelargonium, 'for the whole furniture consisted . . . of varieties of this class of bedding plants, with the exception of a few trivial dots of calceolaria and verbena'.

One of the most dramatic ways of using pelargoniums in a bedding scheme was in pyramid form. Hibberd described it as 'one of the grandest of embellishments, daring, distinct and desirable, if only as a change away from the monotony of flat colourings and imitations of Kidderminster carpets'. He used the pyramid several years in succession in his Stoke Newington garden, originally to use some old plants that had been trained up a wall for several years and would otherwise have been doomed to die. However, he

25. Shirley Hibberd's 'geranium pyramid', a stunning centrepiece to his garden in the 1860s. Plants several years old and 10ft high were used on a wooden framework. *(Shirley Hibberd,* Rustic Adornments for Homes of Taste, *1871/Author's Collection)*

warned that such a structure must be planned in advance, for at least three years, preferably five, and about forty-eight plants would be needed for a pyramid 15 feet in diameter. The plants should be grown in pots in a greenhouse and pruned to encourage the hard wood to develop. Then, when they are about 6 feet tall, a 'wigwam' should be built of strong poles on which to train them, in three concentric circles. They were expected to reach 10 feet or more over the summer.[36]

This elaborate construction would have shocked a correspondent to the *Florist* in 1849, who had heard of the proposal of a pelargonium in pyramidal form, 6 feet in height. He could not conceive of the idea, although to be fair he was actually talking about a single plant being trained round a pyramid-shaped framework. However, his words were strangely prophetic:

> Seriously then, how many generations, let me ask, of long-jointed, weak, weedy, succulent seedlings must be grown, before you can convert this elegant *shrub* into a creeper or semi-creeper? When you have succeeded in altering its whole character, by giving it a habit which would prevent it from standing upright without support, just conceive what an outrage on floriculture you would have perpetuated! Let any unprejudiced person grow a plant that *will* support itself – Beck's Rosy Circle for instance – by the side of one that will not, and let him decide which *is*, or, if the matter is purely conventional, which *ought to be* the habit of the plant.[37]

The habit of the plant was far more varied than the florists could have imagined, and pyramids were only one way of exhibiting them. By the 1860s the scarlet Zonals and deeply coloured Nosegays seemed ready to take the crown as the kings of plants in a Victorian garden – but flower colour was not everything. The pelargonium had another trick to play, which would raise it far above all the other bedding plants, none of which could compete when it came to the colour of the foliage.

7

Flights of Fancy

As the bedding craze developed in the second half of the nineteenth century, emphasis started to be put upon the foliage of plants rather than just the colours of the flowers. Here the pelargonium triumphed again. What other popular plant is grown for both its flowers and its foliage?

Leaves of Many Colours

The mystery of variegation was another unanswered question for the Victorians and there were various theories about how it happened. Some people thought it was a result of feeding or watering the plants in a particular way. In 1844 Henry Groom, a south London nurseryman, and one of the florists who set up the *Florist* magazine, wrote to the *Gardeners' Chronicle* about variegation:

> I have had some of my plants change on the edges of the leaves like the inclosed, giving the plant the appearance of a variegated sort. The leaves appear quite healthy, with a regular pale border, which is principally confined to the old leaves. The only thing I can suppose it to arise from is, that some time since I had the pelargoniums watered with sulphate of ammonia, which had been exposed to the air for some considerable time, and had become quite fluid, and it is possible that it might have been partially decomposed, and a free acid (sulphuric) left, which we know has the power of bleaching vegetable colours.[1]

The editor commented that it was a curious case, the leaves having a pale border about a quarter of an inch deep, 'as regularly limited as if it were really a permanent variegation'. *Henderson's Illustrated Bouquet* attributed variegation to 'some constitutional or occult tendency in the plant'.[2]

It is not certain when the first variegated pelargonium was known, though there is at least one early reference to a plant with coloured leaves. Confusingly, *Pelargonium variegatum*, described by Willdenow in 1800, was so called because of its varicoloured flowers.[3] However, at a slighter earlier date there was a *Geranium marginatum* (later renamed *P. zonale* var. *marginatum*) in existence. Cavanilles knew of it in 1785 and Willdenow in 1800. It was a tricolour-leaved plant, the green leaf having a white or yellowish edge and a dark zone, and it existed in several variations.[4]

The person who worked hardest to create the 'coloured-leaved' pelargoniums was Peter Grieve (1811–95). He was a Scottish gardener who began training with his father, the gardener at Black Adder House, near Allanton, Berwickshire.[5] He then moved several times between private and botanic gardens in Scotland, before eventually becoming employed at Culford Hall near Bury St Edmunds, Suffolk, in 1847. His employer was the Revd Edward Richard Benyon, who had been given the 500-acre estate by his uncle. The grounds had originally been laid out by Humphrey Repton in 1791. Grieve started to experiment with raising pelargonium seedlings in about 1853, and grew double-flowered petunias as well, the plants being marketed by Henderson's nursery in St John's Wood.

Grieve gave an account of his plant-breeding in *A History of Ornamental Foliaged Pelargoniums*, published in 1869.[6] He could not explain the reason for variegation, and also referred to the belief that variegation and double flowers would never be found on the same plant. However, he thought that it would be possible in time. He also distinguished between variegation, which was a

26. The parterre at Eythrope, Buckinghamshire, in about 1890, one of the Rothschild family's gardens. Pelargoniums were one of the main plants used in the bedding. *(Museum of Garden History)*

deficiency in the normal green leaf, and colouration, which, following the *Gardeners' Chronicle*, he termed a 'redundancy' or something added to the green. (This seems to be opposite to the modern meaning of redundancy.)

Grieve then went on to tell how he produced his coloured-leaved plants. He provided some history of pelargoniums, saying that in Philip Miller's *Gardeners Dictionary* a variegated Zonal pelargonium had been mentioned, which was probably the same one found in Loudon's *Hortus Britannicus* under the name 'marginatum'. He assumes that this was probably the first variegated sport known in the genus and was described in Sir Thomas More's *Flower Garden Displayed* of 1734. More said that he had brought the plant into England from Paris, it was easy to grow from cuttings in the

27. Peter Grieve
(1811–95), gardener at
Culford Hall, the breeder of
many of the most
successful coloured-
leaved plants of the 1860s.
*(Carte de Visite/RHS
Lindley Library)*

summer and had flowers of peach-blossom colour. Grieve thought
this was a rare greenhouse plant known as Miller's Variegated, but
more recently a plant known as Lee's Variegated had been grown
in British gardens. Shirley Hibberd, in his lecture in 1880,[7] said
this plant was the only variegated Zonal with bright red flowers
known in 1844. It was probably raised by Mr Bailey, gardener at
Nuneham Park, and produced from Miller's Old Variegated. Lee's
Variegated was used by F.R. Kinghorn of the Sheen Nurseries,
near Richmond, crossed with 'the old Compactum' (mentioned by

Sweet in his last volume as a hybrid produced by Captain Francis in 1828) to produce Cerise Unique and Flower of the Day in about 1847 or 1849.[8] Hibberd says this was: 'the most useful and most famous of all known variegated leaved Zonals. Mr Kinghorn to this day considers this was the greatest advance ever accomplished at one bound in work of this kind, and I thoroughly agree with him.'[9] From Flower of the Day, Kinghorn went on to produce Attraction, the first silver-leaved tricolour. It had a silvery margin and a dark zone, producing red where they met.

Several other raisers then started producing similar varieties. Mr Elphinstone produced Queen's Favourite and Mr Hally of Blackheath produced Burning Bush. This gave Grieve the idea to try something himself. He fertilised Flower of the Day with Tom Thumb (the famous General Tom Thumb, one of whose parents was supposed to have been a 'white Ivy-leaved variety') and raised Culford Beauty, followed in due course by Italia Unita, still the best silver-edged variety known in the 1860s, but now lost.

Next Grieve decided to try something similar with golden-edged varieties. At that stage there was a golden-leaved variety popular for bedding work called Golden Chain. Grieve said it was generally believed to be a sport from *inquinans* that had appeared in 1844,[10] but he thought it might be earlier as he knew that N.S. Hodson of the Botanic Garden, Bury St Edmunds, had a large plant of the variety in about 1822. He also knew that Donald Beaton had used it as a bedding plant at Shrubland Park in 1847. In 1855 Grieve fertilised blooms of an old dark-leaved variety called Cottage Maid with pollen from Golden Chain and produced two new varieties, Golden Tom Thumb and Golden Cerise Unique.

It should be pointed out here that it was common at the time to name a new plant after an older plant that it resembled, distinguishing it with another adjective. It does not necessarily mean that the plants were related. Presumably it was done as a marketing device to persuade buyers that the new plant was as

28. 'Sophia Cusack', described by Peter Grieve as having a bright-flamed scarlet zone on a broken bronze border and yellow margin, from *Ornamental-Foliaged Pelargoniums*, 1863 (reprinted by the British Pelargonium and Geranium Society, 1977, and reproduced with their permission). *(Author's Collection)*

good as the well-known one, but with some crucial difference. It should also be noted that there were in existence at this date both golden-leaved and dark-leaved sorts of pelargoniums, which really come into their own later in the century. This is a pattern constantly repeated. Whenever there is a fashion for a new type of pelargonium, it is not that the new type has just been discovered; it is usually the case that they have appeared before but were rejected as being undesirable or unsaleable. Nurserymen, like all commercial people, will only bother to grow and nurture what they think will sell. For every successful plant there are hundreds,

29. 'Princess of Wales', described by Peter Grieve as having a bright 'vandyked' zone on a yellow ground, from *Ornamental-Leaved Pelargoniums*, 1863 (reprinted by the British Pelargonium and Geranium Society, 1977, and reproduced with their permission). *(Author's Collection)*

if not thousands, of rejects. Sooner or later, the public tires of something done well but done too much, and then the enterprising businessman looks for something new to market. Where does he look? In the case of pelargoniums, it is usually the 'dustheap'.

From this time on Grieve produced many more coloured-leaved plants. In the early 1850s he had produced a seedling called Empress of the French from Cottage Maid and Attraction. It was said to be similar to Cerise Unique, with 'marbled stems'. In 1856 he fertilised Emperor of the French (another seedling from the Cottage Maid × Attraction, and said to be dark-zoned and strong-

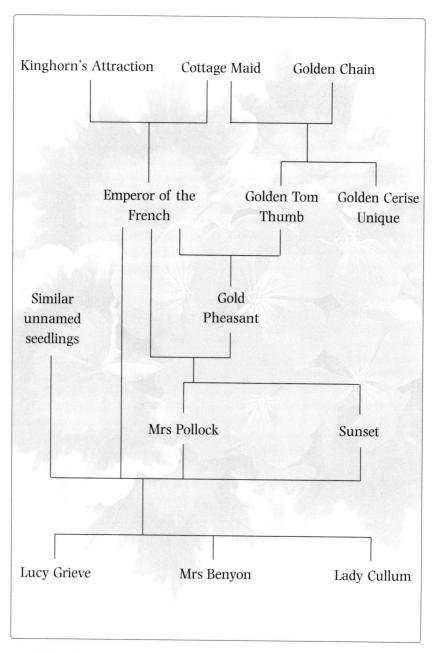

30. Peter Grieve's golden-edged coloured-leaved pelargoniums of the 1850s.

'Mrs Pollock'. *(Vernon Geranium Nursery)*

Mrs Pollock

(Coloured-leaved Zonal)

One of the best known and more enduring of the coloured-leaved pelargoniums, it was created in the 1860s by Peter Grieve, using earlier coloured-leaved hybrids. It has golden-edged leaves and bright scarlet-red, single flowers. It has appeared in catalogues almost continually since its creation.

growing) with pollen from Golden Tom Thumb, which produced Gold Pheasant. In the following two years he fertilised Emperor of the French with pollen from Gold Pheasant and produced his best-known plants, Mrs Pollock and Sunset. Sunset was said to be 'an acquisition of extreme beauty' which surpassed Mrs Pollock in brilliancy.

The *Floral Magazine* compared Mrs Pollock with Sunset, saying that Mrs Pollock was hairy-leaved and a different green.[11] Grieve went on in succeeding years to use Emperor of the French and other similar seedlings (unnamed) with pollen from Mrs Pollock and Sunset to produce Lucy Grieve, Mrs Benyon and Lady Cullum. The coloured-leaved plants provided further new ideas for bedding schemes and were usually grown without their flowers. This required a large workforce to maintain the plants and keep them looking their best throughout the season.

By the late 1850s plants with extended dark zones were being produced, known as Bronze varieties, and these were often combined with the golden leaves, producing Bronze and Gold varieties. Grieve believed these were similar to variegated varieties in that they were caused by a lack of chlorophyll in the leaves, making the green much paler and showing the darker zone to a greater effect. *Henderson's Illustrated Bouquet* admired one called Cloth of Gold because of its dwarf, bushy habit, lack of dark zone, but with the 'broadest bright yellow belt or margin yet known' on its flat, table-like leaves. It was better than Golden Chain because of its freer growth and hardier constitution in 'common garden soil'.[12] Bronze-leaved varieties still commonly grown now are Mrs Quilter and Marechal MacMahon (named after the president of the Third French Republic in 1873), while an easy to acquire yellow-leaved variety is Golden Harry Hieover. A different effect would be achieved by growing Crystal Palace Gem, with its dark green butterfly marking in the middle of a lighter green leaf. Henderson's specified different plants for different purposes, so that some were better for bedding out, others for dwarf ribbon rows, and some for margins or in fancy vases. Clearly, it was important to know your plants (or consult your local nursery, such as Henderson's).

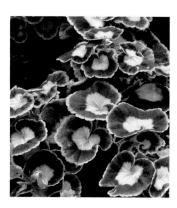

'Mrs Quilter'. *(Author's Collection)*

Mrs Quilter

(Bronze-leaved Zonal)

Mrs Quilter could have been named after the wife of the nurseryman, H.G. Quilter (1824–93) or W. Quilter of Norwood, who employed Samuel Smith as gardener. Although possessing pink flowers, the plant is grown predominantly for its foliage, which is pale greenish-yellow, with a wide bronze zone.

31. Variegated-leaved pelargonium 'Crimson Nosegay' from Peter Grieve, *Ornamental-Foliaged Pelargoniums*, 1863 (reprinted by the British Pelargonium and Geranium Society, 1977, and reproduced with their permission). *(Author's Collection)*

Another diversion from the coloured-leaved plants produced at this time was Beaton's Indian Yellow. This was originally listed with the gold-leaved plants, so that the yellow appeared to relate to the foliage, but later it was apparently claimed to have yellow flowers as well. It was illustrated and fully described in the *Florist* in January 1865, where it was said to belong to a hybrid class of plants they had started calling semi-Nosegays. The raisers had used Nosegays, with their richer range of colours, with ordinary Zonals, to try to produce good bedding plants with more varied colours. It was said to be 'Indian yellow', or have an orangey tint that when put next to scarlets and magentas looked yellow(ish!).

32. Henry Cannell (1833–1914) of Swanley Nurseries, with what may be a pelargonium beside him. As well as creating many new varieties, Cannell kept a large collection of species and early hybrids. *(Carte de Visite/RHS Lindley Library)*

The Florist then described it more as 'an orange-scarlet, with a suffusion of golden yellow, or a wash of the same colour overlaid'[13] (somewhat weakening their case in a fit of conscience, perhaps).

Grieve also attempted to produce variegated varieties of the Nosegays, but with much less success. He used an old variety, Mangles' Variegated,[14] as the pollen parent and an old Nosegay, Mrs Vernon, and produced a plant called Stella Variegata, again annoyingly named after the famous Stella but not apparently related to it. He said, however, that it did in fact resemble sports that had been produced by Beaton's famous Stella. Although he did go on to produce more 'curious and interesting varieties' (not named), Grieve did not have as much success as with the Zonals, due to Nosegays tending to produce little seed or pollen. Yet another category of coloured-leaved plants contained those described as 'marbled', produced by Mr Hally of Blackheath and described as having a pale green centre to the leaves, breaking outwards in irregular blocks or marbly patches. An example was Sheen Rival. They were said to be good as winter plants in a conservatory, presumably because they were interesting even without any flowers.[15]

In 1869 a Pelargonium Congress took place. 'Though rather a high-sounding designation for an unpretentious meeting . . . it was most praiseworthy in its object, that of providing something interesting and instructive to occupy the waste time intervening between the "turning-out" and the "re-admission" of exhibitors on a show morning.'[16] The nurseryman Henry Cannell (1833–1914) of Woolwich proposed a prize essay (£5), and later another prize of £2 was added. Those present included the Revd H.H. D'Ombrain, Maxwell T. Masters (1833–1907) of the *Gardeners' Chronicle* and Dr John Denny (*c.* 1820–81), an amateur grower. Peter Grieve won the £5 prize and delivered a lengthy essay on 'Ornamental-foliaged Pelargoniums', which was the basis for his book described above. This was followed by a discussion on how they should be cultivated: 'for the most part the employment of manure was deprecated, although one of the speakers stated that he had been successful in developing rich colours by using sewage water'. The £2 prize essay was then given by Mr Jonathan Smith of Jersey, on the history and cultivation of pelargoniums with highly coloured leaves.

By the late 1860s there was what could only be described as a 'pelargonium mania'. The *Gardeners' Chronicle* commented:

> At this point of the story the subject becomes too large to be handled on the present occasion, and I shall say nothing of the Tricolours and Bicolours and the Ivy-leaves and the Uniques, that during a period of about ten years overran all the gardens, furnished a common theme for conversation at every table, supplied all the business men and a few peers of the realm with buttonhole flowers, persuaded half the human race that Providence had designed gardens for one tribe of plants alone, and that possibly the Pelargonium itself was the tree of knowledge of good and evil that stood in the midst of the Garden of Eden for the delight and perplexity of the very first of gardeners![17]

Many nurserymen followed the trend of producing coloured-leaved plants and gave each one a new name, though the differences were not very great. It cannot be proved whether the varieties available today are the authentic ones of the nineteenth century, or simply look similar to those that were described in catalogues and magazines.

One famous admirer of pelargoniums was the novelist Charles Dickens, who loved them for their bright colours. His daughter had written: 'He loved all flowers, and scarlet geraniums were his favourite of all. At Gad's Hill there were two large beds of these flowers on the lawn, and when they were fully out, making one scarlet mass, there was blaze enough even to satisfy *him*.'[18] This passage was quoted by a correspondent to *The Dickensian*, who also said that from his own memory Dickens was always seen wearing scarlet 'geraniums' in his buttonhole, and that one of Dickens's other daughters had told him one day that she thought when he was an angel, his wings would be made of looking-glass and his crown of scarlet 'geranium'.[19] He reputedly also had a wreath of his favourite flowers on his coffin. One of the well-known coloured-leaved hybrids is named Dolly Varden after Dickens's character in *Barnaby Rudge*. Perhaps unrelated, but perhaps not, is another well-known coloured-leaved variety, Miss Burdett Coutts, which is named after the Victorian philanthropist Angela Burdett-Coutts (1814–1906), who was a friend of Dickens.

By the 1860s attempts were made by pelargonium growers to bring order out of chaos by officially classifying the recognised groups. In 1866 the *Gardeners' Chronicle* set out the following list of classes:

1. Cape species
This included early hybrids as well as species and was really a miscellaneous selection of all the more unusual plants that were not commonly grown in gardens. The best known and most enduring was *echinitum*.

2. Scented
These were mainly Cape varieties and, being generally easy to grow and propagate, were grown on cottagers' window sills for generations.

3. Show pelargoniums
These were the old florists' pelargoniums, in which nurserymen in the 1860s seem temporarily to have lost interest due to the popularity of Zonals. The typical flower had large blotches on the

upper petals, which were gradually increased to create a dark-coloured petal with a light margin, while the plain lower petals had feathering or a white eye.

4. Spotted or French pelargoniums
These had developed out of the show varieties and had spots or blotches on all five petals. Earlier they had been regarded as two separate sorts, but by the 1860s they seemed to have merged into one.

5. Fancy pelargoniums
These had also been developed by the florists, and were very artificial, round, flat flowers that could have the same colouring on all five petals. By the 1860s they seemed to have gone as far as they could.

6. Hybrid perpetuals
This group contained the failed hybrid bedding varieties that had been superseded as bedding plants by the Zonals and Nosegays; they largely survive as the Uniques. They were also known as 'garden varieties' because they were still grown in gardens, but not for showing.

7. Round-leaved
These were said to be exemplified by Beaton's Indian Yellow, which had also been described as a semi-Nosegay, so were probably hybrids between Zonals and Nosegays.

8. Nosegay
By the 1860s Nosegays were gradually diminishing in popularity. As bedding plants they were being replaced by the coloured-leaved plants, and as large-flowered plants their demise was imminent.

9. Yellow or golden-leaved

These were Zonals and were primarily used as bedding plants or in containers.

10. Golden variegated

This means plants with green and cream foliage, and presumably includes coloured-leaved plants with a cream variegated base.

11. Silver variegated

Similarly, these plants have either green and white leaves or coloured leaves on a green and white base.

12. Ivy-leaved

Not yet a large group in the 1860s, but horticulturalists still thought the various varieties of *peltatum* were separate species.

33. Ivy-leaved pelargoniums in a hanging basket. The Ivy-leaved plants added an extra dimension to gardens, but the early varieties could still be very straggly and difficult to manage. (Thompson's Gardener's Assistant, 1904, *vol. 3/Author's Collection*)

Such classifications were never satisfactory because as soon as they were proposed, some new group was coming to prominence, which would shatter the fragile hypothesis promulgated by those who were trying to bring order to the chaos. That was the fundamental magic and richness of the pelargonium: there was always a new twist still to come.

The Petals Proliferate

After the excitement and novelty of the coloured-leaved plants in the Zonal section, it was time to look at pelargonium flowers again and see what more could be done with them. Nurserymen had been suggesting different uses for pelargoniums in order to sell them more successfully, and it must have occurred to them that more could be done to provide an appropriate plant for vases and urns. The Ivy-leaved or trailing pelargoniums had been used as bedding plants, pegged down into place if necessary, but there would be more scope for them as trailing plants in baskets and pots if they could be trained into more compact shapes. Once again, it was a matter of checking the natural exuberance of the plant.

The Ivy-leaveds were so called because their small shield-shaped leaves, produced close together on trailing stems, were reminiscent of ivy. It will be recalled that the species *P. peltatum* had been known in Holland as early as 1703 and was grown by the Duchess of Beaufort in Britain at the same time (see Chapter 1). However, in its natural state the plant grows very long straight stems, which need support and are really more trouble than they are worth unless ruthlessly cut back. The flowers are also of a limited colour range, either white or pale lilac, although with deep purple markings. The species is variable in the wild and when different plants were introduced into the country during the eighteenth and early nineteenth centuries, they were classified as varieties of at least two different species. L'Heritier described only one Ivy-leaved plant and called it *lateripes*, while Andrews called

L'Elegante

(Ivy-leaved pelargonium)

A hybrid from *P. peltatum* with small silver-edged leaves that turn purple in dry conditions, and large white flowers with purple streaks. It appeared in nursery catalogues from the 1860s and although it sounds French seems to have been first put out by W. Cunningham of Burton upon Trent.

'L'Elegante'. (*Vernon Geranium Nursery*)

his *peltatum* and distinguished another variety which he called *hederinum*, meaning ivy-like. He said that it had been grown in 1787 by the Grimwood and Barret Nursery and was distinguishable from 'the old ivy-leaved pelargonium' (probably meaning L'Heritier's plant). He also listed a variegated version of both plants, with a cream edge. Sweet named the variegated plant *scutatum*, meaning shield-like. There was also another named variety, *P. clypeatum*, which is a softer-leaved variety.

Scutatum, the variegated variety, was thought to be a sport from the species. It seems similar, if not identical, to the commercially successful hybrid named L'Elegante exhibited at the Birmingham Rose Show and at the RHS in 1866 by the nurseryman W. Cunningham of Burton upon Trent.[20] The plant was deservedly popular, and a correspondent to the *Gardeners' Chronicle* in 1866 asked why it had not received a mention there.[21] It was tested in an RHS trial at Chiswick in 1868 and received a First Class Certificate. L'Elegante is still a popular plant today, with its lilac-streaked white flowers, very large in proportion to its small variegated leaves. These have a fleshy but brittle feel to them and

34. Victor Lemoine (1837–1911) of Nancy, a French nurseryman, best known for developing double-flowered and Ivy-leaved pelargoniums. *(Carte de Visite/RHS Lindley Library)*

are mildly scented. Their most striking characteristic, however, is their propensity to develop a deep purple edge, particularly if kept very dry. The origin of the name L'Elegante may be a version of a plant called *Peltatum elegans*, put out by Henderson's Nursery in 1865, described as having bigger flowers than the earlier Ivy-leaved sort and fleshy leaves with dark markings,[22] but in some nursery lists both plants are included at the same time. Perhaps *elegans* was not variegated.

There seems to be even less information about how the Ivy-leaved hybrids were produced than there is about the origins of the other groups, if that is possible. Derek Clifford in 1958 was sceptical that they had been produced from only *peltatum*, considering how varied they became. In 1958 he divided the Ivy-leaveds into three groups: single, large-flowered double and rosette-flowered double.[23] He pointed out that in 1862 the nurseryman John Wills (1832–95) crossed an Ivy-leaved and a Zonal to produce a hybrid, *Willsii rosea*, so there was no reason why other nurserymen should not have done the same. Wills later set up business as a 'floral decorator' under the partnership Wills and Segar of Onslow Crescent, and they specialised in providing magnificent floral displays for exhibitions, shops and railway stations. The theory about hybridising Ivy-leaveds with Zonals is borne out by articles in the Victorian magazines. Shirley Hibberd disapproved of too much crossing with Zonals, as he believed the Ivy-leaveds lost their character as a result.[24] George Gordon, writing in 1880,[25] said that hybrid Ivy-leaveds had started to make the *peltatum* types attract attention from the early 1870s, but it was not until the first double Ivy-leaved appeared that they really became popular. This was a deep lilac flower called König Albert, which was described in 1877[26] as being very useful for bouquets and also for decorative purposes. Several other varieties were also mentioned, including Bridal Wreath and Innocence, which were white with slight pink or crimson markings, and *Peltatum elegans*. The same article mentioned some hybrid sorts as well: Argus (deep rose), Princess Alexandra (salmon pink) and *Willsii rosea*. The hybridising with Zonals therefore increased the colour range considerably and helped to produce more compact, manageable plants.

Ivy-leaved pelargoniums were one speciality of the French breeder, Victor Lemoine (1837–1911) of Nancy, who introduced many new ones in the 1870s and 1880s, although George

Gordon said there was not much to choose between them. He illustrated his article with a fine example of an English variety, Mrs Cannell, produced by Henry Cannell. By the late 1880s, the colours of Ivy-leaveds had been improved beyond all recognition and several sorts still available today were being grown: Abel Carriere (deep fuchsia pink) and Madame Crousse (rich shell-pink rosette-flowered) were mentioned in *The Garden* in 1886,[27] while Shirley Hibberd in *Familiar Garden Flowers*[28] recommended La France (deep lilac) and *Aurea marginatum*, a yellow-edged variegated Ivy-leaved. Millfield Gem is a pink hybrid Ivy-leaved (or Ivy-leaved Zonal cross) which also dates back to this period.

A trial of Ivy-leaved pelargoniums was carried out at Chiswick in 1876, and they were divided into two main categories. Those with peltate leaves were believed to come from the species called *lateripes*, all of which had lilac or white flowers and included L'Elegante. Those with non-peltate leaves, said to be of 'hybrid character',[29] were rose, pale rose, oculate and crimson-edged purple. This seems to be the first mention of 'oculate' or 'eyed' flowers, with a distinct contrasting centre.

'New Life'. *(Gardener's Chronicle, 1877/ RHS Lindley Library)*

New Life

(Single-flowered Zonal)

A sport from a popular red-flowered bedding pelargonium named Vesuvius, New Life has striped red and white flowers and was first described in about 1877. It was also known as Striped Vesuvius and in the United States as Peppermint Candy.

Freak of Nature

(Variegated Zonal)

Described by the *Gardener's Magazine* in 1880 as being the most interesting pelargonium since the tricolours, this plant is predominantly white, with green edges to its leaves. It is slow-growing and needs careful nurturing to keep it in even growth, but will always be a talking point.

'Freak of Nature'. *(Cannell's Floral Guide, 1883/RHS Lindley Library)*

It is easy to forget that flower colours of pelargoniums were not as varied in the mid-nineteenth century as they are now. The Show, Fancy and French sorts, derived as they were from *cucullatum*, tended towards purples, maroons, lilacs and pinks, often with a white background. One of the ambitions of the florists and nurserymen in creating new varieties of these sorts was to produce a scarlet florists' flower, thus combining vivid colour with interesting markings. These had started to appear by the 1860s. The Zonals were predominantly red and pink, although the Nosegays appeared in a larger variety of colours, including richer pinks. By 1861[30] there were flowers of salmon and white 'exquisitely blended', scarlets and crimsons, cerise, rosy red and all shades of pink. Zoned or 'horseshoe'-leaved plants gave further variety, depending on the width and shade, and there were 'novelties' too, such as 'salmon-eyed' flowers, and one of the most important, Madame Vaucher, 'a pure white, with abundant large well-formed flowers in compact trusses, these being well set off by the dark zoned leaves'. This had been produced in France in about

A Happy Thought

(Variegated Zonal)

One of the earliest 'butterfly-zoned' pelargoniums, and although in some Victorian catalogues described as purple-flowered, it is now accepted to be red. The leaf is deep green with an irregular central cream patch. The flowers have straight, narrow petals, and it may be one of the surviving Nosegay pelargoniums of the nineteenth century.

'A Happy Thought'. *(Vernon Geranium Nursery)*

1860, the first round-flowered white, and was used to hybridise many pink varieties.

There had previously been white Nosegays, as described in *Henderson's Illustrated Bouquet* in 1859,[31] but Madame Vaucher seems to have been the first reliable white 'ordinary' Zonal. The production of a successful white led breeders to try harder for other colours. Henry Cannell grew *P. oblongatum* in his nursery, a species with yellow flowers, and he brought out several hybrids which he claimed were yellow, the best one being Jealousy. Others, such as Soleil and Orange Nosegay, were closer to orange than yellow and probably no different from Beaton's attempt. Blue was far less likely, as no species had a blue flower, although some had bluish leaves. Perhaps they felt that that would be a start, and a blue flower may eventually appear. In 1873 Dr Denny of Stoke Newington produced Imogen, described as a 'soft blue-tinted rose' and illustrated in *The Floral World*, though it was said that 'the true colour of the flower is not represented'.[32] Striped or multicoloured flowers were easier. The best 'painted' sort of 1875 was said to be Shirley Hibberd's Alice Spenser,[33] and in 1876 John Wilshire of the Denham Nursery, Buckingham, had bred a striped Zonal from a variety called Lucius.[34] Then in 1877 appeared the famous New Life (also referred to as Striped Vesuvius). This was a sport from a good red single Zonal called Vesuvius, was shown by Cannell's at South Kensington on two occasions,[35] and given a first-class certificate by the RHS as a decorative plant. It was said to have been found by a jobbing gardener on the Isle of Wight and passed on to Cannell's nursery, no doubt for a good price. It was thought so valuable that when a cutting was stolen a reward was offered.[36] Vesuvius, which was probably raised by the nurseryman F.A. Smith,[37] soon became known for its 'sportiveness'. It later produced a white sport (White Vesuvius) and a salmon sport (Salmon Vesuvius), as well as a semi-double scarlet (Wonderful).[38] In *Cannell's Floral Guide* of 1910, West Brighton Gem was listed as a sport from Vesuvius, as was Lady May, while Lady Bess was said to be a sport from West Brighton Gem. Even later, Phlox New Life appeared, which was a single salmon flower with a distinct white patch on each petal like a phlox flower.

'Apple Blossom Rosebud'. *(Vernon Geranium Nursery)*

Apple Blossom Rosebud

(Rosebud or Noisette Zonal)

One of the best-known and oldest of the 'Noisette' or Rosebud-flowered plants of the mid- to late nineteenth century. The double flowerlets never fully open, having the appearance of rosebuds, and the colour is a diffused soft pink. Westdale Appleblossom is a similar variegated plant.

There were other curiosities, too. Dr Denny exhibited a green pelargonium, referred to as a double flower but really an un-developed flower consisting of green scales.[39] More enduring was Freak of Nature, still available today. It was exhibited by Henderson's nursery in 1880 and the *Gardener's Magazine* said 'every leaf has a dark green margin enclosing a space wholly of a creamy-white colour . . . the exact reversal of the usual form of variegation'.[40] It was said to be the most interesting pelargonium since the tricolours. A plant often seen today and, with its straight-sided petals, possibly one of the last remaining Nosegays, is A Happy Thought, unusual in that it has a deep green leaf with a 'butterfly-shaped' cream patch in the middle. It was described in *Cannell's Floral Guide* of 1880 as 'quite another new feature in pelargoniums, and will no doubt lead to other and further strange colouration in this family'. However, the flowers then were described as purple, whereas the plant sold today has scarlet flowers.

A new departure in flowers that appeared in the 1870s, and probably originated in a sport, was the Rosebud or Noisette pelargonium, so called because the flower looked like the half-opened bud of a noisette rose. The best-known plant of this class is Apple Blossom Rosebud, which is a pale, graduated-pink flower that resembles apple blossom. It was called Apple Blossom in the *Gardener's Magazine* of 1875 and described as having 'large trusses that bear close resemblance to large clusters of apple blossom'.[41] Others of this group still grown today are Scarlet Rambler and Red Rambler. John E. Cross, writing in 1965, said that the old pelargonium fanciers used to wear a single floret of one of the Ramblers in the buttonholes of their jackets to confuse the rose-fanciers.[42]

The double-flowered Zonals also started to appear at this date, although Shirley Hibberd, writing in 1880, said that doubles had had a career of at least fifty years, and gave the example of James

35. Wilmore's Surprise, reputedly the
first double-flowered pelargonium,
found in a hollyhock bed in the 1850s.
(Gardeners' Chronicle, *3 July 1880/RHS*
Lindley Library)

Veitch's *veitchianum*, a double purple allied to *barringtonii* of 1828.
It had been depicted by Sweet[43] but was really only semi-double.
He also pointed out Sweet's *implicatum*,[44] which he said was almost
identical to a double *cucullatum* that Cannell's nursery had grown
in the 1870s. Hibberd claimed, however, that the first real double
was Wilmore's Surprise, so called because it was found growing in
the garden of Mrs Wilmore in Strawberry Vale, Edgbaston, among
some hollyhocks,[45] and at the time was thought to be a hybrid
between a hollyhock and a pelargonium. Strangely enough, the
same plant was believed to have been found by Donald Beaton as a
sport from *Diadematum rubescens*, and he named it Monstrosum.
Lee's of Hammersmith exhibited Wilmore's Surprise at Regent's
Park on 30 June 1852, and Mr Beaton suppressed his plant in its
favour. All these plants were of the *cucullatum* or 'Show'
pelargonium type; the double Zonals came later.

In 1864 Victor Lemoine of Nancy produced a double Zonal
hybrid, said to be from a sport found by Henry Le Coq at Clermont

Ferrand before 1862.[46] In 1866 a French Zonal, Gloire de Nancy, was shown, with crimson-scarlet double flowers. This was said by Henri Beurier of Lyons to be a cross between Triomphe de Gregovia (variously spelled Gergoviat, Gergonia, and in other ways) and Beauté de Suresnes, which had been considered the most striking variety of its kind with single flowers.[47] By 1869 there were seventeen double Zonals on display. In that year Lemoine listed seventy. In 1876 the *Gardeners' Chronicle* summarised the progress in doubles. The earliest sorts were by then considered gross, tall and lanky, and not very floriferous, while the Gloire de Nancy types, which were more compact and bushy, were described as 'like a Zonal under powerful stimulants'. A new type was exemplified by Mme Thibault, being dwarf and short-jointed, with a profusion of blooms; and then there was the old double Tom Thumb type, supposedly a sport from the famous Tom Thumb. The best double white of that time was said to be Mme Amalie Baltet.[48] *Cannell's Floral Guide* of 1880 included a 'novel' double pelargonium amusingly called Fright, in which each pip was 'distinctly striped white and scarlet, very striking and unique'. It took longer to produce double flowers in the coloured-leaved groups, something which Peter Grieve had thought would never be possible. By 1910 *Cannell's* listed eleven, including Mrs Parker, a double pink-flowered, silver-variegated plant, still available now.

The classification of 1866 was clearly out of date already, and many people interested in growing pelargoniums thought there should be more organisation in showing the plants and better information for those trying to raise them. The middle of the nineteenth century was a time when many floral and horticultural societies were being formed, taking the place of the old florists' societies on a national scale. With a plant as popular and import-ant as the pelargonium, the formation of such a society was clearly well overdue.

8

Flowers for the Million

The Pelargonium Society

In the 1850s Edward Beck had done much to regulate and improve the growing of pelargoniums by organising shows and promoting good cultivation techniques, but he had not succeeded in creating a society exclusively devoted to the plant. By the 1870s the plants had been transformed, and there was a new generation of growers who were forming societies for all the popular plants. On 2 September 1874 'a few horticulturalists who take particular interest in the pelargonium' got together at the RHS rooms in South Kensington to form a society for its improvement. The promoter of the idea was John Royston Pearson (d. 1876), a nurseryman at Chilwell, Nottingham, who was well known as one of the best growers of Nosegay pelargoniums. Two of his children, Alfred Hetley Pearson (d. 1930) and Charles E. Pearson (1856–1929), carried on the business after him. Charles Pearson's *Essay on the Pelargonium and its Cultivation* was published after it was read out to the Nottingham Horticultural and Botanical Society, in about 1900.[1] John Pearson enlisted the help of two members of the RHS council, R.B. Kellock and F. Webb, as well as Dr Denny, the amateur grower from Stoke Newington. Also attending the first meeting were W.H. Browse of Teignmouth, Devon, Maxwell T. Masters of the *Gardeners' Chronicle*, Thomas Moore (Floral Director of the RHS and Curator of the Chelsea Botanic Garden), and nurserymen Messrs Fraser (of Lea Bridge Road, Hackney), Laing (Forest Hill, south London),

George Smith (Edmonton, north London), Kinghorn (Richmond, Surrey) and J. George (Putney, south London). Mr Webb took the chair and it was decided that the purpose of the society should be to embrace all classes of garden pelargoniums with a view to their improvement, and to determine the relative merits of the species and varieties. The committee was formed of all those present and also Frank Miles and Peter Grieve, who were unable to attend. They compiled a schedule for a competition to be held the following year. There would be prizes for a group of twelve florists' Zonals, another for twelve decorative Zonals, and a third for a collection of thirty distinct Zonals.[2]

This categorisation of show classes immediately suggests how pelargonium growing had moved on. In the 1850s and 1860s there was no such thing as 'a florists' Zonal', and what was 'a decorative Zonal'? It seems that since the advent of the coloured-

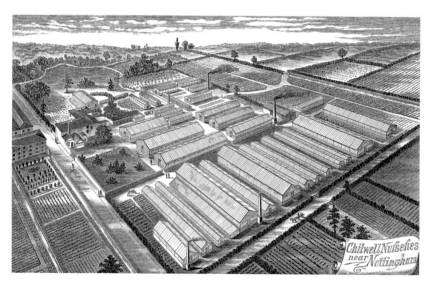

36. John Royston Pearson's Chilwell Nurseries, near Nottingham, which became one of the most important nurseries for pelargoniums in the north of England. (Essay on the Pelargonium, c. 1900/RHS Lindley Library)

37. John Royston Pearson (d. 1876), to whom vol. 29 of the *The Garden* was dedicated in 1886; from the frontispiece. *(Museum of Garden History)*

leaved pelargoniums in the 1860s, growers had taken a greater interest in Zonals, to the comparative neglect of the Show, Fancy and Spotted sorts. In the *Florist* in 1862 'The Plea of the Scarlet Pelargonium' had been published,[3] as if the plant itself were asking to be seen in the same light as the Show pelargonium, and it seems it had now been heard. Inevitably, a 'florists' Zonal' had developed, and any plants that were not considered good enough for the show benches, in other words the florists' rejects, were consigned to the 'decorative' class, which was distinct again from the 'garden' or bedding varieties, which were still holding their own. These decorative plants might be perfectly good plants but they did not conform to the florists' self-imposed rules.

Dr Denny was by now one of the most influential voices in the pelargonium world. He was the resident medical officer at the Stoke Newington dispensary in north London. In 1874 he was 54 and unmarried, and had lived in the large imposing house in the Market Place for eight years.[4] Since moving there, he had taken advantage of the sizeable garden backing on to Abney Park Cemetery, and had started Zonal pelargonium growing to study the effects of selective breeding. In his ten years of cultivating, he sent out sixty commercial varieties from the 30,000 or so varieties he had raised.[5] He explained the attraction of the florists' Zonal, and illustrated what he considered to be one of his perfect plants, Rienzi, in *Floral World* in 1873:

> Time was, when the Zonal geranium afforded but little variety of colour, and certainly no quality of flower. It was then properly regarded as merely adapted for massing for contrast and effect, and not for close inspection. Hence the custom of regarding it as suitable for bedding purposes only; but painstaking and energy have greatly transformed the plant of late, for it may with truth be said now to possess flowers of almost every conceivable colour – colours too that put on their brightest hues in the autumn months, and become the more brilliant as the sun declines. It is then the scarlets stand out the most conspicuous; the crimsons and maroons become shot, as it were, with various hues of purple; the pinks most brilliant, and the various shades of magenta really turn to blue.[6]

The question of blue would not go away, and Denny still believed it would one day be attained. In the meantime, however, he thought he had produced a strain of plants that did not drop their petals, which he felt was breakthrough enough.

Denny used the pages of the *Gardener's Magazine* to elaborate further on the aims of the society. It was clear that they were concentrating their efforts on Zonal pelargoniums and intended to offer their prizes as supplementary to those offered by the RHS for Zonals at their show in July, thereby hoping that the best collection of plants would be brought together on one occasion. This was meant to be an improvement on the previous year, where the competitors for the flowering sections were generally described as being 'most miserable'. Denny wanted the public to see how the Zonals had progressed: 'The flowers of the Zonal section have attained to such a state of perfection as to challenge the criticism of the florists, and the Nosegay varieties produce

38. Dr Denny's 'Rienzi', a florists' Zonal pelargonium of the 1870s. (The Floral World and Garden Guide, *1873/RHS Lindley Library*)

such gorgeous trusses that they require only to be seen to be appreciated.'[7] However, he did not want the society to neglect the other groups. He felt much improvement could be made in the Cape varieties, particularly in enlarging their petals, because he could see that the development of Zonals and Nosegays into florists' flowers meant that they were no longer suitable for outdoor use, and it was 'positive sacrilege' to expose them to 'the buffets of our ungenial clime'. He said that one member of the RHS Floral Committee had remarked a few days before that he knew no more effective variety for bedding than Indian Yellow because the most appropriate plants for that purpose had small flowers and trusses, but were exceedingly floriferous.

Another point made by Dr Denny was that the society should 'take in hand' the matter of classification, which he ventured to call absurd: 'Zonals' frequently had no zone, the term 'Nosegay' was ridiculous, and it was becoming increasingly difficult to demarcate them from Zonals; the old 'large-flowering varieties' were now not much larger than the 'scarlets'; 'Fancies' suggests the question, 'whose fancies?' and many 'French' varieties were raised in England. Lastly, he suggested that all new varieties should be grown together under glass in their first year so they could be properly compared, and then bedded out in their second year for further comparison.[8] By November the society had increased its membership to include two influential editors, Dr Robert Hogg (1818–97) of the *Journal of Horticulture* and the *Florist*, and Shirley Hibberd of the *Gardener's Magazine*, himself a pelargonium grower and a neighbour of Dr Denny, along with Jean Sisley (*d.* 1891), a French grower from Lyons.[9]

In December Shirley Hibberd wrote in the *Gardener's Magazine* that the reason the Zonal pelargonium was now coming into prominence over the Show and Fancy types was because, in addition to its usefulness in the garden as a bedding plant, it was a plant of such variety that growers could not help but notice improvements and then go on to strive for more. Although he knew that blue or yellow flowers would never be a reality, it did not stop people trying to produce them and finding other interesting varieties along the way. However, he felt the most useful improvement was in the widening of the petals, which made the Zonal so much more useful as a show or exhibition plant. He considered it to be 'the most important decorative plant in the English garden'.[10] He then gave further details of the Pelargonium Show to be held in July the following year. There were now to be seven classes:

(1) Twelve distinct varieties of Zonal Pelargoniums, 'Florists' Class', in 8in pots (prizes £8 and £5). This was only to include flowering plants, not those with variegated leaves, and was only for those with 'finely-shaped flowers, according to the florists' model'.

(2) Twelve distinct varieties of Zonal Pelargoniums, 'Decorative Class', in 8in pots (prizes £8 and £5). This class was expressed to be for 'profuse-flowering showy varieties, otherwise known as Hybrid Nosegays'.

(3) Thirty distinct varieties of Zonal Pelargoniums 'irrespective of class' in 6in pots (prizes £6 and £4). Again, no variegated leaves were allowed.

(4) Six Ornamental Cape Pelargoniums, dissimilar (prizes £3 and £2).

(5) Best Hybrid Pelargonium of distinct character (prizes £2 and £1).

(6) Twenty-four Pelargoniums, cut blooms, single trusses, dissimilar (prizes £2 and £1).

(7) Twelve Pelargoniums, cut blooms, single trusses, dissimilar (prizes £2 and £1). Amateurs only.

This show schedule leads to several observations. One is that the 'decorative Zonal' class now seems to be synonymous with something called 'hybrid Nosegays', which leads to the conclusion that by then the Nosegays and the 'ordinary' Zonals (that is, what were presumed to be *zonale* × *inquinans* hybrids) had merged into one class, presumably the class previously referred to as semi-Nosegays. The class of Zonal pelargonium 'irrespective of class' presumably could include bedding varieties. Confusion really sets in, however, when Class 5 is reached with its 'hybrid pelargonium' designation. It seems from the desire of the society to be specially concerned with Zonals, that the 'hybrids' meant here might be a cross between any Zonals and/or Nosegays, but could it also include crossing with 'Cape varieties' or even Ivy-leaved? Non-variegation was not specified either, so perhaps they might have allowed the alien coloured leaves to appear (though in the prevailing climate they would probably not be expected to win). The judges also reserved the right to award an extra prize to any

· PALMAM QUI MERUIT FERAT ·

THE PELARGONIUM SOCIETY
AWARDS THIS
FIRST CLASS CERTIFICATE
PELARGONIUM

RAISED BY

EXHIBITED   BY

CHAIRMAN   SECRETARY

39. Certificate awarded by the Pelargonium Society, with an accurate depiction of the great variety of flowers being grown at the time. *(Gardener's Magazine, 14 February 1880/RHS Lindley Library)*

plant worthy of particular notice and to withdraw any prizes if the plants were not of sufficient merit.[11]

The first Pelargonium Society Show was held on 21 July 1875, staged with the RHS Pelargonium Show in a tent 'several hundred feet in length'. The first prize in the first three sections went to Mr Catlin, a professional gardener from Finchley, north London. The RHS Zonal competition for six and eighteen gold and silver Zonals went to Mr Pestridge of Brentford, and the amateurs' class was won by Mr Lambert.[12] These of course were the growers of the plants, not the raisers of the varieties. A note was given about a new variety called Czar, with a very dark zone and large leaves. A week later, further comments appeared on the success of the show. A.D. wrote that the Pelargonium Society exhibits included no 'flower-bed' plants, and those of the RHS's show should have been 'consigned to the rubbish-heap'. Mr Catlin was said to be the 'prince of pelargonium-growers'. He wonders whether it was possible to go any further with Zonals and Nosegays. Dr Denny was said to be the foremost raiser of Zonals and Mr Pearson of Nosegays, and the Pelargonium Society should think about taking in hand the gold, silver and bronze Zonals, which were 'pretty well played out'.[13]

Later in July the society celebrated its first year's work by dining at The Criterion and added more distinguished names to their number: the nurserymen Andrew Henderson, G.T. Rollisson, B.S. Williams (1824–90), and J.F. West. Mr Pearson took the opportunity to suggest that they fix satisfactory and intelligible names for the different classes instead of 'Fancy', 'Show' and the others, while Mr Cooling mentioned that the first 'Fancy' variety was one called Willoughbyanum, raised in 1835 from one of the ordinary varieties of the time crossed with something like More's Victory or Fair Helen.[14]

By 1877 the Pelargonium Society had extended its aims in spite of there perhaps being a lessening of interest in the plant. The *Gardener's Magazine* remarked that although the pelargonium was not as popular as it had been ten years before, in the whole range of decorative plants, 'there is none more useful'.[15] Charles Turner (1818–85), one of the best pelargonium florist–nurserymen, used a follow-up article in the *Gardener's Magazine* to emphasise the developments of the show pelargoniums since the days of Edward Beck. He reminded readers that in those days there were annual exhibitions and prizes for new seedlings, thought extraordinary in their day, but long since forgotten: 'in size, shape, richness of colour, smoothness, clearness of centre, we have flowers now that were little dreamt of in those, the palmy days of Chiswick'.[16] He went on to say that by this time raisers had managed to produce a highly coloured flower with a clear white centre, and others known as 'scarlets'. Another success had been flowers of a clear white ground with carmine spots on the top petals. Previously all the 'whites' had purple spots until Beck had produced Fairest of the Fair, which although free-flowering, was of 'poor form'. By the 1870s, however, Turner said there were plenty of good plants with carmine markings and other good qualities. It seemed that it was impossible to produce a good pure white if there were purple in the spot, hence the preference for those with carmine markings.

Charles Turner had started as a florist growing pinks, and he trained as a nurseryman, setting up his own business at Chalney, near Windsor, which later became the Royal Nurseries at Slough. By 1849 he was selling pelargoniums from Beck, Foster, Hoyle and all the other top growers. He produced catalogues in spring and autumn, and by 1853 produced a specialist pelargonium catalogue separate from his other florists' flowers. He was scathing about the new French varieties of that time: 'C. Turner has a stock of the French Spotted Varieties of pelargoniums, which are admired by some. They are, however, generally very loose, and of bad form: the best of them being very inferior to the English varieties of the same class such as Sanspareil, Eugenia, etc.' By 1869 his pelargoniums covered sixteen pages of the 55-page catalogue. He continued to be one of the top growers for the rest of his life, and is commemorated by the Ivy-leaved variety Souvenir de Charles Turner.

The mention by the Pelargonium Society of there being 'none more useful' plant than the pelargonium could have been an oblique reference to writers who were beginning to criticise the whole concept of the bedding system and tender plants in general. By this date William Robinson (1838–1935) had established himself as editor of *The Garden* and was promulgating a more natural style of gardening, using only hardy plants. He and Shirley Hibberd (editor of the *Gardener's Magazine*) had started a feud that was to last for well over ten years. Shirley Hibberd, in

40. Charles Turner (1818–85) of the Royal Nurseries, Slough, one of the most successful florist–nurserymen specialising in pelargoniums. *(The Gardening World, 16 May 1885/Museum of Garden History)*

The Amateur's Flower Garden, published in 1872, had actually stressed the importance of growing perennial plants as the mainstay of the flower garden, but it seems that in a perverse way, the more Robinson and his followers veered towards hardy plants and permanent planting, the more Hibberd became a champion of the hybridised, so-called florists' flowers, such as dahlias, chrysanthemums and pelargoniums.

At the end of the article on the Pelargonium Society, reference was made to the subscription to be paid by members, which was a guinea a year. Those interested were instructed to apply to Dr Denny (treasurer) or Thomas Moore (secretary). The *Gardeners' Chronicle,* the paper closest to the RHS, praised the ambitions of the society, pointing out that its object was to improve the different sections of the plant:

> a work best done by specialists, since it requires that the operator should take a special interest in the pursuit and bring to bear upon it the light of special experience . . . That the limit of improvement or of variation has not been reached is quite evident, since scarcely anything has yet been done with the cut-leaved and scented-leaved kinds; and the recent appearance of what have been called 'Regal' Pelargoniums – a variety of great promise in a decorative point of view – affords further evidence of this fact.[17]

That year the society offered twenty-four classes in its show, and prize money of over £100. The classes included Zonals, 'large-flowered Show sorts', 'Fancies', hybrid Ivy-leaved and Cape species. Zonals were again divided into the florists' and decorative sorts (including Nosegays and hybrid Nosegays). In the 'large-flowered or Show types' 'some endeavour' was made to give prominence to the showy, so-called 'Regal' and 'decorative' varieties.[18] The star of the show was Charles Turner, who won the class for six show varieties and was second in the class for four show varieties not yet in commerce, and for six fancies. He then came first in the class for eighteen large-flowered decorative varieties, and in addition exhibited, not for competition, a 'bank' of fifty large specimens of Show varieties. At least someone was still keeping the flag flying for the old varieties! Another prize winner was E.B. Foster of Clewer Manor, who must have been the son of the original Mr Foster. It was clear, however, that despite the efforts of Dr Denny to reorganise the classification of pelargoniums, the situation was getting worse, as the new class of 'Regal pelargoniums' had at last been brought into existence.

The Regals Arrive

By the late 1870s another new pathway was being cleared in the journey to the modern pelargonium. A hundred years had passed since Sir Joseph Banks had sent Francis Masson out to look for plants in South Africa, and now the stage had been reached when one of the most important of the modern groups of plants could take its place in the jigsaw puzzle of pelargonium classification. The Regals seem to have sprung from a group of plants consigned, if not to the rubbish dump, to the next worse thing in the eyes of the nineteenth-century florist–nurseryman: the garden. But this time it was not the garden itself that had become the home of these florists' rejects, it was probably the conservatory, or the inside of the house itself. In Chapter 5 it was explained that the term 'florist' did not mean what it does today, and that the people who sold plants for display purposes were known as 'market florists'. It is now their turn to come to prominence in the story.

Flowers had a special place in Victorian Britain. They were not only used as cut flowers in vases, as they are today, but they were frequently used to decorate clothes and hats. Gentlemen wore buttonholes and ladies carried posies and bouquets, not just at weddings but at balls and other less formal occasions. The 'Language of Flowers' was a diversion among young ladies, who learned to interpret a man's intentions by looking at the meaning behind the flowers he presented to her, much in the romantic way that people read horoscopes today. Flowers had a seasonal significance as well. In the same way that most people were restricted to eating vegetables and fruit that were in season because food preservation and transport from abroad were not as developed as they are now, so the flowers sold in the street were restricted to those available locally in spring, summer or autumn. People made sentimental associations with flowers as representative of the seasons: violets and primroses in spring, roses and lilies in summer and dahlias and chrysanthemums in autumn. Flowers were also subjects for art, not just for painting and drawing but as inspiration for embroidery, woolwork and collage. The Victorians excelled at inventing time-consuming, but largely useless, activities for affluent women who would otherwise be unemployed.

The market florists provided the living plants for decoration and as subjects for art and craftworks. They traded in both cut flowers and potted plants. The demand for pelargoniums was great, because under glass there were varieties that could be obtained almost throughout the year. They are easy plants to grow and quick to propagate, and they do not need tropical heat. Because of the diversity of varieties, special ones were developed for market, differing from those for the garden and the show bench. Gradually,

41. A Victorian street seller of plants for indoor decoration. He holds a pelargonium, and many more are on the cart behind. *(Coloured lithograph/Museum of Garden History)*

these non-show varieties came to be called 'decorative pelar-goniums', because that is what they were. They came into their own as colourful plants that would last well enough in a pot or in water, without having the special attributes that the florists desired, or the tough staying power needed in the parterre. In the ways of the horticultural trade, if something grew, someone would be prepared to let it grow and find a use for it.

The *Gardeners' Chronicle* in 1877 explained the skill of the market florist, which was said to entail 'the successful application of scientific principles'. They felt it would be a lesson to some show exhibitors if they were to see the quality of plants produced 'without stint of labour or time'. These plants had four or five main stems and twenty to twenty-five trusses of blooms. The colours, as mentioned by Charles Turner, seemed to be pre-dominantly white with carmine, rosy-pink or orange.[19] Two varieties mentioned were Triomphe de St Maude (crimson) and Duchess of Edinburgh (light-coloured), and these two were cited a couple of weeks later in the *Gardener's Magazine* as decorative varieties that were all very well in a conservatory, but should not be tolerated in the exhibition tent with the superior 'Show' varieties.[20] The *Chronicle* produced a supplement in June 1877, which featured Zonals grown for market. Vesuvius, Christine and Madame Vaucher were well-known varieties that were popular, with Lemoine's doubles leading the way. One market grower was said to have pelargoniums in 'several houses 200 feet long', including two devoted to Madame Vaucher alone, consisting of 4,500 to 5,000 plants grown from cuttings struck in the spring of the previous year.[21]

By the end of that summer the name 'Regal' was being used by the nurseryman William Bull (1828–1902) for some of the decorative varieties, one of which, Princess of Wales, was illustrated in colour in the *Florist* in September 1877.[22] It was described as a 'crispate' variety, the petals of which gave the

42. A hand-made collage of a pelargonium, probably dating back to the early nineteenth century. The paper for the leaves is scored to produce veining and the petals are carefully inked or painted. *(Author's Collection)*

appearance of a double flower, owing to the frilled edges. Other varieties produced by Bull at the same time were Captain Raikes (fiery crimson), Queen Victoria (vermilion, edged white) and Beauty of Oxton (maroon-crimson, edged white). William Bull had started his career as a traveller or salesman for Rollisson's and Henderson's nurseries before taking over John Weeks's nursery in King's Road, Chelsea. He specialised in new and rare plants, and probably created the name Regal as a marketing tool to sell the hitherto unnoticed market pelargoniums.

Regal[23] was not the name used by all. Some writers and nurserymen still called the new plants 'decorative' or 'market' pelargoniums, or sometimes 'early flowering', but they could not deny their usefulness. Thomas Trussler, a nurseryman from Edmonton, north London, described their virtues:

The more recently-introduced varieties have such a splendid habit and produce flowers of such large size, excellent form, and rich colouring that they may be said to represent a quite new type, and may certainly be described as of the highest possible value. Their neat compact habit is a prime consideration, for with ordinary care they form such dense specimens that not more than three or four sticks will be necessary in training them into shape; the flowers are produced in huge trusses, and if not so smooth as the most perfect of the show varieties, they are very stout in substance and attractively coloured. By very many, more particularly the ladies, the frilled flowers produced by some of the varieties belonging to the section are preferred to those possessing the shape and finish so much appreciated by the true florist; and it is not without interest that they stand when cut very much better than those of either of the other sections, the double Zonals alone excepted; and that for the dressing of epergnes and the formation of hand bouquets they are simply invaluable.[24]

43. *P. album multiflorum*, an early flowering market pelargonium, the type from which the 'decorative' and Regal pelargoniums were produced. *(Gardening Illustrated, 10 December 1892/Museum of Garden History)*

44. William Bull (1828–1902), the nurseryman who first used the name 'Regal' to sell the market or decorative pelargoniums in the 1870s. *(Carte de Visite/RHS Lindley Library)*

NEW REGAL PELARGONIUMS.

This name is applied to that magnificent group of Pelargoniums, the flowers of which are of large size, very rich and showy, and although they are not really double, yet from their fullness of form and the extra number of petals, they have the appearance of being so.

For New Varieties offered for the first time, *vide* page 9.

BEAUTY OF OXTON, a splendid novelty, the flowers of similar form to those of Pelargonium *Queen Victoria*, but of quite a distinct colour. The upper petals are of a very rich maroon colour, darkly blotched; the under petals very dark crimson, shaded with maroon; light centre tinted with rose; all the petals are attractively and regularly margined with white, and beautifully fringed. The flowers are large and very full, the extra number of petals giving them the appearance of being semi-double. 2*s*. 6*d*. and 3*s*. 6*d*.

45. 'Beauty of Oxton', a Regal pelargonium in Bull's catalogue of 1877. *(RHS Lindley Library)*

The mention of three or four sticks, however, should have put the reader on high alert. It seems that although these plants were certainly striking, and could be made to flower early in the season before the Show and Fancy varieties were ready, in order to provide a succession of blooms, carefully regulated artificial heat and special attention in the way of stopping and repotting would have to be lavished on them.

Cannell's Floral Guide of 1880 further explained the attraction of Regals: 'from the fact of their having more scalloped petals, somewhat approaching nearly a double, they retain their petals instead of shedding them as single show flowers, this together with their most brilliant colours, make them quite a necessity for cut flowers'. In the *Gardener's Magazine* several of the best new varieties were recommended, although it was pointed out that many of those being developed would not be widely available for some time. Those that were listed show a rich diversity of colour:

Duchess of Bedford – white, pink blotch on top petals
Duchess of Edinburgh – white, purple blotch
Kingston Beauty – pure white, large purple blotch on top petals
Volonte Nationale – large rich carmine flowers with broad white
    margin
Mrs Lewis Lloyd – bright red, black blotch on upper petals
Leopold – brilliant red-scarlet
The Moor – deep crimson, blackish blotches on each petal
Triomphe de St Mande[25] – deep crimson
Princess of Wales – blush, with crimson markings on each petal
T.A. Dickson – fiery red, blackish blotches on upper petals
Midas – rosy scarlet, white markings
Chancellor – rosy lake, bright maroon markings.

Almost as an afterthought the writer gives the names of just three Show varieties, calling them '*nearly* as free blooming as the very

Geoffrey Horseman

(Regal pelargonium)

Just one of the many Regal pelargoniums grown today, this plant has a deep purple flower, with a lilac margin and distinct feathering. Regals are best grown as pot plants indoors, but can go outside in the summer, making dramatic displays of rich colour with abundant blooms.

Regal 'Geoffrey Horseman'. *(Jean-Patrick Elmes)*

best of . . . the decorative class', and just one solitary Fancy pelargonium:[26] their day was now past.

At this date a different, slightly sinister quality of the pelargonium was noticed in France: 'M. Heckel has been experimenting with the leaves of *P. zonale* by wrapping them around small pieces of meat. After some time an acid secretion was observed, which produced on the meat the same effect as has been observed in carnivorous plants.' This did not happen when the meat was wrapped in leaves of pelargoniums without hairs. The writer said that it seemed to be the glandular hairs alone that were endowed with the property of dissolving nitrogenous matter. 'It remains to be seen . . . of what use the property is. It would seem as if . . . it were a mere luxury, which the plant can perfectly well do without.'[27]

With the brightly coloured Regal pelargoniums, however, at last there was a plant for everyone, not just the florists or the professional gardener providing bedding plants for their wealthy employers. These were plants to be bought from the market by the non-gardener, grown and enjoyed at home, and, perhaps, thrown away at the end of the season. It was the beginning of instant gardening for people with small houses, with small conservatories, who did not grow their own plants or employ their own gardeners to do so, but who nevertheless wanted 'a good show' in the summer months. The pelargonium was the ideal plant for the purpose and was destined to remain so for the rest of the century.

9

The Final Flowering of the Nineteenth Century

As the nineteenth century changed into the twentieth, and the Victorian age gave way to the Edwardian, pelargonium growers continued to exploit any potential they could find for something different. The coloured-foliage plants had lost their novelty value, but the better varieties persisted and are still grown today. Bronze- and golden-leaved plants had been developed which were often dwarf and slow-growing because of the lack of chlorophyll, but this made them very suitable for bedding as they would retain their shapes and need less maintenance. The constantly repeated pattern of the zoning in a bed of coloured-leaved plants gave a rhythm and symmetry to the whole effect, and often the flowers were removed so as not to detract from the green-brown-red-yellow colour scheme.

A more extreme colour effect that came to prominence in the 1890s was the black leaf. Again, the lack of chlorophyll in the plant cells caused growth to be retarded. One of the best-known 'black'-leaved plants (which of course was really just very dark green) was Black Vesuvius, sent out by Cannell in 1889. Whether it was a sport from the very successful Vesuvius of the 1870s is not certain, although it was claimed to be in the 1910 catalogue. As pelargoniums were often named in imitation of other plants, it may be that they were not related but it was called Black Vesuvius because its flowers were of the same vivid scarlet. A similar black-leaved plant called L'Enfer was sent out by Lemoine in 1895, which was not as compact in growth, and a later dark-leaved

Red Black Vesuvius

(Dwarf Zonal)

An early dwarf plant, with almost black leaves and vivid red flowers. It was not a sport from Vesuvius, but was originally named Black Vesuvius for its similar flowers. When a salmon-coloured sport appeared, this plant had 'Red' added to its name. L'Enfer is a similar, larger black-leaved plant.

'Red Black Vesuvius'. *(Author's Collection)*

plant was called Mephistopheles. Whatever its origins, Black Vesuvius did sport later and produced a salmon flower, appropriately named Salmon Black Vesuvius, whereupon the original Black Vesuvius became known as Red Black Vesuvius to distinguish it. At this date also, Distinction appeared in the lists, often with the black-leaved plants. It is not black, although a dark shade of green, but it is distinguished by the very thin line round the edge of the leaf, as if the zone has shrunk and displaced itself, or been drawn round with a pencil.[1] The flowers are a very bright red. It is not a compact plant, but the leaves do stay small. There was also a White Distinction, having a white flower, and at the present time there is a pink-flowered variety too, but this does not appear in the Victorian lists.

Small or miniature plants had periodically appeared throughout the nineteenth century, but there had not been enough of them to constitute a separate class. Some species pelargoniums were naturally smaller than others and considering the average size of the early Zonals, what the Victorians described as compact or dwarf were more like modern 'normal-sized' plants. Andrews had included a *Zonale* variety he called *minima*, but it does not seem to have been used to produce any further hybrids. In 1860 Charles Turner's Lilliput was described as 'a little gem' in the RHS report on pelargonium plants. It was very dwarf with a distinct zone and bright scarlet flowers.[2] Henderson's had brought over a group they called Lilliputian Zonals, originally produced in Saxony. They were illustrated in the *Gardeners' Chronicle* in 1868 and described thus:

> These novelties are said to be as free growing as the ordinary larger bedding varieties, and to have foliage of diminished size, proportionate to their dwarf habit, but flowers equally large with those of the ordinary kinds. Their small size, free compact habit, and abundant bloom, should make them useful plants for the edges of flower beds, or for ribbon borders, while the colours, consisting of various shades of scarlet and rose-colour, are just those which come in useful in bedding combinations.[3]

There were also small French plants. In 1884 Paul Bruant of Poitiers sold five so-called miniatures and a variegated plant first named Le Nain Blanc, later renamed Madame Salleroi (or Salleron). It was a tufty spreading plant which never flowered. This plant, or one like it, may have been seen as far back as 1861 by John Salter, who knew it as Variegated Dandy or Little Dandy, which he said he had been told was a sport from a normal-sized plant.[4] It was identified as Madame Salleroi by Albert Hosking (*c.* 1874–1938) of the John Innes Horticultural Institute in 1923, who said it produced green, variegated or white sports, and that the flowers, when they appeared, were no different from those of Mangles' Variegated.[5] This was confirmed by John E. Cross who wrote in 1951 that a 'taller variety' of Dandy is known as Little

Madame Salleron

(Variegated Zonal)

Originating in the middle of the nineteenth century, probably a sport from a flowering variety, this plant never flowers. With its small size and delicate, heart-shaped leaves, it is ideal for edging beds and can be quickly multiplied from cuttings to provide a constant display in garden or greenhouse.

'Madame Salleron'. *(Author's Collection)*

Trot.[6] Victor Lemoine of Nancy also sent over Madame Fournier, another dwarf plant, in 1895. However, H. Dauthenay dates the plant to 1877 when Pierre Mathieu, gardener to Mr Salleron, found in a border of Mangles' Variegated a plant that 'appeared to be sick' and which formed a clump, of a different form than the rest. He took it up and grew it on, naming it after the mistress of the house.

There were further advances in unusually shaped flowers. Henderson had included in their catalogue in 1869 plants with 'fringed petals' and by 1878 had a whole category of 'frilled or fringed petals'. These may have been the forerunners of 'carnation-flowered' plants with serrated petals. They may have had a similar appearance to plants like Skelly's Pride available now and described as having 'fimbriated' petals. A type that is easier to define is the 'cactus-flowered', also known as poinsettia-flowered, and so called because the flowers were thought to resemble the cactus-flowered dahlias that were popular at the time. The first was Fire-Dragon of 1899,[7] which later produced a sport known as

Chinese Dragon. By 1907 Cannell had twenty-eight sorts. In 1905 cactus varieties were also produced by Lemoine and they were assessed by the RHS scientific committee in 1913–14.

Another novelty, this time in flower colour, was the 'bird's egg varieties' with speckled flowers. The Royal Horticultural Society grew five varieties in 1898. Cannell had listed Little Dear in 1869. There were also 'oculated' flowers, with contrasting centres to the flowers, also known as 'Cyclops types'. Cannell included four varieties with variegated foliage in 1883, including Mrs J.C. Mappin, 'a splendid white bloom and pink eye . . . the habit and appearance is the same as the well-known favourite, Flower of the Spring'.[8]

At the same time as the dwarf varieties were being developed, there were moves in the opposite direction. From the 1870s Bruant had been developing a new 'giant' race of plants with fleshy stems and leaves, which probably originated from a sport from an ordinary Zonal. The first was called Bruant, which was closely followed by Beauté de Poitevine and many more. In France they were described as being of 'grand bois' (great or large wood) rather than the normal Zonal type. In Bruant's catalogue of 1899 it was remarked that they were particularly popular in America, and that they were well able to stand strong sunlight. In about 1908 new strains were developed from the Bruants, known as Fiats. These had serrated petals and a bluish tint to the foliage.

The French growers had been sending plants over to Britain since the middle of the nineteenth century, first making their impact with the spotted Fancy varieties and later introducing the best whites and doubles. They certainly brought fresh blood and new ideas into pelargonium breeding, but the view of the British writers was that the French plants were never as strong and well formed as the British ones, and the British breeders soon outclassed them once they got their hands on the plants. The trade went the other way too, and many British varieties were known in France and other parts of Europe from the middle of the nineteenth century. The contemporary French view of Zonal pelargoniums was summarised by H. Dauthenay in 1896 in *Les Geraniums*, and his work has now been analysed and translated into English by Richard Clifton.[9] In the book Dauthenay wanted to provide a definitive guide to the varieties, so as to identify and distinguish them, and also to provide the best examples for different uses. As such, he was the first person to attempt to do so since the time of Sweet, but even he could see that the whole subject of pelargoniums would be too vast, so he confined himself to the *zonale/inquinans* hybrids, of which he estimated there were about 3,000 known at the time. He was writing his book principally for the specialist breeders, to whom he gave a new name, 'pelargonistes'.[10]

Dauthenay begins his book with a summary of the early history of the Zonal pelargonium, which largely corresponds with what is known today. The French, he writes, did very little hybridising between 1834 and the 1850s, so that of the best varieties of 1855 over half were British. He gives as examples Cerise Unique, Flower of the Day, Tom Thumb (known as Tom Pouce) and Shrubland Scarlet. By the late 1850s, however, there were many good French varieties, although Mrs Pollock also made her mark in France in 1863. Two varieties of the time that were to come to prominence later for hybridising were Madame Vaucher and Beauté de Suresnes. At this point the French became confused like the British, when the same name was used for different plants of different types. In 1867 M. Barillet, Gardener in Chief to the town of Paris, instigated a commission of horticulturalists to try to unravel the problem and classify the plants. They resolved that it would be impossible to divide the plants between *zonale* types and *inquinans* types, so instead they divided them into groups, largely dependent on colour, which were then subdivided as follows:

46. A French Bruant pelargonium 'de grand bois' which were stronger and larger than the British sorts. They became popular in the United States, where they were used for further hybridisation. *(Catalogue from Bruant's nursery, 1899/RHS Lindley Library)*

(1) Deep red to salmon to white, subdivided into:
- (a) deep red to white (including Tom Thumb and Frogmore);
- (b) red salmon (including Beaton's Indian Yellow, which casts some doubts as to the claims made for it);
- (c) rose salmon;
- (d) red-orange, pink, pale, lined and dark;
- (e) white tinted (including Madame Vaucher, which was not, therefore, totally white); and
- (f) white.

(2) Red-carmine
(3) Rose, subdivided into:
    (a) unicoloured; and
    (b) with white 'onglet', translated as 'claw'.
(4) Nosegays
(5) Varieties with highly coloured leaves.

It seems that the commission found the work almost beyond them, as sections 4 and 5 did not appear.

The plants then went into abeyance in the 1870s due to war and to the increased popularity of other plants, such as begonias. In 1874, however, the first plants of 'grand bois' appeared, which were the forerunners of Bruant, described as the classic variety of 1882. France still took note of British plants too, and Dauthenay named New Life, the first striped flower, as an introduction in 1877. In 1883 Victor Lemoine carried out a trial of over 500 of the best varieties, planted out for the summer, to test their qualities.

As to Nosegays, Dauthenay's view is that they represented the most ancient hybridisation between *zonale* and *inquinans*, the first providing the irregular corolla, the narrow petals and the zoned leaves, the second the upright form, general vigour and size. He thought they then went out of favour in 1878 due to the intro-duction of double flowers and the Bruant race, and lost their purity of character through the subsequent crossing with those plants. He divides the Nosegays into *nineteen* sections, defined by colour. Considering that we do not recognise the Nosegay at all today, it seems incredible that such a huge range could have existed just over a century ago. Dauthenay's colour definitions were very detailed and, as he himself admits, largely personal. They include the usual pinks and reds, such as salmon, rose, carmine, scarlet and cerise, but also grenadine, solferino, vermilion, cinnabar, copper, red lead and brick. The pale pinks

47. *Carte de Visite* of a gardener holding a pelargonium as one of his 'tools of the trade', *c*. 1900. *(Museum of Garden History)*

NEW ZONATE PELARGONIUMS,

RAISED BY SHIRLEY HIBBERD, ESQ., OF STOKE NEWINGTON

OFFERED FOR SALE BY

ROBERT OUBRIDGE (Sole Agent),

CHURCH WALK NURSERY, STOKE NEWINGTON, LONDON, N.

CRIMSON BANNER.—Very distinct; makes a gorgeous bed. The leaves are sulphur yellow; the flowers rich magenta crimson, produced in very large trusses. This fine Geranium affords the novel feature of a bed of golden leaves dotted with huge rosettes of the richest crimson flowers. Price 5s. each, seven for 30s.

GOLDEN BANNER.—Surpasses everything of the class of which "Goldfinch" has long been the type; and, by its free growth, and stout, slightly-convex leaves, richly and uniformly coloured, may be pronounced the best yellow-leaved Bedding Geranium extant. Price 5s. each, seven for 30s.

MULBERRY ZONE.—Small, neat leaves, disc and margin clear sulphur-yellow, changing with age to rich gold colour, the zone on the young leaves mulberry colour, changing to chesnut. A fine bedding plant. Price 5s. each, seven for 30s.

WHITE WONDER.—A neat free flowering variety of the type of Madame Vaucher, but far preferable to that variety for bedding, as it does not become stained in hot weather. Price 5s. each, seven for 30s.

GENERAL COLLECTION.

Strong Plants, 1s. 6d. each; the set of fifteen for £1.

1. **KATE ANDERSON.**—Scarlet.
2. **MAY QUEEN.**—Rosy pink.
3. **ANDREW MARVEL.**—Intense fiery scarlet.
4. **H.W. LONGFELLOW.**—Deep salmon, shaded with vermilion.
5. **MAGNA CHARTA.**—Deep vermilion-red colour.
6. **MRS. SPENCER.**—Delicate flesh, shading to carmine.
7. **THOMAS MOORE.**—Flowers as round and large as "Richard Headly," of a lighter shade of scarlet. Makes a wonderful bed.
8. **HIBBERD'S ORANGE NOSEGAY.**—Flowers intense fiery-orange, leaves bluish.
9. **TRISTRAM SHANDY.**—Light cerise-scarlet. A model bedder where colour is a desideratum.
10. **RICHARD HEADLY.**—The finest scarlet Geranium for pot culture and for plunging.
11. **DR. M'DONNELL.**—Vermilion-shaded.
12. **JAMES CRUTE.**—Crimson-shaded.
13. **ROSE OF ALLANDALE.**—Shaded pale pink and blush. A gem for pot culture.
14. **ISABELLA.**—Margin pure white, centre rich deep carmine, rose.
15. **LION HEART.**—Rosy salmon.

GERANIUM SEED, saved from Hibberd's Strain, in sealed packets, free by post, 2s. 6d. per packet. Geranium Seed may be sown at any time; and if sown from May to August, requires no artificial heat. If sown early in heat, and grown on freely under glass, the seedlings begin to flower in July of the same season.

48. Advertisement for New Zonate Pelargoniums raised in Stoke Newington, north London, showing the variety of colours available. *(Rustic Adornments for Homes of Taste, 1871/Author's Collection)*

include dawn, perhaps meaning 'flushed', and, rather alarmingly, 'carne' or meat (which could, perhaps, be translated as either flesh or blood, but it is difficult to know which). The more purple shades are very enticing: magenta, violet, amaranth, fuchsine, amethyst and 'water-of-wine'. His descriptions produce an overwhelming feeling of regret, just as Sweet's do, that these sumptuous plants have been irretrievably lost. Dauthenay was obsessed with colour, writing his own book on the subject and commissioning standardisation of the terms, which was never used because of the poor quality of colour printing at the time. Dauthenay then describes the plants of 'grand bois' or 'great wood', which became particularly associated with Bruant. They had very large flowers and thick, leathery leaves, characteristically scalloped, with stems about 4cm in circumference. Bruant's branching and vigorous plants became particularly popular in

America, where they were capable of covering large areas and could tolerate heat and sun. This export would lead in due course to new races of plants.

Dauthenay felt English plants earned their place in French gardens because they were robust and floriferous. A French nurseryman, Rozain, son-in-law of Boucharlat, took to crossing the English and French varieties, to keep the English form but produce better flowers with a bigger eye in the eyed varieties. Lemoine also did the same, and one of the varieties thus produced was Paul Crampel of 1893. It was described as 'umbel enormous . . . colour vermilion flagrant . . . foliage ample and vigorous'. This was to become one of the most important varieties for bedding well into the twentieth century.

Next Dauthenay dealt with 'varieties with large white centre, and novelties with multi-coloured flowers'. The 'oculated' flowers included Souvenir de Mirande, which was obtained as a seedling in 1886 and was followed by several similar plants from other raisers. Better plants were produced by hybridising these together. Bruant, of course, had to go one better, and produced flowers with stippling and shading, eventually producing two plants that caused 'a sensation': Madame Bruant and Fleur Poitevine. The first was white with rose-lilac stippling and rose veining. The second was pale rose with carmine veining and speckled all over.

In writing about double flowers, Dauthenay gives an account of the first French double, embellishing the story told earlier by Henri Beurier.[11] He says M. Le Coq, director of the Clermont Ferrand Botanic Garden, had seen growing in the garden there a semi-double plant, called Triomphe de Gergonia. M. Ambland, a nursery-man, took seeds from it and raised Gloire de Clermont, exhibited in 1863. It was vermilion with a white centre. Various cuttings found their way into the trade and Van Houtte sold it as *Ranunculaeflora plenissima* (or 'very double buttercup-flowered'). In 1863 Emil Chate purchased Ambland's plant and Lemoine obtained from him one stamen, which he used to fertilise Beauté de Suresnes. A seedling produced by that cross turned out to be a full double flower of a rich red shade, and he called it Gloire de Nancy (1865). Lemoine produced the pink double, Madame Lemoine, and the first white double was Aline Sisley, from Jean Sisley in about 1872. Two of the best varieties by Dauthenay's time were Madame Thibaut[12] and F.V. Raspail, a crimson purple.

Dauthenay divides dwarf plants into four sections: Nosegay-derived plants, which he exemplifies with La Destinée, and in which he includes Harry Hieover; *inquinans*-derived plants, such as Tom Thumb; *zonale* Lilliput-derived plants; and Bruant's dwarfs. The resurrection of Tom Thumb is a great surprise, as the plant had hardly been mentioned in English magazines after the 1850s, although of course it could easily have survived in many gardens. It seems that in a letter to the *Revue Horticole* in 1875, Comte d'Epremesnil related how a Mr Leclerc of Fécamp had two great tubs of Tom Thumb plants, which had been untouched for forty years and which measured, apparently, 20m, although he gives another height of 1.5m which sounds more likely. As Tom Thumb was not produced until 1842, it is likely that the plants classified by Dauthenay are simply the *inquinans* type, and as seen previously, many plants of that type were claimed to be Tom Thumb, whether they were or not.

As to the 'Lilliput' race, Dauthenay says they were obtained from seed by Edouard Pynaert, nurseryman of Gand, in 1881, and other French raisers. They were 12–18cm high, compact and short-branching, and mainly single-flowered. He does not mention any connection with the plants from Saxony put out by Henderson's nursery. Bruant's dwarfs were typified by Philemon, produced in 1888, and were 15–20cm high. As an afterthought in this chapter Dauthenay mentions hybrids between *peltatum* and *zonale*, both double, but he says they have not produced descendants and are seldom used.

The last section is on coloured-leaved plants. Dauthenay uses Grieve's book to explain their origin, and says that the classification used then did not take account of the newer black-leaved plants. He also adds a section on Mangles' Variegated-derived plants. He does not know the origin of Mangles' Variegated, but confirms that Madame Salleron (also known as Le Nain Blanc) was a sport from it. The story came from Mr Menard, nurseryman from Melun, who first sold the plant.

In the last years of the nineteenth century, the older types of plant were not totally forgotten. Some of the Uniques were still going strong. Richard Dean (1830–1905) in the *Gardeners' Chronicle* in 1876 had referred to the usefulness of Rollisson's Unique, which was in danger of being gradually 'elbowed out of existence'. His view was that it was a hybrid between *quercifolium* and another Cape variety and was the forerunner of the race of hybrids from the Old Unique and its sports. He gives no basis for this story, and presumably is just reflecting what had been written earlier. He did, however, name the other Uniques as Aurora, Conspicuum, Crimson Unique, Diadem, Lilac Unique, Scarlet

'Scarlet Unique'. *(Author's Collection)*

Scarlet Unique

(Unique pelargonium)

One of the Victorian Uniques of uncertain origin, this plant has frilled, deeply indented foliage with a pungent, acrid scent, and clusters of beautifully marked flowers. It is easy to grow and, like the other Uniques, if kept indoors in winter can grow into a shrub of large proportions.

Cannells' Floral Guide, 1910.

PINK, SHADED PURPLE.

858. **LILACINA IMPROVED**—In several respects a decided advance in this class; fine bold trusses; well above the foliage. 9d.

859. **LILACINA**—Dwarf habit; of a pleasing shade of soft lilac-pink; immense flowers. 9d.

360. **MAUD OF WALES**—Flowers of the most perfect form and immense size, equal to any of the scarlet section.

361. **MRS. DAVID SAUNDERS** — Habit dwarf and very free, grand trusses standing well up above the foliage.

All varieties not priced 6d. each (in 60's).

DEEP PINK AND ROSE-COLOURED.

362. **SYDNEY** — Of a very light pink colour, quite a pleasing shade; good sized flowers. 1s.

363. **CARONIA** — Bright rosy-pink, immense flowers, bold trusses; good habit. 1s. 6d.

364. **HATFIELD**—Bright rose pink, of a very pleasing and attractive colour; large individual flowers; fine. 1s.

365. **HENRY COMPTON**—Large trusses of a pretty shade; habit vigorous and branching; free.

366. **MRS. B. W. CURRIE** — Soft rosy pink, flowers large and very circular, enormous trusses, robust habit; a fine introduction.

367. **MRS. BROWN-POTTER**—Decided advance for size of flowers and trusses; clear bright pink; very effective; good habit; free. 1s.

368. **MRS. WILLIAMS**—Clear rose-pink, small white blotch at base of upper petals; a grand flower in size and substance. 1s.

369. **COUNTESS OF BUCKINGHAM**—Producing flowers of a deep rose-pink; of extra size and bold trusses; beautiful and refined shape; vigorous but spreading habit.

370. **PINK DOMINO** — Splendid dwarf bushy habit; broad circular flowers, bold trusses; attractive.

371. **ETHEL LEWIS**—Rose-pink, distinct white blotch on upper petals; habit dwarf.

372. **DUCHESS OF PORTLAND**—Bright rosy pink, colour clear and distinct; of good form, immense trusses.

WHITE.

. **VENUS**—Of the purest possible white and fine large flowers; habit very regular. 1s. 6d.

373. **CLAREMONT** — A fine bold clear white; a fine improvement on *Niagara*. 1s.

374. **GOODWOOD**—Of the purest possible white, and of the most correct form; free flowering; dwarf habit. 1s.

375. **SNOWSTORM** — Splendid habit; dwarf and branching; free flowering, and of the purest possible white. 1s.

376. **MARY BETON**—A fine flower of the purest white; bold trusses. 9d.

377. **MARY E. WILKINS**—Blush white, pretty shade; large and well formed. 9d.

378. **NIAGARA**—Of the finest form and size; of the purest white.

380. **DUCHESS OF YORK**—Large pure white; good vigorous habit, large trusses.

381. **SNOWDROP**—Snow white; of perfect form and size; very pure; dwarf and free.

383. **ALBION**—A decided improvement on *Swanley Single White;* very dwarf habit.

384. **WHITE LADY**—Large flowers of the purest white; very dwarf.

. **WHITE VESUVIUS; WHITE WEST BRIGHTON GEM**—Sports from the parents. 6d. each.

HYBRID NOSEGAY, GIGANTEA SECTION.

HERE we have a great move onward in the size of pips and trusses, for they produce immense flowers, measuring 2¾ in. over, and although they are of the Nosegay section their petals are very broad, strong growers, individual pips far beyond any hitherto seen in England, and are evidently the beginning of again enlarging the size of our Zonal Pelargoniums.

389. **BRUSSELS**—Blush pink of a pretty shade; dwarf and robust; distinct. 1s.

390. **MME. F. CARNOT**—Light rosy pink, enormous trusses. 1s.

391. **VOIE LACTEE**—Pure white very large trusses, the only one of its colour in this section.

393. **BELLEROPHON**—Large flowers of a bright scarlet shade; enormous trusses.

394. **GENERAL DODDS**—Equal in size of flowers to any in this class, and of a bright scarlet.

395. **MRS. MAYES**—Flower nearly three inches across; light salmon, shaded with cream.

396. **MRS. E. G. HILL**—Soft salmon, deeper centre.

897. **AURORE BOREALE**—Light scarlet, tinged salmon; flowers immense.

49. A page from *Cannell's Floral Guide* of 1910, showing the huge variety of plants still available before the First World War. *(Reprinted by the British Pelargonium and Geranium Society and reproduced with their permission/Author's Collection)*

Unique (also known as Macbeth) and White Unique, which, he says, was not frequently met with.[13] It seems that White Unique, or a plant very like it, was rediscovered in a derelict greenhouse in 1957 by Peter Abbott, a gardener and nurseryman who specialised in Scented-leaved plants.[14] Of the others, Aurora is probably the one grown now as Aurora's Unique (or Unique Aurora), which is sometimes confused with *ignescens*.

Uniques had also been mentioned in an article by John Walsh in the *Gardener's Magazine* in 1876, on pelargoniums useful for bouquets. He included them as scented-leaved varieties, and said the best were Crimson Unique, Scarlet Unique and Unique Diadem.[15] He also mentioned a similar pelargonium called Lothario, which had rosy-crimson flowers spotted with blackish maroon, and had been distributed by Cannell. In the 1880s *Cannell's Floral Guide* listed eight Uniques, including Unique Diadem (rich violet crimson with dark blotches and feathers) and Mrs Kingsbury[16] (magenta crimson, possibly named after the wife of James Kingsbury (*c.* 1822–85), a nurseryman). The French growers sent over at least one more Unique in the later part of the nineteenth century. Madame Nonin or Monsieur Ninon (or interchangeable variations of the two) has a strikingly beautiful deep pink ruffled flower and pungently scented (not very pleasantly), finely cut leaves. Some nurseries distinguish the two depending on the deepness of the flower colour, but no one really knows the true original. There is, however, a flatter-petalled flower of a similar pink, called Paton's Unique, which is probably a sport from the original, and it is known in the United States as Apricot. Further, there is a variegated-leaf plant with a similar flower, called Phyllis.

The scented-leaved plants mentioned by John Walsh included Pheasant's Foot, which may have been another disregarded Unique, as it had been listed as a hybrid bedding pelargonium in 1861. It is said to have elegantly cut foliage, and be suitable for vase use. He also mentioned *denticulatum, quercifolium minor*, 'a small form of the oak-leaved geranium' and *grandis odorata*, with large oak-shaped leaves. For highly scented foliage, he recommended *radula* and Prince of Orange. In the same article Walsh also mentioned some useful 'Cape' varieties for bouquet use. He pointed out that the flowers of these were useless as far as florists were concerned, but that the plants were worth growing for the versatility of their flowers and foliage for decorative purposes, and that it should be possible to fit them in somewhere without taking up the room needed for choicer varieties. He mentioned *P. echinatum* as a well-known plant, from which many hybrids had been produced. In particular he illustrated Spotted Gem, with neat growth and profuse flower trusses, although he pointed out that the flowers were more elegant and produced on more slender stems than the picture suggested. *Compactum multiflorum* was also said to be compact and free with rose-purple flowers, spotted with crimson. Similarly Rosy Morn was rose-carmine with dark crimson spots. It seems that these were both hybrids from *echinatum*, but this was not mentioned specifically. The flowers of the species were readily available, however: 'As they are not to be met with generally in trade collections, it may save some trouble if it is added that stocks are held by Mr Cannell, who deserves the warmest thanks for having prevented their being practically lost to cultivation.'[17]

Henry Cannell had by that date moved his nursery to larger premises in Swanley, Kent, further away from the pollution of London. It became known as the 'Home of Flowers' for the great variety of florists' flowers and the chrysanthemums, which were one of the specialities.[18] Certainly all pelargonium lovers should have been grateful to Mr Cannell and any other of his contemporaries who made the effort to keep the old varieties alive. Unfortunately, at the end of the nineteenth century none of them could foresee the disasters of the next century that would make it even less likely that these plants would survive in cultivation.

10

Demise and Renaissance

The beginning of the twentieth century saw the triumph of nature over formality best seen in the classic English gardens of Gertrude Jekyll. The exquisite herbaceous borders and seemingly endless pergolas covered in scented rambling roses replaced the carefully calculated parterres of half-hardy plants that had dazzled a previous generation. The pelargonium did not have a place in these predominantly perennial gardens, although they were still grown in conservatories and in tubs on terraces. However, they did come into their own in public parks and municipal gardens, where their bright colours and constant flowering throughout the summer made them indispensable.

The most successful variety for bedding became Paul Crampel, which had been raised in the late 1890s by Victor Lemoine and which gradually superseded previous good bedding varieties such as Henry Jacoby and F.V. Raspail. One story is that the plant was recognised as being so good that a huge stock of plants was built up by the nursery without allowing them to flower so as to avoid anyone stealing them and selling them off. They were then released on the public and sold at £1 each.[1] Whatever the facts of its raising, Paul Crampel represented fifty years of hybridising since the 'beauties run wild' had led to such despair for the Victorian gardeners. It was so successful that no one wanted to grow anything else and this led to the popular idea that that was all there was to pelargoniums: just rows and rows of uniform red-flowered bedding plants. As demand for Paul Crampel grew in every parks department, the stocks of the plant deteriorated, either due to other varieties being wrongly passed off, or because the plant was allowed to revert back to one of its parents.

Outside Great Britain the pelargonium was still of interest, particularly to botanists. In 1912 Reinhard Knuth (1874–1957), a German botanist whose doctoral thesis had been on the Geraniaceae and who was later professor of botany at Berlin, revised the family as part of a larger work comprising the whole plant kingdom.[2] Knuth followed the classification of Harvey in 1860 and included some new species, but his divisions have been amended again since that date. Perhaps of more interest to horticulturalists was the work of the American botanist, Liberty Hyde Bailey (1858–1954), who was the son of a Michigan farmer and had an early interest in plant taxonomy. He became a professor at the Michigan State Agricultural College and later at Cornell University, New York. In 1916 he created names for the two main groups of pelargoniums, the Zonals and the Regals. Those derived largely from *P. zonale* he named *P. × hortorum* (meaning 'of gardens'), and those derived largely from *P. cucullatum* he named *P. × domesticum* (meaning 'domestic' or 'homely'). The official naming did not really change anything in the pelargonium world because everyone knew that the two groups of plants were distinct, and as Bailey did not name the hybrids derived from *P. peltatum*, it did not advance a 'global' classification of the whole genus. The name *hederinum* (meaning ivy-like) has been suggested for that group and perhaps should be adopted.

The Demise

Everything changed in gardening during the First World War (1914–18). The young men who would have been the next generation of gardeners went away to the trenches, and many never returned. Fuel restrictions meant that greenhouses could not be heated. These factors together led to a decline in the interest in

50. A novelty bedding display in Weston-super-Mare in the early twentieth century, featuring Zonal pelargoniums for their brightness and reliability. *(Museum of Garden History)*

greenhouse plants, nurserymen gave up specialising in pelar-goniums and new varieties were not introduced. There was even more reason for Paul Crampel and his allies to be perpetuated every year, as there was little chance of acquiring anything else. When gardeners started to rethink gardening without the large workforce that had been available before the war, they looked for something new. There were improved varieties of 'mignon' dahlias, which lasted better through the winter, and new hybrid antirrhinums in a wide range of colours, and the pelargonium was largely ignored.[3]

But gardeners have long memories and occasionally a spark of interest was kindled. In 1922 John Heal commented in the *Gardeners' Chronicle* that although the Show pelargoniums were no longer popular, and no one knew their true history, they were still valuable as conservatory plants in the winter. He referred to the whole group of Show and Fancy hybrids as 'rough-leaved' varieties, presumably to distinguish them from the Zonals, and he gave a list of recommended varieties, which shows that at least some of them must still have been available.[4] The following year, however, another writer commented that in the immediate neighbourhood of London Zonal pelargoniums were hardly worth growing for winter flowering because one night's fog was sufficient to ruin them.[5]

By the 1930s it seemed that some gardeners were beginning to miss their old friends. An 'anonymous grower' in July 1933 predicted a revival with a new dwarf variety (unnamed) being introduced, and a pink one expected, as if the world had never seen such a thing before. He thought there was a chance that even the Ivy-leaveds and tricolours might find favour again. He mentioned the merit of growing double-flowered and cactus-flowered sorts and named Clorinda as a scented-leaved type worth growing.[6] In August another correspondent commented that when he heard people say 'they hate geraniums', he reminded them that Gertrude Jekyll would always say that a bedding plant was a plant long before it was misused for bedding in Victorian times.[7]

In October 1933 a correspondent to the *Gardeners' Chronicle* observed that it was a continued source of astonishment to him that one never saw pelargoniums exhibited at the RHS shows. He had recently seen only one display, the year before at the Chelsea show, where a Mr Clifton had been allowed 'about six inches of space' in which to exhibit 'something quite extraordinary in the way of varieties', which it had taken him thirty years to get together. He hoped the RHS would allow the pelargonium more prominence, 'particularly the unique varieties'. One wonders whether he meant the 'Unique' varieties, but that the editor or the typesetter did not know the significance of the name.[8] The Mr Clifton referred to was William Alvared Rae Clifton of Chichester (d. 1962), who asked in an advertisement in *Amateur Gardening* in 1935, 'Why not make your greenhouse gay with our superb geraniums?'[9] He was the only specialist grower of pelargoniums throughout the interwar period, having started collecting them in 1902. He ran Cherry Orchard Nursery and published a series of pamphlets, starting with *The Geranium, its History and Cultivation* in 1935.[10] Judging by the several editions and reprints, there must have been quite a few 'closet' pelargonium growers who needed information. Mr Clifton raised the Ivy-leaved pelargonium Mrs W.A.R. Clifton, still available in catalogues today.

In 1935 *Amateur Gardening* asserted that there really was no substitute for the traditional plants:

It is indeed a difficult task to find a plant which will provide a braver show than the pelargonium. A more brilliant or longer-lasting effect than that which is made by scarlet Paul Crampel is hard to imagine. Some plants are vastly improved in association with others of contrasting or harmonising colour, but this variety is one of those that are almost too brilliant to mix readily, and it is usually considered best to plant it alone. Another good kind, but in a more companionable shade, is the salmon King of Denmark. This is a strong grower, and the same might be said for Flower of the Spring, which has pink flowers and white and green leaves; with a groundwork of blue lobelia, it is really delightful. The tricolours, with their ornamental foliage, have never regained their popularity, and it is questionable if even the variety Mrs Pollock is now in keen demand. Where they are grown, however, this is the variety to choose. Of the ivy-leaved kinds, Charles Turner is still supreme, with its deep rose flowers, and the pink Madame Crousse is also striking when planted with a ground work of heliotrope. Both varieties are excellent for draping window boxes.[11]

None of these varieties was new, but it seemed that there was no need to invent any more bedding varieties when the old ones were perfect.

There was still a minority who wanted to know the origins of the plants. A series of letters to the *Chronicle* in 1935–6 concerned the silver-leaved, white-flowered, variety, Mrs J.C. Mappin (sometimes wrongly referred to as Mrs Mapping). Albert Hosking of Guildford summarised the different stories in January 1936, which seemed to agree that the plant originated in the garden of Mr Mappin of Netherfield Court, Battle, near Hastings, in about 1878, although there were different accounts of the raiser. He also gave further details of Flower of the Spring, the red-flowered variety, of which Mrs Mappin was believed to be a sport, as well as comments on sports and variegation generally.[12]

In June 1936 Gerald Wynne Rushton made a valiant attempt to summarise the history of pelargoniums with a full-page article in the *Gardeners' Chronicle*, even suggesting data for a graph to be made of the vicissitudes of the pelargonium in public esteem. He felt that their eclipse was partly due to the chaotic condition of their nomenclature, but does not help his case by going on to refer to Show or Regal sorts and Scented-leaveds as 'pelargoniums proper'. He refers to the brilliant colours of Show pelargoniums, comparing them to Sweet's illustrations, and attributing the colours to the use of *P. ignescens* as a parent, seeming to imply that that is a species. He guesses that the 'great enthusiast' Edward Beck used *ignescens* sparingly, by the appearance of his seedlings, but feels there would be room for the hybridists to regain the colour of the classic Show varieties if they were to use *ignescens* again. But where, he asks, is *ignescens* now?[13] Worse was to come. Mr Wynne Rushton then went on to wonder how he could positively identify the well-known 'Rose Geranium' of his grandmother's day, when the writers at the beginning of the century had declared it impossible to connect their plants with those of Sweet. Miss Henrietta White of Dublin was thought at that date (1935) to have one of the best private collections of pelargoniums. She had been principal of Alexandra College, Dublin, from 1890 to 1932, where she had encouraged horticultural education for girls. She had previously agreed with her two friends, Miss Ellen Willmott (1858–1934) and Mr Vicary Gibbs (1853–1932), who also possessed comparable collections, to use the same names for their scented varieties so as to maintain consistency. Wynne Rushton pointed out that the chaos regarding names had been mentioned in 1870 by Miss Hope (Frances Jane Hope, who was referred to in connection with Rollisson's Unique in Chapter 6, though was probably mistaken in what she said in that context) and repeated in 1904 by Miss White, who had said that she had been unable to identify *any 1* of the 50 varieties in her collection as any of the *500* described by Sweet.

The mention of Miss Willmott exemplifies the way that great plant collections were being broken up at that date, seemingly without a thought. People at the time did not seem to understand that a great plant collection is in many respects unique and to let it be dissipated and, what is probably even worse, to allow the collectors' records to be lost, is as bad as allowing a work of art, such as a painting or a sculpture, to be destroyed. Ellen Willmott was an enormously rich heiress who maintained not just her own home garden at Warley Place, Essex, but gardens in Italy and France as well, so that almost her entire fortune was spent on them. As she never married, Warley was sold after her death and demolished, the site intended for development. However, luckily, the Second World War (1939–45) intervened and afterwards the land was protected from being used for building, so that today the remains of the garden are being recovered by the Essex Wildlife Trust. Unfortunately the pelargoniums she grew have long gone, unlike her daffodil collection which has partly survived in the ground.

Wynne Rushton had similar problems to those of Miss White when comparing the list of pelargoniums in the Glasnevin collection (in Dublin) to Sweet's books. He gives the example of Fair Rosamund, which Sweet shows as large and white with carmine blotches, while the current plant was small, dull pink, and with no blotch. He had also looked at public collections to see which varieties were still grown. Although Glasnevin had sixty-five species and Kew had a good collection, Cambridge had none. At this point it is not clear whether he is referring to Scented-leaved plants only, or all pelargoniums. He said that Brooklyn had three species, Paris had seven species and a large collection of Zonals, Ghent one or two species and a number of Zonals, and La Mortola had ten or fifteen varieties but they were mostly 'badly under a cloud'. He had asked all these gardens to identify the Rose Geranium and had been told variously *capitatum*, a hybrid between *filicifolium* and *grandifolium* (presumably they meant *grandiflorum*), *graveolens*, and *radula*. Wynne Rushton then went on to recount the difficulties in producing oil of geranium. At the end he gave a list of all the different scented sorts, not names of varieties but types of scent, and said how hard they were to find in Britain. Apparently, however, they were much more readily available in the United States, where they had been cherished more carefully. The Garden Club of America had staged an exhibit of Scented-leaved plants at the International Flower Show in New York in 1936. There did, therefore, seem to be some hope.

There were still some independently minded amateurs pursuing their own interests in the pelargonium, waiting for their day to come again, and it was the Scented-leaved group that provided the inspiration. The first attempts at developing a new group, later to be known as Angel pelargoniums, had been made in about 1913–14. This group is sometimes referred to as dwarf or miniature Regals, but has a separate ancestry and can be traced to a specific breeder. Arthur Langley-Smith (d. 1953), a schoolmaster

'Catford Belle'. *(Author's Collection)*

Catford Belle

(Angel pelargonium)

The first of the 'Langley-Smith hybrids' bred by Arthur Langley-Smith in south London in the 1920s and 1930s, by hybridising *P. crispum* and Regals. The plant is small and delicate, with bushy growth, and the flowers are pinkish-purple. They were named Angels after an eighteenth-century plant, Angeline.

from Catford in south London, started to create a line of hybrids using *P. crispum*, one of the lemon-scented pelargoniums with small 'crisp' leaves and an upright habit. He is believed to have crossed *crispum* with a Regal called 'The Shah', but to have gone on to use other species, Regals and hybrids, as well as crossing his own hybrids together. The first hybrid was not introduced until 1935, and was named Catford Belle; later ones included Mrs Dumbrill, Mrs H.G. Smith, Rose Bengal, Shirley Ash and Solferino.[14] They were first known simply as Langley-Smith hybrids and in the books of the 1950s were categorised as Scented-leaved plants. They do not seem to have been very well known at that time. John E. Cross, in 1951, when reviewing all known pelargoniums, described Catford Belle as 'an old variety', so he could not have been familiar with its origin.[15] In 1952 he described it as having a scent like turpentine.[16] They were given the name Angels in 1958 by Derek Clifford, who likened them to a plant named by Andrews as Angelina.[17] Sweet had renamed the plant *P. dumosum*,[18] and its parents may have been *P. betulinum* and possibly *P. crispum*, although no leaf scent is mentioned in the description. This eighteenth-century plant was white with maroon blotches on the upper petals.[19]

There was little attempt to take pelargonium breeding further after Langley-Smith had first introduced his new plants because flower gardening again went into abeyance during the Second World War. It was to be the 1950s before gardeners had enough time and money to start taking much notice of what might be thought of as luxuries when they were digging for victory in their allotments and struggling against fuel restrictions, lack of housing and continued rationing in the late 1940s.

The Renaissance

The first book in Britain in the twentieth century to provide a detailed study of pelargoniums and their history, as well as explaining how to grow them, was *The Book of the Geranium* written in 1951 by John E. Cross, a BBC television producer. He tried to show that there was more to the plants than just scarlet bedders, thought by many to be coarse and vulgar. He based his information largely on the collection of W.A.R. Clifton, listing all the varieties he could find, which was about 350 in total, although he noted that he had since received more nursery catalogues with names he had not been able to include. He divided them into (1) bedding varieties (including Zonals, variegated-leaveds and species, and Ivy-leaveds); (2) greenhouse varieties (including Zonals, Ivy-leaveds, scented-leaveds, cactus varieties, hybrid Ivy-leaveds, dwarf varieties, and unclassified varieties and species); and (3) greenhouse Regal or Show varieties. He then reprinted the whole of Cannell's 1910 catalogue (consisting of over 700 varieties) to show what had been lost in pelargoniums, and in the hope that more lost varieties might be found. He also suggested the formation of a pelargonium society, as no one had any records of the previous one.

Cross suggested that the renewed interest in pelargoniums may have been partly due to a display of many different varieties bedded out together at Kew in 1950, which had been described in a leading article in *The Times*. This said that it was 'stimulating to find Kew trumpeting defiance at the anti-geranium ranks by growing not a few cautious plants, but a hearty eighty-yard belt of them in many shades and varieties of leaf. Indeed, we now see that we never really knew our gardens, even though it is the flower of summer in the London streets.'[20] Also W.A.R. Clifton had shown 'brilliant' displays at Chelsea in 1939 and 1949, at the second of which Eleanor Sinclair Rhode (1881–1950), the gardening writer and historian, had made the following comments:

> I was delighted to find those Victorian favourites, geraniums, in a remarkable range of colours. Geraniums will, I think, once more become a cult. Big bowls of them in mixed colours are so old-fashioned that they appear ultra-modern, and no other flowers light up with such remarkable brilliance in artificial light.[21]

The beginning of the 1950s was exactly the right time to try to give a new look to pelargoniums, at least as bedding plants. J.R.B. Evison, writing in *Amateur Gardening* in 1952, attributed the renewed interest to the displays that had been seen at the Festival of Britain, saying that those who said they were monotonous and vulgar were not familiar with the number of varieties available.[22] The following year was the Coronation and the opportunity for every park and garden horticulturalist to create the greatest displays of their lives. The royal parks in London raised 20,000 plants of Gustav Emich alone, created 300 4ft standards and 600 3ft standards, as well as producing pink and white varieties and Ivy-leaveds for the hanging baskets adorning the lamp-posts along the procession route.[23] By the 1950s Gustav Emich had taken over

51. The inside of an
amateur's greenhouse in
1904 with a fine collection
of pelargoniums. *(Amateur
Gardening, 27 February
1904/Museum of Garden
History)*

from Paul Crampel as the most reliable red bedding variety. Originally raised at the end of the nineteenth century, it was rediscovered in the 1940s under the name of Lord Kitchener and, conveniently for the Coronation, exactly matched the guardsmen's tunics when planted outside Buckingham Palace.[24] D. Giffard in *Amateur Gardening* was of the prevailing view that there was 'more pomp and circumstance about [the pelargonium] than any other species put together'.[25]

This renewed interest caused the Geranium Society to be formed in 1951,[26] becoming the British Pelargonium and Geranium Society in 1964. Articles in magazines became a little more frequent and there was still the occasional mention of history. In 1953 there was some correspondence in the *Gardeners' Chronicle* relating to the origin of the Ivy-leaved pelargoniums Madame Emille [sic] Gallé and Galilee. All correspondents speculated that it or they had been introduced around the turn of the century and had fallen into abeyance due to the recent lack of interest in growing pelargoniums in private gardens. Actually they both appear in *Cannell's Floral Guide* for 1882, Galilee being described as pale lilac and Madame E. Galle [sic] as white. However, Mr H. Broomfield of Bristol hoped that in the Coronation year there might be a resurrection of the old garden favourites.[27]

The next writer to do justice to the pelargonium was Derek Clifford (1915–2003). Clifford was a writer and nurseryman, as well as a collector of pottery, carpets and paintings, all of which he wrote about. His first book on pelargoniums, alarmingly called *Geraniums*,[28] came out in 1953. It was a vignette of pelargonium growing in the midst of its decline, when the author was clearly collecting as many varieties as he could find and testing their worth as garden plants. In 1958 he published the much more comprehensive *Pelargoniums, including the popular 'Geranium'*[29] (the title showing that publishers still did not think it feasible to sell a book on pelargoniums without the magic 'G' word in the title).

Clifford made interesting speculations on the origin of plants such as Nosegays and Uniques, as well as the Regals and Zonals, and named the Langley-Smith hybrids Angels in order to show that they were related to an earlier group of plants. He gave detailed information on all the varieties he mentioned, to try to identify them correctly and show their raisers. Clifford carried on the movement to rehabilitate the pelargonium and restore it to its rightful place in the garden and conservatory, and once more it started to become the subject of horticultural literature.[30]

While the pelargonium had been slow to make progress in Britain, there were developments in the United States. Dauthenay had said that the large Bruant-type plants from France had proved popular in America, partly due to their resistance to strong sunlight. Charles Behringer, a hybridiser in Ohio, had used them to produce a new strain of Zonals called Irenes, which were named after his wife and introduced in 1942. A British nursery-man, Sidney Lake of Rotherfield, Sussex, imported four varieties into Britain in about 1959. In spite of 500 of the 800 plants that were flown across the Atlantic freezing in mid-air, those that survived were propagated and Mr Lake started to develop his own varieties.[31] Two other American growers, Frances Hartsook and F.A. Bode, developed Irenes further in the 1960s, using more French varieties to enhance the semi-double flowers,[32] so that by the 1970s there were about forty-five varieties. The plants are fleshy and vigorous, and leaves green with no zone. They are dramatic plants if given the room to grow, but few people have enough space and they generally went out of favour when people preferred to grow several smaller plants instead of one Irene. New influences came from Europe as well. In 1968 Ken Gamble of Derbyshire introduced what were known as Swiss varieties, although actually from Austria, the best known being Burgenland Girl and Regina. He used these to produce new varieties, leading to his Highfields strain.

Patricia Andrea

(Tulip-flowered pelargonium)

The tulip-flowered pelargoniums were produced in the United States in the 1960s, probably from a sport from a Fiat plant, hybridised from French 'Bruant' types, produced near the end of the nineteenth century. The frilled-petalled flowers never fully open, giving the plant a tulip-like appearance.

'Patricia Andrea'. *(Vernon Geranium Nursery)*

Helen Van Pelt Wilson produced *The Joy of Geraniums* in 1946, giving some history of the plants as well as cultural instructions. The book had been reprinted three times by 1965. She filled in some details of the development of pelargoniums in the United States, and made it clear that there was just as much interest there in the French plants in the 1860s as there was in Britain. American growers also developed Regals. They had been grown in the United States since the 1870s where they were known as Martha Washington or Lady Washington pelargoniums, probably after a cultivar of that name. In Germany in the 1920s Carl Faiss had produced new hybrids with more ruffled petals and a more compact habit. The Americans had used these to produce further refinements. William E. Schmidt of Palo Alto, California, started developing new Regals in the 1940s, particularly trying to increase their flowering period. One of the best varieties, and one still grown today, was Grand Slam (1950), and a sport, Lavender Grand Slam, appeared in 1953. Pink Bonanza appeared in 1966.[33]

The large Fiat types were also used to produce tulip-flowered plants, which appeared in 1966 in the USA and were introduced into Europe in the 1980s. They were hybridised by the Andrea family in Boston, probably from a Fiat sport, and the first was named Patricia Andrea.[34] The flowers have six to nine petals, but they never open properly, giving them the appearance of a tulip. The foliage is characteristically crinkled and the flower colour is carmine red. The plants frequently revert back to the Fiat type and have not been bred extensively.

Australia is another country where pelargoniums were developed in the 1960s. In the 1950s Ted Both used an unusual pelargonium, known as Chinese Cactus (also known as Fiery Chief), to hybridise with a Zonal. He believed Chinese Cactus was similar to a species named by Sweet as *P. staphysagroides*,[35] which was said to have been grown from seed, probably sent from South Africa. The plants produced therefore became known as 'Both's Staphs' and were introduced into Europe in 1966. There were thirty original hybrids in many colours. Unusually, both the

Stellar 'Arctic Star'. *(Vernon Geranium Nursery)*

Arctic Star

(Stellar pelargonium)

The original plant from which the Stellar pelargoniums were hybridised was thought to be a species, but later research failed to find such a species in the wild. Both the flowers and leaves have an irregular pointed shape, probably caused by a virus. They are similar to the Formosa or Fingered-flowered hybrids.

flowers and the leaves were pointed and had the appearance of being star-shaped. Further investigations were made in Britain and in South Africa, however, and it was discovered that there was no such plant as *P. staphysagroides* growing in the wild, and therefore the one known by Sweet must have been a hybrid. It was assumed that the strange shape to the leaves and flowers came from a virus. The plant actually looks similar to the Harlequin grown by Edward Beck in 1848 (see Chapter 5), which he said had no redeeming features as a florists' flower, although its unusual appearance had attracted the attention of Queen Victoria. In 1969 Ted Both's plants were renamed *P. × palmatifolium* by Rob Swinbourne in the *Newsletter* of the South Australian Geranium and Pelargonium Society.[36] When they were introduced into Europe and the United States they were given the name Stellar Pelargoniums. Ted Both was responsible for another new breeding line in Australia, known as zonquils (or zonquels). These were hybrids between Zonals and *P. quinquelobatum*. Only a few were ever produced.

A similar type of plant to Stellars, but smaller, was introduced into the United States in the 1960s. An American, Milton Arndt

'Deacon Lilac Mist'. *(Vernon Geranium Nursery)*

Deacon Lilac Mist

(Double dwarf Zonal)

The Deacon hybrids were developed in the 1960s by the Revd Stringer of Suffolk. He hybridised miniature Zonals with Ivy-leaved plants to produce a small, bushy, compact plant, ideal for small gardens. This variety is white with a rosy-purple edge.

'Rouletta'. *(Author's Collection)*

Rouletta

(Ivy-leaved pelargonium)

Rouletta was discovered in Mexico in the 1960s, believed to be a sport from a red-flowered variety called Mexican Beauty. Its originality lay in its red and white striped petals. Rouletta was grafted on to other Ivy-leaved varieties to produce the Harlequin series of cultivars.

of New Jersey, was on holiday in the Baja California region of Mexico and found growing in the courtyard of a hotel a strange type of pelargonium, from which he took a cutting, which he brought home. When he asked where the plant had come from, he was told that it was thought to have come off a Japanese ship that may have been to Taiwan, then called Formosa. He therefore called the plant 'Formosum'. It was almost like the story of the 'Indian cranesbill', back in the 1630s. It seems that later the story of the Japanese ship was discounted, and another American, Holmes Miller, named the plants 'Fingered-Flowers' when they were introduced into commercial catalogues in 1964.[37] Although Stellars and Fingered-Flower plants are not identical, they have been hybridised together, which shows they have some genes in common, and it seems to be something of a coincidence that both 'Chinese Cactus' and 'Formosum' mysteriously appeared from nowhere and yet both had links to the Far East.

In the 1960s more experiments with small plants were taking place, this time in Britain. The Revd Stanley T. Stringer of Suffolk (d. 1986) used a plant that he thought was Red Black Vesuvius with 'a geranium of the primitive type' to develop the 'Alde' strain of seeds in different shades of red.[38] He produced several other strains of miniature plants in different colours, some with double flowers, and some more he named as 'micro-miniatures'. Later, the Deacon series of dwarf plants was introduced into commercial production, from crosses with Ivy-leaved plants and miniature Zonals. The Revd Stringer introduced eighteen in the next ten years and twenty-four altogether. They appeared at the Chelsea Flower Show for Wick Hill Geraniums in 1970 and also became known as Floribunda pelargoniums because of their profuse flowering.

During the second half of the twentieth century more variation was produced in flower and leaf patterns. Striped flowers originated with an Ivy-leaved plant with white petals, edged in red, named Rouletta. This was believed to be a sport from a red-flowered plant, Mexican Beauty, found by William Schmidt. Mexican Beauty was itself a sport from Comtesse de Grey, introduced by Milton Arndt in the 1950s.[39] In 1977 Rouletta was introduced into Europe, where it was called Mexikanerin or Mexicana, but it should now be known as Rouletta. Rouletta was grafted on to other Ivy-leaved plants to produce the Harlequin range of striped flowers in the 1970s and 1980s.

The stripe in Rouletta is believed to be caused by a virus, which is the explanation also given for leaves that have developed a 'meshed' or 'laced' appearance when the veins turn cream or white. The first such plant that was commercially produced was The Crocodile in 1957 in Australia, an Ivy-leaved plant with fine cream meshing and a deep pink flower. It was introduced into Britain in 1964. A similar cultivar was named White Mesh by Ted Both, which he sent to the Southern California Geranium Nurseries and there it was seen by Sidney Lake in 1962. He arranged for some cuttings to be sent to him in Sussex. Once again, disaster befell the plants, this time due to a delay at customs, and very few could be salvaged from the lifeless, dried-up specimens (another

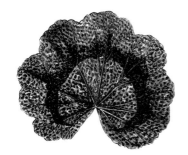

Reticulatum

(Zonal pelargonium)

Reticulatum was pictured by Peter Grieve in 1869, but The Crocodile was the first modern commercially produced 'mesh-leaved' plant, the appearance probably caused by a virus. White Mesh or Sussex Lace is a similar variety and further hybrids have been produced with striped flowers.

'Reticulatum', meshed-leaf pelargonium. *(Peter Grieve*, Ornamental-Foliaged Pelargoniums, *1863, reprinted by BPGS, 1977/Author's Collection)*

reminder of the iron-like constitution of the pelargonium: remember Tom Thumb being rescued from the dust-heap?). Three cuttings survived and one was grown on; that developed a new kind of patterning, and it was named Sussex Lace. Its flower was later seen to be a paler pink than The Crocodile. This story was told in the *Gardeners' Chronicle* in 1967,[40] in which the different characteristics of the plants were defined. The Crocodile had been raised by Mr Robinson of Keiraville, New South Wales, and one parent was called Sallen. There was red veining on the green leaf. White Mesh, on the other hand, was produced from Madame Crousse, and it seems that Sussex Lace is probably the same plant.

By the late 1960s pelargonium growing was once again flourishing in Britain. In 1970 another society was formed in Manchester, the British and European Geranium Society, which was affiliated to the North West Geranium Society. Shows and exhibitions were being held and it became obvious that with the introduction of so many new cultivars and classes of plants something should be done about standardising the names. Other petal colours and patternings were being developed during the twentieth century, although most had appeared from time to time in previous centuries. Bird's Egg varieties had been popular at the beginning of the century, but later, so-called eggshell varieties appeared. There were also 'paintbox' flowers in the 1980s, speckled or freckled flowers probably not very different from the 'painted' flowers of the Victorian era. The 'phlox-flowered' plants, which have a dark-coloured disc in the centre of a single white Zonal flower, were also developed in the twentieth century, but originated as yet another sport from New Life of the 1870s. From the United States there came a flower with a thin white margin round each red petal, named Mr Wren. These were all attractive in their own way, but were still only superficial subdivisions of Zonals.

There were some genuinely new developments in the twentieth century though. In the 1950s F_1 hybrids were developed in America. The term means hybrids from two known, true-breeding cultivars that produce the same plant every time. The first

'Sparkle'. *(Jean-Patrick Elmes)*

Sparkle

(Paintbox Zonal pelargonium)

The paintbox Zonals are another kind of the bird's egg or eggshell varieties produced since the nineteenth century and often marketed as new plants. They are also known as speckled or freckled flowered, but however classified, they represent novelties that will always be popular.

commercially produced strain was called Carefree and became available in 1967. Later, European firms began to produce more and they appeared to be an attractive proposition for many gardeners, who did not want to have to take cuttings and needed plants for one season only. They conform to the desire for compact, reliable plants, good for bedding, and that are disease resistant. The range is limited, however, and mainly consists of single-flowered Zonals. Unfortunately the plants are usually marketed as 'geraniums', which is unnecessarily misleading.

There was also an advance in using the lesser known pelargonium species for hybridising. *P. frutetorum* was hybridised to create some scrambling, trailing varieties, useful for window boxes on balconies or in other situations where they can ramble profusely. The foliage is dark and zoned, and the flowers are different shades of pink. One popular variety was called The Boar. These plants are sometimes known as Cascade types but should not be confused with some of the Ivy-leaved plants also used for balconies and hanging baskets and also called Cascades. These were sometimes referred to as Decoras and Balcons and have been particularly popular in Europe where balconies become almost an art form in summer. The Ivy-leaved varieties were also further developed to create smaller, dwarf and miniature varieties.

Angels were developed again in the 1980s by Jan Taylor and Ray Bidwell, who recognised their usefulness in being smaller than Regals and their distinctive, delicate appearance. They were originally found only in shades of white, purple and lilac, but later varieties have extended the colour range. The characteristics of Angels, which can be seen to have come from their *crispum* ancestry, are their upright habit and their manner of holding the flowers outwards so as to cover the foliage evenly. They also have a longer flowering period than the early Regals. In the United States a separate group of pelargoniums had developed, known as 'pansy-faced cultivars'. Although they looked similar to Angels, they originated from a French variety, Madame Layal, known in about 1870. Further similar varieties were hybridised in the USA in the 1950s and 1960s, but when Angels were exported there, the pansy-faced plants were eclipsed as a separate group. Although Angels are not miniature Regals, there are a few Regals classified as miniatures, usually originating from sports from Regals, and sometimes the two groups are combined in show classes.

Another species that has been hybridised for centuries but is still used to create new plants for a modern world is *P. tricolor* (also known as *P. violareum*), from which has been produced Splendide and Renate Parsley (named after a South African pelargoniste), as well as a hybrid with *P. tomentosum*, Islington Peppermint. Nor were the days of new discoveries over. In 1930 a seedling was discovered at the Royal Botanic Gardens, Kew, with narrow deep red petals, recognised as being a new primary hybrid. The parents were likely to have been *zonale* and *scandens*, and the plant was named *P.* × *kewense*. It was popular when introduced commercially and a sport emerged later with variegated leaves that became known as Silver Kewense.

With the renewed interest in pelargoniums in the second half of the twentieth century, attention was eventually turned back to their home, South Africa. In 1977 the first in a three-volume series of books describing the pelargonium species of southern Africa appeared. The author was Professor J.J.A. van der Walt of the University of Stellenbosch, joined in the later volumes by P.J. Forster, and with illustrations by Ellaphie Ward-Hilhorst.[41] This is the definitive guide to the species, giving descriptions and details of habitat, and some information on the history and medicinal and traditional uses of the plants. In 1996 a one-volume book on Pelargonium species was published, written by Diana Miller of the RHS's Wisley garden, and this too included some information on early hybrids.[42]

Some breeders looked back to the old classes of plants in order to develop new ones. In the United States Frances Hartsook developed new varieties by crossing some of the old Uniques with Regals, intended to be specially adapted to the desert conditions which she found not conducive to some of the other pelargonium varieties. She created Bolero, Carefree, Hula, Mystery, Polka and Voodoo in the 1960s. In the 1980s Ian Gillam of Vancouver created two more, Sweet Memory and Sweet Success.[43] Roller's Satinique also appeared in the catalogues in 1986, believed to be a seedling from Voodoo, found in California in 1982 by Carol Roller.

In 1988 the National Collection of Pelargoniums was established by Hazel Key of Fibrex Nurseries, in Warwickshire. It brought together as many species, early hybrids and modern varieties as could be found, and at the time of writing includes about 2,000 sorts. However, such a number of varieties does raise again the problem of classification of pelargoniums, and how, in particular, some of the older hybrids, such as the Scented-leaved varieties and Uniques, can best be identified.

11

Regaining the Treasures of the Past

This story of the pelargonium has spanned nearly 400 years and it is clear that many of the interconnecting links between the plants have been lost. Those we grow today must retain genes from the species from which they are derived and perhaps one day someone will do the work to reveal exactly what they are. There is no other way to confirm their ancestry as any records that were kept have mostly been lost and the confusion in naming old varieties, and lack of illustration, means that much of the evidence is unreliable. However, the hybridisers left a trail behind them of rejected plants that they did not consider suitable for further development, and some of these can be gathered up and preserved as 'missing links' by those who feel conservation is worthwhile. It is from the so-called 'Scented-leaved' group and the Uniques that many of these precious remnants come.

The Scented-leaved plants seem to exist in a parallel universe and in a different time scale to the other groups of pelargoniums. Many of them are species or primary hybrids, and some are naturally occurring hybrids. Because their flowers were less impressive than those of the species used by florists and gardeners to create specialised plants for exhibition or garden decoration, they were only hybridised intermittently and on a small scale. They therefore tend to be closer to the species. Some seem to have been grown indefinitely, many for centuries, without ever being properly identified. There lies the problem: because they have been largely ignored by horticulturalists, they have been given common names and passed on informally to friends and relatives under those names, which are therefore perpetuated and lead to confusion when an enterprising collector wants to be systematic and tries to identify and label them. Many of the collectors of Scented-leaved plants were women, which is perhaps not surprising because the plants seem to have been grown traditionally on window sills in a domestic setting. They became part of the home, almost part of the furniture, as indoor or 'house' plants often do. It may have been more appropriate to have given the name *P. × domesticum* to these, rather than to Regals. Although these plants were not hybridised for their flowers, people liked them for their scent and foliage. Some varieties are supposed to be good as fly repellents, others can be used like herbs in cooking. The so-called 'lemon geranium' has a place in every home, office or Chinese restaurant, and no one ever bothers to find out its 'proper' name, many people not realising there are many varieties, not just one.

Periodically, attempts were made to try to classify the Scented-leaved plants. In response to the article by Gerald Wynne Rushton in the *Gardeners' Chronicle* in 1936,[1] a correspondent called F.A.B. of Dumbartonshire sent out a plea for their recognition:

One wonders sometimes how it is that such an appealing race of plants should come to be regarded with almost complete indifference by the majority of present-day plant lovers, and whether the increasing quest for 'something new' is after all an unmixed blessing. The trend of fancy that allows such charming plants to slip into oblivion without an effort to arrest their passage must surely suggest some lack of good taste, and I would like to suggest that an eleventh hour effort be made to rehabilitate the scented-leafed Pelargoniums in public favour. Probably the best way to do this would be to create an interest in them by means of displays in the greenhouses of some of the large public parks.[2]

The writer gave some advice on cultivation and then mentioned some of the fourteen varieties he or she grew. These included Fair Emily, Endsleigh, Fair Ellen and Little Gem, as well as *P. echinatum*. The last variety was the subject of an article in 1937 by the American correspondent T.H. Everett of the New York Botanic Gardens, who wrote that he had received a richly coloured specimen from Kew in 1935.[3] As Wynne Rushton had pointed out, there was more interest in the Scented-leaved plants in the United States. This was confirmed by John E. Cross in 1951, when he wrote that there were eighty varieties on sale there.[4]

There had been an earlier attempt to try to produce order out of chaos, at a time when there had been more chance of contacting growers of the plants in the nineteenth century. In 1911 Miss M.C. Troyte-Bullock, a Fellow of the RHS, wrote an article in the *RHS Journal* in which she related her experience of collecting the plants. She cited a list of 111 varieties grown by Lord Ilchester at Melbury House, Dorchester, in 1817, and divided them into groups depending on the species she thought they were descended from. A comprehensive table was then drawn up by Miss E.A.V. Brenan.[5] They were divided into three main groups:

(1) *capitatum* types, including Attar of Roses, *radula*, *graveolens* (including Lady Plymouth), *blandfordianum*, *rapaceum* (including Little Gem and Spotted Gem), Scarlet Pet and Lothario ('of Miss White');

(2) *citriodorum* types, including *grossularioides*, *crispum*, Lady Scarborough, Prince of Orange and Lady Mary (*hirsutum*); and

(3) *quercifolium* types, including Fair Ellen, *pencillatum*, *glutinosum*, *denticulatum*, *filicifolium*, *pinnatum* and Pheasant's Foot.

Following these came the Uniques. They included many that are known today, such as Monsieur Nonin, Purple Unique (listed as or with *conspicuum* of 1810), White Unique, Scarlet Unique,

Variegated Lady Plymouth

(Scented-leaved pelargonium)

Lady Plymouth is a grey-leaved variety of *P. × graveolens*, and this is a variegated version of the grey leaf. It has a rose-lemon scent and the striking lilac flowers are beautifully set off by the foliage.

'Variegated Lady Plymouth'. *(Author's Collection)*

Rollisson's Unique, Claret Rock, Mrs Kingsbury and Shrubland Rose (but not Shrubland Pet). There were several names also known today, or already mentioned in this book, but not normally considered Uniques, such as Clorinda, Lothario, and *P. diadematum*, as well as others not so familiar. Finally came a list of miscellaneous scented plants, such as *abrotanifolium*, *fragrans*, *tomentosum*, *cucullatum*, *ardens*, *ionidiflorum*, *carnosum*, *tetragonum*, Fair Rosamund, More's Victory and *echinatum album* and *rubra* (known as Moulton Gem and Ariel).

Miss Troyte-Bullock seems to have had some thrilling experiences while amassing her collection, some of which came from abroad:

> Do let me point out that one of the chief charms of a collection such as mine is that money cannot buy most of the varieties; barely one dozen of my hundred varieties have come from nurserymen. They are the spoils of about ten years' careful – and let me add, sometimes extremely exciting – search and exchange. What triumph of orchid hunter in Borneo can beat the thrill of

joy with which from the depths of a dirty and disreputable cabaret in the heart of the Ardennes one emerges with a treasure in one's arms, fruit of a long and stormy bargaining with M. and Mme les Proprietaires? As to exchange – words will not express my gratitude to the many kind and generous fellow-collectors to whom I am indebted. From the old village postman (whose gift of a sprig of *gratum* practically started my collection) to the courteous Curator of Kew Gardens, all have combined to overwhelm me with kindness. My *best* friend was the result of answering a chance advertisement in a garden paper! From that generous Irish lady, my collaborator in this article, whose collection puts mine to shame, nearly half my specimens have come. We have never met, and that is the case with many another 'friend by post', but the kind letters I receive from my unknown correspondents form not the least of the pleasures of my collection.[6]

The following year Miss Troyte-Bullock read a paper at the RHS.[7] She expanded on her original information, naming Mr Dorrien-Smith's garden at Tresco Abbey, Isles of Scilly, as the only place where one of the old collections of pelargoniums still existed, although she thought that there might be remnants of Lady Scarborough's collection in the cottages surrounding 'the old house'.[8] Lady Scarborough's name was given to a Scented-leaved hybrid, sometimes said to be reminiscent of strawberries. Miss Troyte-Bullock quoted Sweet[9] as saying that many of the species grown originally had become scarce, as people were only interested in the ones used for hybridising, but she felt there were many more still to be found in country places. She referred also to Donald Beaton's Shrubland plants, which she named as Shrubland Pet, Shrubland Rose and Shottisham Hero.[10] These may have been related to Lothario and Touchstone, which she considered to be scented plants. She repeated her view that it was impossible to buy the plants from nurseries, not just because they

Lady Scarborough

(Scented-leaved pelargonium)

Known by Robert Sweet in the 1820s as Lady Scarborough's Storksbill, this is one of the most enduring Scented-leaved plants still grown today. It has lemon-scented foliage and beautifully marked pinkish-lilac flowers, although is sometimes described as smelling of strawberries.

'Lady Scarborough'. *(Sweet, Geraniaceae, plate 117/Author's Collection)*

did not have many, but because they were often wrongly named. (There was nothing new in that!) She gives more detail on her own classification, but to expand on it here would simply confuse the efforts that have since been made to rationalise the group. She suggested that it was up to the RHS at Wisley to take on the job, but her pleas went in vain.

When pelargonium growing revived in the 1950s it was as much as the enthusiasts could do to try to rationalise the Zonals, Regals and Ivy-leaveds without straying into the more obscure territory of the Scented-leaveds and Uniques. Both Cross and Clifford dutifully mentioned them and admired them but probably felt it was beyond the scope of their work as practising nurserymen to attempt to unravel their ancestry.

In 1964, Edna Knowles wrote a series of articles in the *Gardeners' Chronicle*[11] on the Scented-leaved plants, commenting again that there were many more hybrids, and more information on them, in the United States. Ms Knowles was writing when Harvey's classification was still being used, so the terminology is confusing for a modern reader. She also commented that Clifford did not cover the group in any detail and tried to relate hybrids to species and common names to botanical names. Much of her speculation does not stand up to more recent work, but it shows which plants were still known at that date.

It was not until 1993 that Richard Clifton and David Barrett produced the pamphlet *Pelargoniums with Scented Leaves*,[12] which listed all the varieties they could find with all the information available on their origins and common names. This was followed in 1994 by Peter Abbott's *A Guide to Scented Geraniaceae*,[13] a collection of information on, and descriptions of, scented species and hybrids in both genera Pelargonium and Geranium. Peter Abbott (b. 1923) had trained as a gardener and had collected the Scented-leaved plants all his life. He ran the Cedar Nursery and acquired plants from all over the world, but particularly from the USA. In some cases he discovered that old plants he had known in his youth had been exported to the United States, renamed, and then sent back to Britain under the new name. By growing all the varieties he could find over many years he managed to clearly define which plants were known under synonyms and which were separate varieties. Abbott also listed the Uniques in his book and attempted to define them. Considering that the United States has been cited so often as having the best collection of Scented-leaved plants, it seems surprising that no American author seems yet to have written a book on them. Faye Brawner, in her *Geraniums, The Complete Encyclopaedia*,[14] has a long section listing the plants in groups according to their scents, but does not give much detailed information on their ancestry.

While they may have been overlooked, it would be wrong to think that Scented-leaved plants are dull and monotonous in flower size and colour. There are many hybrids with bright red, deep pink or purple flowers, several with two-coloured flowers, and most will flower profusely all summer. Clorinda has a large-flowered deep pink flower with light green leaves; Copthorne a delicious cedar-scented plant with a large purple, *cucullatum*-type flower; Concolour Lace, probably the same as the old Shottisham Pet, has a plethora of small red flowers and finely cut foliage; Brunswick, a red, almost Unique-type flower; Islington Peppermint and Renate Parsley have small dual-coloured flowers; the list goes on so that an enthusiast will soon build up a collection until the greenhouse overflows.

One amateur grower who researched some of the old hybrids, and the Uniques in particular, is Penelope Dawson-Brown. She wrote several articles in the 1990s,[15] trying to revive the interest at Stourhead in collecting the plants associated with Sir Richard Colt Hoare. She illustrated the pelargonium herbarium of Thomas Moore[16] of the Chelsea Physic Garden, found in the 1990s, and also researched and wrote about the life of Robert Sweet.[17] When

Clorinda

(Scented-leaved pelargonium)

One of the spectacular large-flowered, Scented-leaved plants known before 1900. It has cedar-scented foliage and large pink flowers, and will grow tall and sturdy. Golden Clorinda is a later golden-leaved variety.

'Clorinda'. *(Author's Collection)*

the Geraniaceae Group was started in 1981, one of its aims was to try to re-create some of Sweet's hybrids that had been lost, and they had some success. In Australia, Cliff Blackman has produced many hybrids in the 'Lara' series, using species such as *cortusifolium*, *echinatum* and hybrids derived from them. The Geraniaceae Group has produced the *Checklist of Pelargonium Species* and lists of early cultivars, to ascertain which are true species, and to establish the ancestry of early hybrids. The information on the old plants is therefore available for anyone who wants to find it.

However, there is still no 'official' list of pelargonium cultivar names and probably never will be. Back in the 1970s the Australian Geranium Society was appointed as the International Registration Authority for pelargonium cultivars. Parts one and two of a projected work in ten parts were produced by 1985, covering the letters A to F.[18] The lists include brief descriptions and are apparently based on old catalogues and books, but cannot have covered every source as these had not all been found. Unfortunately, the coordinator died before completion of the work and, while the work in progress was handed on to the British and European Geranium Society, it remains unfinished. Obviously, many more names would by now have to be added to the lists already published. Indeed, a list of names alone would serve little purpose, other than to prevent the names being used again, yet for many of the Victorian cultivars there is little or no description, just lists of names, and many names are repeated again and again. It is simplistic, however, to think that there is only a purpose in classifying plants being grown today, as what would happen when an unknown old variety crops up? There must be a record of old, forgotten varieties, in order to know when one has been found. A further complication is the issue of Plant Breeders' Rights, whereby cultivar names can be registered and plants under that name cannot be sold by anyone else without permission. Clearly, a name used in the past could be registered for a modern variety, and then if an old one were identified and revived, it would have to be renamed.

It is not an idle hope to think that old varieties will be found. While searching for illustrations for this book I visited Southend Borough parks nursery in Essex, and much to my amazement found that they were growing a collection of Victorian bedding and coloured-leaved varieties, Uniques, scented-leaved plants, and Regals dating back to the 1960s when they had regularly shown at Chelsea and other shows. Because the borough had not had the finance to purchase new plants, they had simply continued propagating the old ones. There were several names on the plants that I could not trace, and one that I greeted like an old friend, Pheasant's Foot. Could it be the forgotten Unique or hybrid bedding pelargonium last heard of in 1861? Peter Abbott mentioned Pheasant's Foot in his book on scented-leaved plants as a synonym for *glutinosum* or *viscossimum*. He describes it as having pink flowers and finely cut leaves with a balsam scent. Miss Troyte-Bullock and Miss Brenan also listed it with the *quercifolium* types. The *Gardener's Magazine* in 1877 described it with *denticulatum* as having 'finely-cut foliage'. This plant has very stiff, pungently scented leaves, with elongated sharp lobes and a thin black line down the centre. They have the appearance of a bird's foot, or perhaps even a stag's horn fern. Could there be a connection and confusion somewhere with the other lost hybrid bedding pelargonium, Antler?[19] This may be too much of a leap in ideas, almost as bad as Shirley Hibberd saying Tradescant brought back *Pelargonium triste* from North Africa. However, the plant is not like any other that I have seen described and certainly merits further investigation. It is also possible to find pressed flowers dating back many years. The Museum of Garden History received an anonymous gardener's notebook, probably dating back to the 1840s, and inside was a collection of pressed pelargonium flowers. They are mostly unnamed, but are clearly florists' varieties.

52. A collection of pressed pelargonium flowers found in a gardener's notebook and believed to date back to the mid-nineteenth century. The flowers are mostly unnamed but include florists', Show and French types. *(Museum of Garden History)*

The purpose of this book has been to bring together the historical information on pelargoniums into one place, to encourage gardeners to enjoy the modern plants and conserve what remains of the old varieties. Today, pelargonium societies flourish again, species collected in their native habitats are grown all over the world and new varieties are constantly being developed. With climate changes due to global warming, it may become easier to keep pelargoniums through the winter in northern Europe and as a plant certainly suited to drought conditions, the pelargonium seems to be a plant of the future. In 2007 one can choose from thousands of plants, scented or non-scented, plain-leaved, zoned or coloured, with flowers of every colour, except the elusive blue. From its first appearance in Europe, nearly 400 years ago, the pelargonium has established itself as an indispensable part of our gardens, and we should continue to admire and celebrate it.

53. A prize-winning poster for the Liverpool International Garden Festival in 1984. The bright red Zonal pelargonium was naturally chosen to depict city gardening. *(Museum of Garden History)*

Appendix 1

Botanical Classification of Pelargonium Species

This book does not aim to present a complete account of the taxonomy of pelargoniums, as this is comprehensively covered by others. However, it would be negligent not to give details of the present-day classification of the plants for readers who are interested. Some history of how the classification developed is referred to in the text as an important part of the story of the plants, but here the general division of the genus into sections is set out, with examples of species referred to in the text.

The classification of pelargoniums by European botanists began in the early 1600s when they first observed the plants brought from South Africa. They could only describe them in relation to plants they already knew, and they saw they were similar to the geraniums that they were already familiar with, which they called cranesbills after the shape of the seed pod (*geranos* being the Greek word for crane). Later, as more plants appeared, they began to see there were consistent differences in the flowers of the 'African geraniums' compared to the European ones, and some botanists were prepared to divide them into different groups. However, Linnaeus, when he introduced his new system of classification in 1753, did not consider the African species to be different enough to be put into a new genus, and he kept them within Geranium. The first botanist to use the Linnaean system for classification *and* to call the plants pelargonium (*pelargos* being the Greek word for stork) was L'Heritier in the 1790s. Throughout the next 200 years several botanists, including Sweet, de Candolle, Harvey and Knuth, reassessed the pelargonium sections, adding to them and amalgamating them by turn, until today there are generally accepted to be fourteen sections. There are, however, still disputes and discussions, and species are sometimes moved from one section to another. In the second half of the twentieth century, research into chromosomes and DNA, as well as chemical analysis of plant tissue, changed classification methods previously based on plant structure and habitat. It is a testament to the work done by the early botanists that very few species were moved from their original sections, rather it was the sections themselves that were reassessed. For detailed descriptions of the plants, see J.J.A. van der Walt's *Pelargoniums of Southern Africa* or Diana Miller's *Pelargoniums*. To check species names, and how they have changed over the years, see Richard Clifton's Geranium Family *Species Check List, Part 4, Pelargonium*.

The Sections of the Genus Pelargonium

Campylia

The name, meaning curved, was introduced by Sweet and used by de Candolle and Harvey. It includes the species *tricolor* and *ovale*, which were used to hybridise 'Splendide'; and also *incarnatum* and *elegans*.

Ciconium

The name was used by Sweet and Harvey, and the section includes several species used for hybridising by horticulturalists, such as *peltatum* (also known as *lateripes*), *zonale* and *inquinans*. Other species in this group are *frutetorum*, *alchemilloides*, *stenopetalum*, *acetosum* and *quinquelobatum*.

Cortusina

The section was introduced by Harvey and consists of desert species, such as *crassicaule* and *cortusifolium*, many of which are succulent. The best known is *echinatum*, dating back to 1795, when it was described in *Curtis's Botanical Magazine*.

Glaucophyllum

Harvey first defined this section which, as its name suggests, consists of plants with glaucous (greyish-green) leaves. The species in this section most likely to be encountered are *fruticosum*, *grandiflorum* and *lanceolatum*.

Hoarea

Sweet named this group after Sir Richard Colt Hoare of Stourhead. It was amalgamated by de Candolle with two other of Sweet's groups, Seymouria (named after Mrs Seymour, a collector from Woburn in Bedfordshire) and Grenvillea. Harvey split them again into Hoarea and Seymouria, but they are now both classified under the name Hoarea. They are all geophytes, which become dormant during unfavourable conditions and appear to be dead. They are not therefore much in demand for general horticultural use, but are fascinating to collectors with the facility for keeping them.

Isopetalum

This section was named by Sweet as a separate genus, but retained by de Candolle and Harvey as a section. It consists of only one slow-growing species, *cotyledonis*, which comes from the island of St Helena.

Jenkinsonia

Sweet introduced this section as a new genus, named after Robert H. Jenkinson. De Candolle divided Sweet's genus into three sections, Jenkinsonia, Chorisma and Myrrhidium. Harvey amalgamated the first two back to Jenkinsonia. The plants have a top pair of petals, very obviously different from the others, an example being *tetragonum*. Two species are native to the Middle East (which makes them hardy in some parts of Britain), and one to East Africa.

Ligularia

Harvey used this name for a section that was enlarged by Knuth. Its many varied plants include *fulgidum*, *alpinum* and *spinosum*.

Myrrhidium

This was the section divided by de Candolle from Sweet's genus, Jenkinsonia. It includes the species *myrrhifolium*, with very divided leaves and proportionately large flowers.

Otidia

This is a small section, named by Sweet and retained until the present. The plants are succulent and slow-growing and include *carnosum*.

Pelargonium

This large section was named by Sweet, but the group went through many changes until it reached its present status. It includes many species useful to horticulturalists, such as *quercifolium*, *capitatum*, *tomentosum*, *crispum*, *cucullatum* and *betulinum*. Most of these species have scented leaves and many have been used to create cultivars. More examples are *denticulatum*, *radens*, *panduriforme*, *vitifolium*, *cordifolium*, *papilionaceum* and *greytonense*.

Peristera

This section was subdivided by de Candolle from Sweet's Pelargonium genus. It was then retained by later botanists with variations. They are short-lived plants which are native to Australia, East Africa, Madagascar and Tristan da Cunha, as well as southern Africa. *Grossularioides* is one species relatively easy to find.

Polyactium

This section was a subdivision by de Candolle from Sweet's Pelargonium genus. They are tuberous plants, which allows them to store water underground, and may also have thickened stems above ground. The section includes well-known species such as *triste* and *gibbosum*, both of which are night-scented. Other interesting species with attractive flowers are *caffrum, bowkeri, schizopetalum* and *lobatum*. This section, more than any, gives the collector a chance to show the uninitiated just what pelargoniums are capable of.

Reniformia

This section was named by Knuth to include some plants from the earlier Cortusina and Ligularia sections, according to their habitat. Many have small, scented leaves, such as *odoratissimum, fragrans, dichondrifolia, ionidiflorum, sidoides, abrotanifolium* and *exstipulatum*. The species with the same name as the section, *reniforme*, has outstanding deep magenta flowers.

Appendix 2

Horticultural Classification and Glossary

Horticulturalists classify their plants in a different way to botanists as they are more concerned about the appearance and use of the plants than their origins. Many gardeners would not be interested in whether a plant were a species or a hybrid, although they would find it useful to know if they wanted to reproduce it. Also, as has been seen in this book, the names of the groups have changed through history as more specialised hybridising took place and different uses were made of the plants.

There is no universal classification of pelargoniums, other than the botanical one set out in Appendix 1. Societies that run shows use their own classifications, which may be broadly similar to others, but tend to reflect the interests of those exhibiting and competing in that particular society. Nursery catalogues usually divide the plants into similar groups to the show groups, but also according to uses and sometimes according to colour, often with a miscellaneous group including species, early hybrids and plants that don't fit in anywhere else. It very much depends on what their specialities are and what their customers want. Some plants can appear in more than one group: for instance, Uniques are sometimes grouped with Scented-leaved plants; Coloured-leaved varieties are also Zonals. It is therefore difficult to divide pelargoniums into mutually exclusive groups. Terminology, as well as common names, also vary in different countries, so referring to a book written in the United States or Australia can be confusing to British readers if they are not aware of the differences.

Hybrids and cultivars (intentionally produced hybrids) have been named in different ways throughout the 300 years of pelargonium growing. The early hybrids were generally given Latin names in the same way as the species, partly because they were not necessarily known to be hybrids and partly because it was the convention of the time. Gradually, as more plants were produced intentionally by nurserymen and their commercial potential was visualised, the growers began to use names they thought would help the plants to be marketable.

During the nineteenth century there were few sanctions against retailers passing off any product as another, and there was little 'quality control' or 'consumer protection' in any type of goods. It was quite common for nurseries to use the same name for a plant as that from another nursery. As plants were often named after historic or fictional characters, or patriotic concepts such as 'Victory', it was common for a plant to be known by the raiser as well as the name, such as 'More's Victory' or 'Henderson's Efulgence' to distinguish them from a plant of the same name from another raiser. Similarly, the same name might be used by the same nursery for different plants in different categories, such as a Zonal and an Ivy-leaved. Again, as some varieties only lasted a season or two, the name might be repeated a few years later for a different plant. There is therefore huge scope for confusion when trying to trace back plants to discover their history. Such research is not helped by the lack of illustrations in early magazines. Added to this is the common habit of nursery-men naming a plant after another famous plant, whether or not they were related. The bright red Zonal, Vesuvius, produced many sports, so it was logical to call the white sport White Vesuvius. However, Black Vesuvius appeared to be named because it had black leaves and bright red flowers, thought to be as good as those of Vesuvius.

When pelargonium growing was revived in the mid-twentieth century it was difficult to be certain about the true origins of cultivars, and nurseries probably adopted old names for plants that they thought they recognised. As time went on it became important to some growers to try to rationalise the names and standardise the groups of plants. However, as new groups were continually appearing it became an ongoing task. In the 1970s the British Pelargonium and Geranium Society produced a checklist which was used internally but was not published. In the late 1950s or early 1960s a list was compiled in the United States, known as the Spalding List, although no one seems to know why. If there was a Mr or Ms Spalding, he or she has not been identified. This was never published and as it contains so many mistakes it was probably a draft list, possibly circulated originally for approval or addition. It relied on nursery catalogues and H. Dauthenay's list of 1897. It divided plants into the following categories: Species, Zonals, Variegated-Leaved, Domesticum (Regals), Ivy-Leaved, Scented-Leaved, and Old (miscellaneous plants listed by the nurseryman Van Houtte). For each plant a 'Raiser' and/or 'Originator' is given, often with a date, as well as a description.

In about 1970 a more concerted effort was made to compile a cultivar list by Mrs Jean Llewellyn of the Australian Geranium Society. She intended to produce a ten-part register. By 1985 she had published two parts (up to Fynn) and had compiled the other eight before her death in 1999, but at the date of writing (2006) these eight have still not been published.

In 2001 Richard Clifton of the Geraniaceae Group published a checklist of pelargonium cultivars from 1840 to 1959. This is based on the Spalding List, with corrections and additions. It is complementary to his previous 'Decadic' (ten-yearly) lists for the years 1450 to 1839 and his Species Checklist, and is the most complete list in existence.

Lists of pelargonium groups have appeared in several books for horticulturalists. One of the most comprehensive was Derek Clifford's in 1958, and more recently Hazel Key's *1,001 Pelargoniums* in 2000. However, although they give good descriptions of plants known at the time the books were written, they only give sketchy information on the history and origin of the plants.

Glossary

The following is a glossary of names used in the past and the present, at home and abroad, rather than a definitive list of groups only found today.

Angel pelargoniums – originally known as **Langley-Smith hybrids**, named Angels by Derek Clifford in 1958. Hybrids from *P. crispum* and **Regals**, named after 'Angelina' of the eighteenth century. Appearance similar to miniature **Regals**.

Balcons – trailing ivy-leaved pelargoniums, also known as Cascades or Decoras.

Bird's egg pelargoniums – **Zonals** with flowers speckled like a bird's egg, known in the 1890s.

Bruant pelargoniums – **Zonal** hybrids raised by Paul Bruant of Poitiers in the late 1800s; also known as 'grand bois' (large wood) type.

Butterfly-zoned pelargoniums – variegated **Zonals**, having an irregular 'butterfly'-shaped cream or white patch in the centre of a green leaf, e.g. A Happy Thought. The name can also be used for plants with leaves of two shades of green with similar markings, e.g. Crystal Palace Gem.

Cactus-flowered pelargoniums – developed in the late nineteenth century, **Zonals** with twisted petals, likened to cactus-flowered dahlias. Also known as **Poinsettia-flowered** or **Quilled**.

Cape pelargoniums or species – name used in the eighteenth and nineteenth centuries for species or early hybrids.

Carnation-flowered pelargoniums – **Zonals** with serrated petals, first produced in the late nineteenth century.

Coloured-leaved or Fancy-leaved pelargoniums – **Zonals** with variegated and zoned leaves, which together produce patches of reds and browns as well as green and cream or white, extensively bred in the 1860s.

Cyclops pelargoniums – see **Painted Lady**

Deacon pelargoniums – dwarf or miniature **Zonals** raised by S.T. Stringer of Suffolk, with a branching, upright habit.

Decorative pelargoniums – in the nineteenth century, the name originally meant **Show pelargoniums** not considered good enough for the show bench, so used as decorative plants for conservatories; later described as **Regals**. The term is used now by some nurseries for a particular type of **Regal** thought to be closer to the old types.

Dwarf, miniature and micro-miniature pelargoniums – **Zonals** of small habit, generally classified as:
   Dwarf – not above 8–10in (200mm) high
   Miniature – not above 5in (125mm) high
   Micro-miniature – not above 3in (75mm) high

Fancy pelargoniums – nineteenth-century group developed out of **Florists' pelargoniums**, smaller and more delicate than **Show pelargoniums**, with round, flat flowers, generally veined or feathered on the lower petals and blotched or margined on the top.

Fancy-leaved pelargoniums – see **Coloured-leaved**

Fiat hybrids – large **Zonals** developed from **Bruant** types *c.* 1908, with frilled petals.

Fingered-flowered – see **Formosa** hybrids

Five-fingered pelargoniums – see **Formosa** hybrids

Florists' pelargoniums – plants derived from *cucullatum, fulgidum,* and many other species and early hybrids, developed by florists in the early nineteenth century for competitions. They later evolved into **Show, Fancy, French** and **Spotted** sorts.

Formosa or **Formosum** hybrids – developed from a plant found in Mexico, believed to be from Formosa. Later named **Fingered-flowered** or **Five-fingered**.

Freckled varieties – see **Paintbox Zonals**

French pelargoniums – used in the mid-nineteenth century to refer to French types of **Florists' pelargoniums** with markings or 'spots' on all five petals; see also **Spotted pelargoniums**.

Frutetorum hybrids – hybrids developed from *P. frutetorum,* also known as Cascades.

Grandiflorum pelargoniums – name used in Germany and Holland for **Regals**.

Hybrid bedding pelargoniums – a nineteenth-century classification for hybrids used for bedding before the **Zonals** were fully developed for the purpose.

Hybrid – Ivy-leaved pelargoniums – hybrids between **Ivy-leaved pelargoniums** and **Zonals**, with characteristics more like **Zonals**.

Hybrid – Zonal pelargoniums – hybrids between **Zonals** and **Ivy-leaved pelargoniums**, with characteristics more like **Ivy-leaveds**.

Irene hybrids – **Zonals** developed *c.* 1940 in the USA from **Bruant** types, with the same large, vigorous habit.

Ivy-leaved pelargoniums – hybrids produced from *P. peltatum*, probably through hybridising in the nineteenth century with **Zonals**.

Langley-Smith hybrids – see **Angels**

Martha Washington pelargoniums – American name for **Regals**, probably named after an early variety.

Meshed pelargoniums – **Ivy-leaved** pelargoniums with light-coloured veining on the leaves producing a 'meshed' appearance, caused by a virus.

Micro-miniature pelargoniums – see **Dwarf pelargoniums**

Miniature pelargoniums – see **Dwarf pelargoniums**

Noisette pelargoniums – see **Rosebud**

Nosegay pelargoniums – nineteenth-century type of **Zonal** with narrow petals but large heads of flowers, said to be descended from *P. fothergillii* and/or *P. crenatum*.

Oculated pelargoniums – flowers with a distinct contrasting centre, first listed in the late 1800s.

Paintbox Zonals – flowers covered in dots and streaks of a darker colour, originating in the nineteenth century.

Paintbrush Zonals – with spiky petalled flowers like a paintbrush – also known as **Fingered-flowered**.

Painted-lady pelargoniums – **Zonals** with an appearance of being airbrushed, whiter at the centre, darker at the outside.

Palmatifolium – name given to **Stellar pelargoniums** in Australia.

Pansy-faced cultivars – American name for plants similar to Angels, descended from Madame Layal.

Phlox-flowered pelargoniums – flowers with a ring of colour round the florets' centre.

Picotee Zonals – flowers with a pencilling effect round the edge of the petals.

Poinsettia-flowered pelargoniums – see **Cactus-flowered**

Quilled pelargoniums – see **Cactus-flowered**

Regal pelargoniums – large-flowered pelargoniums developed in the late nineteenth century from **Decorative** or **Show pelargoniums**, classified as *P. × domesticum*. There are also **Dwarf** and **Miniature Regals**.

Rosebud pelargoniums – **Zonals** with large heads of tightly packed double petals which never fully open, developed in the late nineteenth century. Also known as **Noisettes** after their similarity to Noisette roses.

Scented-leaved pelargoniums – plants grown mainly for their scented leaves rather than their flowers. However, some **Uniques** with scented leaves are sometimes included. Many scented-leaved plants are species or early hybrids.

Show pelargoniums – the large-flowered pelargoniums developed in the mid-nineteenth century from **Florists' pelargoniums**, and from which the **Regals** were eventually produced.

Spotted pelargoniums – **Fancy pelargoniums** developed in the mid-nineteenth century from the **French** varieties, with spots or marks on all five petals.

Staphs – see **Stellar pelargoniums**

Stellar pelargoniums – plants with star-shaped leaves and flowers, first bred by Ted Both in Australia in the 1950s, known as **Staphs** because believed to descend from *P. staphysagroides*.

Tulip-flowered pelargoniums – **Zonals** developed from **Fiats**, with petals that never open fully, and each floret has the appearance of a tulip flower.

Uniques – hybrid pelargoniums, many of which date back to the eighteenth century, named after an unidentified plant known as 'the old Unique', and included in the **Hybrid bedding pelargoniums** of the early nineteenth century. In the twentieth century a new group of Unique hybrids was developed in the USA.

Variegated pelargoniums – plants with cream or white markings on the leaves (also known as **Gold** or **Silver-leaved**).

Appendix 2

Zonal pelargoniums – hybrid pelargoniums generally believed to have originated from *Zonale* and *inquinans*, which may have single, double or semi-double flowers, classified as *P.* × *hortorum*.

Zonquil pelargoniums – hybrids between **Zonals** and *P. quinquelobatum*.

Appendix 3

List of Suppliers and Organisations

Specialist Pelargonium Nurseries
Barnfield Scented-leaf Pelargoniums
Barnfield, Wilnecote Lane, Belgrave, Tamworth, Staffordshire B77 2LF
01827 250123   brianandjenniewhite@hotmail.com

Fibrex Nurseries Ltd (holder of National Collection of Pelargoniums)
Honeybourne Road, Pebworth, near Stratford-upon-Avon,
Warwickshire CV37 8XP
01789 720788   www.fibrex.co.uk

Fir Trees Pelargonium Nursery
Stokesley, North Yorkshire TS9 5LD
01642 713066   www.firtreespelargoniums.co.uk

Oakleigh Nurseries Ltd
Petersfield Road, Monkwood, Alresford, Hampshire SO24 0HB
01962 773344   www.oakleigh-nurseries.co.uk

Brian and Pearl Sulman
54 Kingsway, Mildenhall, Bury St Edmunds, Suffolk IP28 7HR
01638 712297   www.sulmanspelargoniums.co.uk

Swanland Nurseries
Beech Hill Road, Swanland, North Ferriby, Hull, East Yorkshire
HU14 3QY
01482 633670   www.swanlandnurseries.co.uk

Vernon Geranium Nursery
Cuddington Way, Cheam, Sutton, Surrey SM2 7JB
0208 393 7616   www.geraniumsuk.com

Organisations
British and European Geranium Society
Membership Secretary: 8 Roses Close, Wollaston, Wellingborough,
Northamptonshire NN29 7ST
www.begs.org.uk

British Pelargonium and Geranium Society
Mrs Gwen Ward, 'Lyneham', Hullbrook Lane, Shamley Green,
Guildford, Surrey GU5 0UQ
www.bpgs.org.uk

The Geraniaceae Group
Membership Secretary: Peter Starling, 22 Northfields, Girton,
Cambridgeshire CB3 0QG
www.geocities.com/RainForest/Canopy/3139

International Geranium Society
IGS Membership, Dept. WWW, PO Box 92734, Pasadena, CA 91109-
2734, USA
www.geocities.com/RainForest/2822

Notes and Sources

Introduction

1. Not all pelargoniums are native to southern Africa. Some come from other parts of Africa, mainly along the eastern side, and some are from the Middle East, as well as Australia, and one species is from St Helena, but most of the species used for hybridising are from the Cape area of South Africa.
2. *Geraniaceae Group Associated Note 10* (Dover, Geraniaceae Group, 2001), p. 3.

Chapter One

1. Thomas Johnson, *Gerard's Herball* (1633), p. 948.
2. Miles Hadfield, *A History of British Gardening* (Penguin Books, 1985), p. 89; Maggie Campbell-Culver, *The Origin of Plants* (Headline, 2001), p. 140; Anna Pavord, *The Naming of Names* (Bloomsbury, 2005).
3. The name storksbill is used here for the geranium as an alternative to cranesbill, but cranesbill was, and still is, the name commonly used. Storksbill was later adopted for the pelargonium.
4. *Gardeners' Chronicle*, 3 July 1880, p. 5. The lecture was given on 29 June 1880, on the occasion of the Pelargonium Society's annual exhibition.
5. *Ibid.*, p. 6.

6. The Wardian case was a closed, glazed box which protected living plants on the decks of ships and provided a microclimate in which they could survive voyages through varying latitudes.

7. J.J.A. van der Walt and P.J. Vorster, *Pelargoniums of Southern Africa* (3 vols, Cape Town, Purnell & Sons S.A. (Pty) Ltd, 1977, 1981, 1988), vol. 1, p. 46.

8. R.T. Gunther, *Early Botanists and their Gardens* (Oxford University Press, 1922); Marjorie F. Warner, 'The Morins', *National Horticultural Magazine* (July 1954), p. 168.

9. Jacques Cornut, *Canadensium Plantarum, Historia* (Paris, Simonem Le Moyne, 1635), p. 109.

10. In South Africa the plant is used to treat diarrhoea and dysentery: see van der Walt and Vorster, *Pelargoniums of Southern Africa*, vol. 1, p. 46.

11. J. Harvey, *Early Nurserymen* (Chichester, Phillimore & Co. Ltd, 1974), p. 148.

12. Diana Miller, *Pelargoniums: A Gardener's Guide to the Species and their Hybrids and Cultivars* (London, B.T. Batsford Ltd, 1996), p. 15. The plants would have been given descriptions in Latin, according to the convention of the time. As botanical names had not been standardised and no illustrations were given, it can only be guessed which plants they were. However, botanists have agreed that *cucullatum* is likely to have been one of them.

13. Jan and Caspar Commelin, *Horti Medici Amstelodamensis Rariorum Plantarum Descriptio et Icones* (1682–1710).

14. See generally O. Wijnands, *The Botany of the Commelins* (Rotterdam, A.A. Balkema, 1983).

15. *Ibid.*, pp. 106–9. According to Wijnands, the others were *acetosum, auritum, myrrhifolium* (var. *fruticosum*), *pinnatum* and *rapaceum*.

16. Information given here on Bentinck's life comes from Marion E. Grew, *William Bentinck and William III (Prince of Orange)* (John Murray, 1924).

17. At least one writer has asserted that their relationship was even closer and that they were lovers: see Robin Brooks, *The Mystery of the Portland Vase* (Duckworth, 2004), p. 156.
18. For further details of the gardens, see David Jacques and Arend Jan van der Horst, *The Gardens of William and Mary* (Christopher Helm, 1988).
19. R.T.F. Clifton, *Geranium Family Species Checklist*, Part 4: *Pelargonium* (The Geraniaceae Group, 1999), pp. 21, 22.

Chapter Two

1. Diana Miller, *Pelargoniums: A Gardener's Guide to the Species and their Hybrids and Cultivars* (London, B.T. Batsford Ltd, 1996), p.121; J.J.A. van der Walt and P.J. Vorster, *Pelargoniums of Southern Africa* (3 vols, Cape Town, Purnell & Sons S.A. (Pty) Ltd, 1977–88), vol. 1, p. 17.
2. For some biographical information, see Sally Festing, 'The Second Duchess of Portland and her Rose', *Garden History*, Spring (1985), p. 195.
3. Robin Brooks, *The Mystery of the Portland Vase* (Duckworth, 2004).
4. George Rude, *Hanoverian England* (Stroud, Sutton Publishing, 2003), p. 67.
5. At this date all pelargoniums were still called geraniums.
6. Ruth Hayden, *Mrs Delany, Her Life and Her Flowers* (London, British Museum Press, 1980), p. 131.
7. A. Llanover (ed.), *Autobiography and Correspondence of Mary Granville, Mrs Delany* (6 vols, Richard Bentley, 1861). I am grateful to Derek Adlam of Welbeck for informing me of this reference.
8. The collage, including 'scarlet geranium', is on p. 29 of volume VI of the British Museum collection of Mrs Delany's collages (ref. 1897–5–5), and is numbered 529*. Unfortunately, although the 'scarlet geranium' is illustrated on p. 131 of Ruth Hayden's

book, it has been wrongly captioned as being described by Mrs Delany as Bloody Cranesbill (which could mistakenly be thought to mean scarlet geranium), which words do not appear on the original collage. The confusion probably stems from the fact that 'bloody' cranesbill (*Geranium sanguineum*) sounds as if it is red, whereas the 'bloody' refers to its traditional use for staunching wounds; the flower of *G. sanguineum* is actually purple.

9. Hayden, *Mrs Delany*, pp. 114–15.
10. Howard was a member of the Earl of Suffolk's family, a relative of Anne, the first wife of William Bentinck.
11. R. Hingston Fox, *Dr John Fothergill and his Friends* (Macmillan and Co., 1919), p. 183.
12. *Ibid.*, chapter 10.
13. In *ibid*, p. 202, it is stated that the pelargonium appears in Kerner's *Hortus Sempervirens*, 1795, vii, tab. 469. However, tab. 469 is not in vol. vii, which is in the RHS's Lindley Library, but would be in a later volume, which is not in the Lindley and probably not in any other library in Britain. A plant under this name is described in Robert Sweet's *Geraniaceae* (figure 226 of 1825 (vol. 3)) but there is no certainty that it is the same plant.
14. Francis Masson, 'An Account of Three Journeys from Cape Town into the Southern Parts of Africa', *Philosophical Transactions*, LXVI, Third Journey, 29 February 1776.
15. *Ibid.*, pp. 295–6.
16. *Ibid.*, pp. 306–7.
17. *Ibid.*, Second Journey, 3 January 1776.
18. Henry C. Andrews, *Geraniaceae* (1792), figure 26.
19. *Curtis's Botanical Magazine*, vol. 9, figure 315 (1795).
20. William John Burchell, *Travels in the Interior of South Africa* (2 vols, 1822–4, repr. Batchworth Press Ltd, 1953).
21. *Ibid.*, vol. 1, p. 72.

22. *Ibid.*, vol.1, p. 149. The word means 'kidney-leaved', from the shape. However, *renifolium* is the recognised name of an Australian species. The South African kidney-shaped-leaved pelargonium is properly called *reniforme*, which is a striking magenta-flowered plant with soft greyish leaves.
23. *Ibid.*, vol. 1, p. 161.
24. *Ibid.*, vol. 2, p. 70.

Chapter Three

1. For further details, see R.T.F. Clifton, *L'Heritier: Geraniologia – Discussion and Index of the Figures* (Dover, The Geraniaceae Group, 1996). A facsimile edition of the plates was published in Holland by Boerhaave Press in 1978.
2. Details of Curtis's life are from W. Hugh Curtis, *William Curtis 1746–1799, Botanist and Entomologist* (Winchester, Warren and Son Ltd, 1941).
3. It continued until 1983, well over a century longer than its rivals, and in 1995 the name was revived for the *Kew Magazine*.
4. There is a detailed plan and drawing of the inside of Banks's house in H.B. Carter, *Sir Joseph Banks* (British Museum (Natural History), 1988), but unfortunately it could not be reproduced here as the copyright could not be ascertained.
5. Further details of the dispute over the Dombey herbarium can be found in Carter, *Sir Joseph Banks*.
6. Patrick O'Brian, *Joseph Banks, A Life* (Collins Harvill, 1989), pp. 206–7.
7. *Ibid.*, pp. 207–11.
8. In my experience these plants are often found in the front window of Chinese takeaway restaurants. I would love to know why.
9. See R.T.F. Clifton, *Geranium Family Species Check List, Part 4: Pelargonium* (Dover, The Geraniaceae Group, 1999), p. 118.
10. British Library, ref. c.23.fff.17(3).

11. The other numbers of Curtis's plates of pelargoniums are 136, 143, 148, 165, 201, 240, 309, 315, 413, 477, 493, 518, 524 and 547.

12. This is now known as *P. radens*. See J.J.A. van der Walt and P.J. Vorster, *Pelargoniums of Southern Africa* (3 vols, Cape Town, Purnell & Sons S.A. (Pty) Ltd, 1977–88), vol. 1, p. 38.

13. See further, Robin Brooks, *The Mystery of the Portland Vase* (Duckworth, 2004), pp. 114–19. As to Emma Hamilton, see Kate Williams, *England's Mistress, The Infamous Life of Emma Hamilton* (Random House, 2006).

14. *Curtis's Botanical Magazine*, vol. 45, pl. 1983 (1828).

15. *Gardener's Magazine*, vol. 8 (1832), pp. 476–81.

16. For further details of Andrews's eccentricity in botanical terminology, see R.T.F. Clifton, *Henry Andrews and Geraniaceae, 1798–1828; Index and Discussion*, 2nd edn (Dover, The Geraniaceae Group, 2000), p. 2.

17. Henry C. Andrews, *Monograph of the Genus Geranium* (1805), Introduction.

18. Henry C. Andrews, *Botanists' Repository*, vol. III, pl. 499 (1802).

19. See Clifton, *Henry Andrews*, p. 3.

20. See Ray Desmond, *A Celebration of Flowers, 200 Years of Curtis's Botanical Magazine* (Royal Botanic Gardens, Kew, and Collingridge, 1987), p. 57.

21. See Clifton, *Pelargonium Species Check List*, p. 23.

22. *Ibid.*, p. 119.

Chapter Four

1. Most of the information on Sweet and his trial is based on the account of his life given in Penelope Dawson-Brown, 'Robert Sweet FLS, 1783–1835', *The Linnean*, vol. 12, no. 4 (January 1997), pp. 29–34.

2. John Harvey, *Early Nurserymen* (Chichester, Phillimore & Co. Ltd, 1974), p. 130.

3. *The Times*, 3 February 1824.
4. Robert Sweet, *Geraniaceae, The Natural Order of Gerania* (5 vols, 1820–30), vol. 3, no. 212.
5. *The Times*, 3 February 1824.
6. *Ibid.*, 26 February 1824.
7. Colt Hoare had a conservatory leading off his library, the ultimate luxury for the studious plant collector. It was demolished long ago, and the reconstructed greenhouse today housing pelargoniums at Stourhead was brought in from a different garden.
8. For the information given here on Colt Hoare's manuscript, I am very grateful to Richard Soar.
9. Clifton gives several different varieties and explains the relationship with 'Splendens': see *Geranium Family Species Check List, Part 4: Pelargonium* (Dover, The Geraniaceae Group, 1999), pp. 72–4.
10. There are various spellings for More, but this one is used consistently in this book.
11. Sweet, *Geraniaceae*, vol. 1, fig. 23; Clifton, *Pelargonium Species Check List*, pp. 45–6.
12. *Ibid.*, pp. 44, 119.
13. *Ibid.*, p. 94.
14. *Ibid.*, p. 38.
15. *Ibid.*, p. 41.
16. *Ibid.*, p. 88.
17. *Ibid.*, p. 59.
18. Robyn Marsach, *My Garden, Letters of Mary Russell Mitford* (Sidgwick and Jackson, 1990).

Chapter Five

1. For the history of amateur gardening, see Anne Wilkinson, *The Victorian Gardener* (Stroud, Sutton Publishing, 2006).
2. Ruth Duthie, *Florists' Flowers and Societies* (Princes Risborough, Shire Publications, 1988).

3. *Gardeners' Chronicle*, 3 July 1880, p. 6.
4. *Floricultural Cabinet*, September 1834, plate facing title page. The quality of the picture shows the difference between the botanical drawings of the eighteenth century and the horticultural drawings of the nineteenth.
5. *Ibid.*, June 1835, pp. 139–40.
6. A guinea was £1 1s. In pre-decimal currency twelve pence (*d*) made a shilling (*s*) and twenty shillings made a pound (£).
7. As explained before, this was probably *lobatum*.
8. *Floricultural Cabinet*, November 1840, p. 242.
9. R.T.F. Clifton, in *Geranium Family Species Check List, Part 4: Pelargonium* (Dover, The Geraniaceae Group, 1999), says Prince Regent is mentioned by Sweet (*Geraniaceae*) in fig. 81 of 1821 (vol. 1) as a parent of *P. calycinum*, and Commander-in-Chief is *P. involucratum*, var. *incarnatum* (Sweet's fig. 33 of 1820 (vol. 1)). It is pink, with a medium-sized spot, veined dark red.
10. *Floricultural Cabinet*, January 1837, p. 8.
11. *Ibid.*, July 1838, p. vii. The plant may be the same as Efulgens listed in R.T.F. Clifton, *Decadic Pelargonium Cultivars, Part 4* (Dover, The Geraniaceae Group, 2000–2), but there was also a later plant, Fulgens, from Wilson's, said to be a fine scarlet crimson, the top petals dark with a light centre: see *Floricultural Cabinet*, May 1841, p. 119.
12. *Gardeners' Chronicle*, 2 October 1841, p. 643.
13. Sweet's and Andrews's hybrids had generally not been produced from the Zonals or Ivy-leaveds. As to the oak-leaved, various different plants had been described as such. 'Quercifolium' means oak-leaved, but it was seen in Chapter 3 that L'Heritier confused the species which was so named and the confusion has lasted to this day.
14. *Gardeners' Chronicle*, 29 January 1842, p. 68.
15. *Ibid.*, 2 October 1841, pp. 643–4.
16. *Ibid.*, 15 January 1842, p. 37.

17. *Floricultural Cabinet*, September 1841, p. 212.

18. *Gardeners' Chronicle*, 1 July 1843, p. 447.

19. It may be that Thurtell's name was later corrupted to Turtle, as several pelargoniums are named as 'Turtle's'.

20. *Floricultural Cabinet*, September 1843, p. 201.

21. *Ibid.*, September 1840, p. 191, sent in by S.A.H. of Arundel.

22. *Gardeners' Chronicle*, 30 September 1843, p. 681.

23. *Ibid.*, 9 March 1844, p. 151. This is clearly related to the medicinal use for *Geranium sanguineum*, 'the bloody cranesbill'.

24. *Ibid.*, 21 September 1844, p. 637.

25. *Ibid.*, 24 October 1846, p. 710.

26. *Ibid.*, 5 December 1846, p. 806.

27. *Floricultural Cabinet*, October 1843, p. xii.

28. Information of Beck's life was found in newspaper cuttings and census returns in the Hounslow Record Office.

29. *Gardeners' Chronicle*, 4 November 1848, p. 735.

30. *Ibid.*, 2 January 1847, p. 4.

31. *Ibid.*, 30 January 1847, p. 70; 13 February 1847, p. 102.

32. *Ibid.*, 26 June 1847, p. 420.

33. *Ibid.*, p. 419.

34. Wilkinson, *Victorian Gardener*, pp. 35–40.

35. *Gardeners' Chronicle*, 20 November 1847, p. 763.

36. There were two George Gordons who were writers in the nineteenth century, possibly father and son. This was the older one, as the later one's dates were 1822–1914.

37. This might have referred to the plant known as Shepherd's Queen Victoria from Henderson's Nursery (see text, above).

38. There is a *P. sanguineum*, as well as the better known *Geranium sanguineum*: see Clifton, *Pelargonium Species Check List*, p. 128.

39. *Gardeners' Chronicle*, 4 December 1847, p. 799.

40. *Florist*, July 1848, p. 169.

41. *Ibid.*, November pp. 301–4, 320–1.

42. *The Garden*, 30 October 1886, p. 415.
43. This was not the same Upton Park where Fothergill had lived, but was south-west of London, near Windsor and Slough.
44. i.e. £1.50 in decimal currency.
45. *Florist*, July 1849, pp. 170–1.
46. *Floral Magazine*, 1862, plate 75.

Chapter Six

1. *Floricultural Cabinet*, January 1837, pp. 53, 57. From this date onwards, names are less often written as botanical names in italics.
2. E. Adveno Brooke, *The Gardens of England* (T. McLean, *c.* 1856); *Cottage Gardener*, 23 September 1856, pp. 452–4.
3. *Proceedings of the RHS*, 1861, p. 434, 1862, p. 128; *Gardeners' Chronicle*, 6 April 1861, p. 313, 15 February 1862, p. 139. For a complete list of pelargoniums appearing in RHS trials from 1859 to 1901, see R. Clifton, *Geraniaceae Group, Associated Note 25* (The Geraniaceae Group, October 2006).
4. The main problem with bedding out Uniques, particularly in a wet summer, is that they grow enormous and produce a lot of foliage at the expense of flowers. Trying it for yourself will show why the Victorians hybridised the modern bedding pelargoniums.
5. *Gardeners' Chronicle*, 9 November 1861, p. 968.
6. *Cottage Gardener*, 1 April 1856, p. 4.
7. These various references to Purple Unique were gathered together in the *Gardeners' Chronicle*, 22 December 1923, pp. 364–5, when there was a renewed interest in the plant.
8. *Ibid.*, 26 October 1861, p. 945.
9. *Ibid.*, 9 November 1861, p. 968.
10. Derek Clifford, *Pelargoniums, Including the Popular 'Geranium'* (Blandford Press, 1958), p. 130.
11. R.T.F. Clifton, *Geranium Family Species Check List, Part 4: Pelargonium* (Dover, The Geraniaceae Group, 1999), p. 36.

12. R.T.F. Clifton, *Decadic Pelargonium Cultivars, Parts 1–5* (Dover, The Geraniaceae Group, 2000–2), Part 1, p. 50.

13. *The Garden*, 24 November 1877, p. 491.

14. *Gardeners' Chronicle*, 5 February 1876, p. 180.

15. *RHS Journal* 1861, vol. 1, p. 200.

16. *Floricultural Cabinet*, April 1847, p. 84.

17. Clifton, *Pelargonium Species Check List*, describes several early hybrids as Zonal cultivars, but they cannot be distinguished.

18. *Floricultural Cabinet*, September 1840, p. 205.

19. Shirley Hibberd, *Familiar Garden Flowers*, 2nd series (Cassell and Co. Ltd, *c.* 1880), p. 38.

20. *Gardeners' Chronicle*, 13 October 1866, p. 973.

21. *Ibid.*, 7 February 1846, p. 85. Some years later Shirley Hibberd referred to Trentham Scarlet as 'True Tom Thumb', which was not explained: *Gardener's Magazine*, 21 July 1877, p. 352.

22. *Florist*, July 1849, p. 171.

23. *Henderson's Illustrated Bouquet*, vol. II, 1859–61, plate L.

24. It seems to be the Unique story all over again!

25. *Cottage Gardener*, 21 October 1856, p. 41.

26. Clifton, *Decadic Pelargonium Cultivars* lists a Stella, probably raised by Beaton before 1854, and a Stella Nosegay, as a Zonal from Beaton, undated. Cybister is listed as an orange-scarlet Nosegay type, attributed to Beaton before 1869. The other two are not listed.

27. See *Cottage Gardener*, 6 October 1863, p. 266, 3 November 1863, p. 349, 24 November 1863, p. 415, referring to Beaton's autobiography in the *Cottage Gardener*, 28 November 1854, p. 153.

28. *Floral Magazine*, 1865, vol. V, p. 317. Presumably this was not the same Duchess of Sutherland listed in the *Floricultural Cabinet* in 1835: see Chapter 5.

29. *Henderson's Illustrated Bouquet*, vol. III, 1861–4, Plate LXXXIII.

30. However, Andrews gives Bath Scarlet as another name for

crenatum, which is supposed to be one of the origins of the Nosegays – so the story goes round in circles once again.

31. Clifton, *Pelargonium Species Check List*, gives *fulgens* as *formosissimum* of Sweet and Andrews, which is probably descended from *betulinum* (see p. 58). There is no indication of a connection to the Efulgence or Efulgens referred to in Chapter 5, note 10.

32. Kinghorn was a Scottish gardener who later worked at Twickenham, before opening the Sheen Nursery. Later, he was frequently a judge at competitions and a member of the RHS Floral Committee: see *Gardeners' Chronicle*, 18 June 1887, vol. 1, p. 817.

33. *Ibid.*, 10 May 1856, pp. 322–3.

34. *Cottage Gardener*, 23 September 1856, pp. 452–4.

35. Shirley Hibberd, *The Amateur's Flower Garden* (Groombridge and Sons, 1871). The instructions, and several more, appear in Chapter II.

36. Shirley Hibberd, *Rustic Adornments for Homes of Taste*, New Edn (Groombridge and Sons, 1870), pp. 310–14.

37. *Florist*, October 1849, p. 269.

Chapter Seven

1. *Gardeners' Chronicle*, 7 September 1844, p. 605.

2. *Henderson's Illustrated Bouquet*, vol. III, 1861–4, plate LXXXIII.

3. R.T.F. Clifton, *Decadic Pelargonium Cultivars, Parts 1–5* (Dover, The Geraniaceae Group, 2000–2), Part 1, p. 7.

4. *Ibid.*, p. 6.

5. Details of Grieve's life come from E.J. Willson, 'Peter Grieve' in E.J. Willson (ed.), *Fancy-leaved Pelargoniums, Peter Grieve and After* (British Pelargonium and Geranium Society, 1990), p. 21.

6. Reprinted by the British Pelargonium and Geranium Society 1977.

7. *Gardeners' Chronicle*, 3 July 1880, p. 5.

8. Kinghorn recounted the story himself in *ibid.*, 15 September 1866, p. 876, referring to the parent plant as Globe Compactum.
9. *Ibid.*, 3 July 1880, p. 7.
10. *Ibid.*, p. 628. He gives the reference for this as a lecture given by John Wills, then gardener at Huntroyde, to the Royal Horticultural Society on 21 May 1867.
11. *Floral Magazine*, 1862, plate 101.
12. *Henderson's Illustrated Bouquet*, vol. II, 1859–61, plate LII.
13. *Florist*, January 1865, pp. 1–2.
14. There is little information on this plant, although it is often quoted as a parent. There were several members of the Mangles family connected to gardening and plant collecting in Australia, the best known being Capt James Mangles (1786–1867).
15. *Gardeners' Chronicle*, 28 January 1865, p. 74.
16. *Ibid.*, 29 May 1869, pp. 582–4.
17. *Ibid.*, 3 July 1880, p. 7.
18. *Cornhill*, January 1885, quoted in *The Dickensian*, 1907, p. 55.
19. *Ibid.*, 1948, p. 251.
20. Diana M. Miller, 'Pelargonium "L'Elegante"', *The Garden* (September 1996), p. 560.
21. *Gardeners' Chronicle*, 14 July 1866, p. 660.
22. *Floral Magazine*, vol. V (1865), p. 257.
23. Derek Clifford, *Pelargoniums, Including the Popular 'Geranium'* (Blandford Press, 1958), pp. 39–40.
24. *Gardener's Magazine*, 21 July 1877, p. 352.
25. *Ibid.*, 17 January 1880, pp. 26–7.
26. *Ibid.*, 24 March 1877, p. 128.
27. *The Garden*, 19 June 1886, p. 582.
28. Shirley Hibberd, *Familiar Garden Flowers*, 2nd series (Cassell and Co. Ltd, *c.* 1880), p. 129.
29. *Gardener's Magazine*, 21 April 1877, p. 179.
30. *Gardeners' Chronicle*, 15 February 1862, pp. 139–40.
31. *Henderson's Illustrated Bouquet*, vol II, 1859–61, plate L.

32. *Floral World*, December 1873, p. 353.
33. *Gardener's Magazine*, 28 August 1875, p. 443.
34. *Gardeners' Chronicle*, 30 September 1876, p. 425.
35. *Gardener's Magazine*, 14 April 1877, p. 171, and also 10 November 1877, p. 558.
36. *Gardeners' Chronicle*, 13 January 1877, pp. 203–4, referring to vol. VI (1876), p. 398.
37. *Gardening World*, 10 January 1885, p. 302.
38. *Gardener's Magazine*, 10 November 1877, p. 558.
39. *Gardeners' Chronicle*, 12 August 1876, p. 200.
40. *Gardener's Magazine*, 26 June 1880, p. 317.
41. *Ibid.*, 28 August 1875, p. 443.
42. John E. Cross, *Pelargoniums for all Purposes* (W.H. & L. Collingridge Ltd, 1965), p. 18.
43. Robert Sweet, *Geraniaceae, The Natural Order of Gerania* (5 vols, 1820–30), supplementary volume (1830), no. 81.
44. *Ibid.* (1830) no. 86.
45. See *Gardeners' Chronicle*, 3 July 1880, p.7, referring to ibid, 17 August 1850, figs. 1,2.
46. Clifford, *Pelargoniums*, pp. 243–4; Faye Brawner, *Geraniums, The Complete Encyclopaedia* (Altglen, PA, Schiffer Publishing Ltd, 2003), p. 6.
47. *Gardener's Magazine*, 6 March 1875, p. 109.
48. *Gardeners' Chronicle*, 18 November 1876, p. 650.

Chapter Eight

1. A copy can be read in the RHS Lindley Library.
2. *Gardener's Magazine*, 5 September 1874, p. 475.
3. *Florist*, June 1862, p. 83.
4. The old dispensary building is still there, but is now a solicitors' office.
5. *Gardener's Magazine*, 26 November 1881, pp. 681–2; *Gardeners' Chronicle*, 3 July 1880, p. 7, 26 November 1881, p. 702.

6. *Floral World*, 1873, p. 355.

7. *Gardener's Magazine*, 12 September 1874, p. 486.

8. *Ibid.*, p. 487.

9. *Ibid.*, 14 November 1874, p. 616.

10. *Ibid.*, 12 December 1874, pp. 661–2.

11. *Ibid.*, p. 662.

12. *Ibid.*, 24 July, 1875, pp. 366–7.

13. *Ibid.*, 31 July 1875, p. 389.

14. *Ibid.*, p. 380. It seems that Mr Cooling may have had too much from The Criterion's wine cellar, as I can find no reference anywhere to 'Willoughbyanum'.

15. *Ibid.*, 10 March 1877, p. 99.

16. *Ibid.*, 24 March 1877, p. 124.

17. *Gardeners' Chronicle*, 17 March 1877 (vol. VII), p. 340.

18. *Ibid.*, p.340.

19. *Ibid.*, 2 June 1877, p. 685.

20. *Gardener's Magazine*, 23 June 1877, p. 308.

21. *Gardeners' Chronicle*, supplement for 9 June 1877, p. 685 (viii).

22. Princess of Wales in still available, and must therefore be one of the oldest Regals. It is sometimes confused with a similar variety, Prince of Wales.

23. It has sometimes been suggested that the name Regal, meaning royal, was used for the plants because they were grown at the royal family's home at Sandringham. I have not found any reference to Regals at Sandringham until the 1950s: see *Amateur Gardening*, 15 July 1952, p. 16.

24. *Gardener's Magazine*, 7 February 1880, p. 60.

25. The *Gardeners' Chronicle* of 1 July 1876 (p. 16) was still perplexed about classifying this plant: 'we require a distinct classification of this section [decorative pelargoniums]'. It was said to have a generally robust habit and be grown more easily than the more delicate, higher-bred varieties, by those whose house accommodation is limited. The name is variously spelled St Mande and St Maude.

26. *Gardener's Magazine*, 5 June 1880, p. 271.
27. *Gardeners' Chronicle*, 2 June 1877, p. 694.

Chapter Nine

1. A pelargonium species with a similar leaf is *P. alpinum.*
2. *Proceedings of the RHS*, 1861, p. 441.
3. *Gardeners' Chronicle*, 18 April 1868, p. 405.
4. *Ibid.*, 2 November 1861, p. 968.
5. *Ibid.*, 22 December 1923, p. 365.
6. John E. Cross, *The Book of the Geranium* (Saturn Press, 1951), p. 93.
7. Faye Brawner, *Geraniums, The Complete Encyclopaedia* (Altglen, PA, Schiffer Publishing Ltd, 2003), p. 58.
8. See *Cannell's Floral Guide*, 1883.
9. R. Clifton, *Zonal Pelargoniums: A History at 1896, from 'Les Géraniums' by H. Dauthenay* (Dover, The Geraniaceae Group, 2006). Dauthenay referred to several books in French: see J. De Jonghe, *Traite Methodique de la Culture du Pelargonium* (Brussels, J.B. Tircher, 1844); M. Malet and B. Verlot, *Culture Pratique des Pelargonium* (Paris, E. Donnaud, undated); and also Boucharlat, *Culture du Pelargonium a Grande Fleurs*, 2nd edn (Lyon, published by author, 1875). These are all in the RHS Lindley Library, as is Dauthenay, *Les Géraniums.*
10. He attributed the name to Carrière, who was presumably a French nurseryman after whom the Ivy-leaved plant Abel Carrière was named.
11. See Chapter 7.
12. This name was later given to a Regal.
13. *Gardeners' Chronicle*, 2 December 1876, p. 714.
14. Peter Abbott, *A Guide to Scented Geraniaceae* (Angmering, Hill Publicity Services, 1994), p. 189.
15. *Gardener's Magazine*, 24 March 1877, p. 128.
16. In the author's experience Mrs Kingsbury and Jessel's Unique

are identical, but that may be because of misidentification by nurseries.

17. *Gardener's Magazine*, 24 March 1877, p. 128.
18. *Gardeners' Chronicle*, 31 October 1914, p. 300.

Chapter Ten

1. This story is related in John E. Cross, *The Book of the Geranium* (Saturn Press, 1951), p. 18, but refers to the raiser being named Paul Crampel and gives the date of release as 1903. These details are corrected in Cross's later book, *Pelargoniums for All Purposes* (1985).

2. See R. Knuth, 'Geraniaceae', vol. IV of A. Engler, *Das Pflanzenreich* (Germany, 1912). The work was written in German and Latin.

3. *Gardeners' Chronicle*, 1 July 1933, p. 6.
4. *Ibid.*, 9 December 1922, p. 342.
5. *Ibid.*, 27 January 1923, p. 49.
6. *Ibid.*, 1 July 1933, p. 6.
7. *Ibid.*, 26 August 1933, p. 167.
8. *Ibid.*, 28 October 1933, p. 333.

9. See classified advertisements in *Amateur Gardening*, 22 and 29 June 1935.

10. Published by B.H. Gadd, Worthing, and available in the RHS Lindley Library, together with the accompanying letters by the author.

11. *Amateur Gardening*, 30 March 1935, p. 1019.
12. *Gardeners' Chronicle*, 18 January 1936, p. 42.
13. *Ibid.*, 13 June 1936, p. 386.

14. See Faye Brawner, *Geraniums, The Complete Encyclopedia* (Altglen, PA, Schiffer Publishing Ltd, 2003), pp. 90–5. Unfortunately, although several books give these details on the Langley-Smith hybrids, I have not managed to find any direct information about their introduction or Langley-Smith himself.

15. Cross, *Geranium*, p. 102.
16. *Amateur Gardening*, 2 December 1952, p. 23.
17. Derek Clifford, *Pelargoniums, Including the Popular 'Geranium'* (Blandford Press, 1958), p. 44.
18. Robert Sweet, *Geraniaceae, The Natural Order of Gerania* (5 vols, 1820–30), vol. 1 (1820), fig. 19.
19. R.T.F. Clifton, *Geranium Family Species Check List, Part 4: Pelargonium* (Dover, The Geraniaceae Group, 1999), pp. 12, 50.
20. *The Times*, 21 September 1950, p. 5.
21. Quoted in Cross, *Geranium*, pp. 113–14.
22. *Amateur Gardening*, 12 February 1952, p. 18.
23. See T. E. Atkins, *ibid.*, 29 May 1953, p. 23.
24. John E. Cross, *Pelargoniums for all Purposes* (W.H. & L. Collingridge Ltd, 1965), p. 18; Clifford, *Pelargoniums*, p. 99.
25. *Amateur Gardening*, 15 May 1953, p. 22.
26. *The Times* praised this development: see 9 August 1952, p. 6.
27. *Gardeners' Chronicle*, 28 February 1953, p. 80.
28. Published by Ernest Benn Limited, 1953.
29. Published by Blandford Press, 1958.
30. Another writer of the same era who helped to popularise pelargoniums was Anthony C. Ayton: see his lecture 'The Modern Pelargonium', *RHS Journal*, vol. 88 (August 1963), p. 326.
31. *Gardeners' Chronicle*, 25 January 1964, p. 57.
32. Brawner, *Geraniums*, p. 8.
33. For further details of British and American breeders in the period 1950s to 1980s, see Alan Shellard, *Geraniums for Home and Garden* (Newton Abbot, David and Charles, 1981).
34. Brawner, *Geraniums*, p. 61.
35. Sweet, *Geraniaceae*, vol. 5 (1830), fig. 498.
36. See South Australian Geranium and Pelargonium Society *Newsletter*, Summer 1970.
37. The plants are sometimes known as 'Five-Fingered' and also continue to be known as Formosa hybrids.

38. *Gardeners' Chronicle*, 22 February 1967, p. 10.
39. It seems that this also came from Mexico, but whether Mr Arndt went there regularly or managed to find both this and the plant supposedly from Formosa at the same time has not been verified. These stories appear in several books on pelargoniums but no source is ever given for them.
40. *Gardeners' Chronicle*, 22 February 1967, p. 10.
41. J.J.A. van der Walt and P.J. Vorster, *Pelargoniums of Southern Africa* (3 vols, Purnell & Sons S.A. (Pty) Ltd, 1977, 1981, and 1988).
42. Diana Miller, *Pelargoniums, A Gardener's Guide to the Species and their Hybrids and Cultivars* (B.T. Batsford Ltd, 1996).
43. Brawner, *Geraniums*, pp. 63, 64.

Chapter Eleven

1. See Chapter Nine.
2. *Gardeners' Chronicle*, 11 July 1936, p. 24.
3. *Ibid.*, 13 March 1937, p. 169.
4. John E. Cross, *Book of the Geranium* (Saturn Press, 1951), p. 101.
5. Both articles are in the *RHS Journal*, vol. 37 (1911–12), pp. 103–7.
6. *Ibid.*, pp. 104–5.
7. *Ibid.*, vol. 38 (1912–13), p. 497.
8. Presumably somewhere in Yorkshire.
9. Robert Sweet, *Geraniaceae, The Natural Order of Gerania* (5 vols, 1820–30), vol. 3, p. 299, under *P. odoratissimum*.
10. Shottisham Hero could be the same as Shottisham Pet.
11. *Gardeners' Chronicle*, 17 October 1964, p. 398; 31 October 1964, p. 445; 14 November 1964, p. 493.
12. The pamphlet is available in the RHS Lindley Library.
13. Peter Abbott, *A Guide to Scented Geraniaceae* (Angmering, Hill Publicity Services, 1994).
14. Faye Brawner, *Geraniums, The Complete Encyclopedia* (Altglen, PA, Schiffer Publishing Ltd, 2003).

15. Penelope Dawson-Brown, 'Unique Display', *Country Life* (26 January 1995), p. 36; Penelope Dawson-Brown, 'A Plantsman's Passion Revived at Stourhead', *Country Life*, 8 June 2000, p. 200.

16. Penelope Dawson-Brown, 'Unique Origins', *The Garden*, November 1996, p. 694.

17. Penelope Dawson-Brown, 'Robert Sweet FLS, 1783–1835', *The Linnean*, vol. 12, no. 4 (January 1997), p. 29.

18. See Jean Llewellyn *et al.*, *A Check List and Register of Pelargonium Cultivar Names*, Part 1 (A and B), Part 2 (C–F) (Australian Geranium Society Inc, 1978, 1985).

19. For an illustration and comments on this variety, see *Geraniaceae Group News*, Summer 2006, pp. 6, 7.

Bibliography

The place of publication is London, unless otherwise stated.

Books

Abbott, Peter. *A Guide to Scented Geraniaceae*, Angmering, Hill Publicity Services, 1994

Andrews, Henry C. *Monograph of the Genus Geranium*, 1805

Ayton, Anthony C. 'The Modern Pelargonium', *RHS Journal*, vol. 88 (August 1963), p. 326

Bailey, Henry. 'The Pelargonium, Culture of the Various Classes', *The Garden*, 1880

Beck, Edward. *A Treatise on the Culture of the Pelargonium*, Chapman & Hall, 1847

Boucharlat, M. *Culture du Pelargonium a Grandes Fleurs*, 2nd edn, Lyons, 1875

Brawner, Faye. *Geraniums, The Complete Encyclopaedia*, Altglen, PA, Schiffer Publishing Ltd, 2003

Brooke, E. Adveno. *The Gardens of England*, T. McLean, *c.* 1856

Brooks, Robin. *The Mystery of the Portland Vase*, Duckworth, 2004

Brown, Mary and Kevin. *Isleworth: The Second Selection*, Tempus Publishing, 1998

Burchell, William John. *Travels in the Interior of South Africa*, 2 vols, 1822–4, repr. Batchworth Press Ltd, 1953

Burmann, J. *Rariorum Africanarum Plantarum*, 1738

Campbell-Culver, Maggie. *The Origin of Plants*, Headline Book Publishing, 2001

Carter, H.B. *Sir Joseph Banks*, British Museum (Natural History), 1988

Bibliography

Clark, David. *Pelargoniums (Kew Gardening Guides)*, The Royal Botanic Gardens, Kew, with Collingridge Books, 1988

——. *The Pelargonium Guide*, Alresford, Oakleigh Publications, 1990

Clifford, Derek. *Geraniums*, Ernest Benn Ltd, 1957

——. *Pelargoniums, Including the Popular 'Geranium'*, Blandford Press, 1958

Clifton, R.T.F. *Decadic Pelargonium Cultivars, Parts 1–5*, Dover, The Geraniaceae Group, 2000–2

——. *Geraniaceae Group Associated Notes: 5, 10, 20, 22, 24, 25* Dover, The Geraniaceae Group, 1999–2006

——. *The 'Geraniaceae' of Robert Sweet, 1820–1830, Index and Discussion*, 2nd edn, Dover, The Geraniaceae Group, 1998

——. *Geranium Family Species Check List, edn IV, Part 4: Pelargonium*, Issue 4, Dover, The Geraniaceae Group, 1999

——. *Henry Andrews and Geraniaceae, 1798–1828; Index and Discussion*, 2nd edn, Dover, The Geraniaceae Group, 2000

——. *L'Heritier: Geraniologia – Discussion and Index of the Figures*, Dover, The Geraniaceae Group, 1996

——. *Pelargonium Bibliography, Part 1*, Dover, The Geraniaceae Group, 1998

——. *Zonal Pelargoniums: A History at 1896, from 'Les Geraniums' by H. Dauthenay*, Dover, The Geraniaceae Group, 2006

Clifton, W.A.R. *The Geranium, its History and Cultivation*, Worthing, B.H. Gadd, 1935

Coats, A.M. *The Quest for Plants*, McGraw Hill, 1970

Cornut, Jacques. *Canadensium Plantarum, Historia*, Paris, Simonem Le Moyne, 1635

Cross, John E. *The Book of the Geranium*, Saturn Press, 1951

——. *Pelargoniums for all Purposes*, W.H. & L. Collingridge Ltd, 1965

Curtis, W. Hugh. *William Curtis 1746–1799, Botanist and Entomologist*, Winchester, Warren & Son Ltd, 1941

Dauthenay, H. *Les Géraniums*, Paris, O. Doin et Fils, et Librairie Agricole, 1897

Dawson-Brown, Penelope. 'A Plantsman's Passion Revived at Stourhead', *Country Life*, 8 June 2000, p. 200

——. 'Robert Sweet FLS, 1783–1835', *The Linnean*, vol. 12, no. 4, January 1997, p. 29–34

——. 'Unique Display', *Country Life*, 26 January 1995, p. 36

——. 'Unique Origins', *The Garden*, January 1996, p. 694

De Jonghe, J. *Traite Methodique de la Culture du Pelargonium*, Brussels, J.B. Tircher, 1844

Delany, Mary. *Letters*, Longman, Hurst, Rees, Orme & Brown, 1820

Desmond, Ray. *A Celebration of Flowers. 200 Years of Curtis's Botanical Magazine*, Royal Botanic Gardens, Kew, and Collingridge Books, 1987

——. *Kew, The History of the Royal Botanic Gardens*, Harvill Press, 1995

Dillenius, J.J. *Hortus Elthamensis*, 1732

Duthie, Ruth. *Florists' Flowers and Societies*, Princes Risborough, Shire Publications, 1988

Esser, Mia. *Pelargoniums*, Lisse, Netherlands, Rebo Productions Ltd, 1998

Festing, Sally. 'The Second Duchess of Portland and her Rose', *Garden History*, Spring 1985, p. 195

Fisher, John, *The Origins of Garden Plants*, Constable, 1982.

Gilmour, J.S.L. (ed.), *Thomas Johnson, Journeys in Kent and Hampstead*, Pittsburgh, PA, Hunt Botanical Library, 1972

Grew, Marion E. *William Bentinck and William III (Prince of Orange)*, John Murray, 1924

Grieve, Peter. *A History of Ornamental-foliaged Pelargoniums*, 2nd edn, 1869, repr. British Pelargonium and Geranium Society, 1977

Gunther, R.T. *Early Botanists and their Gardens*, Oxford University Press, 1922

Hadfield, Miles. *A History of British Gardening*, Penguin Books, 1985

Harvey, John. *Early Gardening Catalogues*, Phillimore & Co., 1972

——. *Early Nurserymen*, Chichester, Phillimore & Co. Ltd, 1974

Hayden, Ruth. *Mrs Delany, Her Life and Her Flowers*, The British Museum Press, 1980

Hibberd, Shirley. *The Amateur's Flower Garden*, Groombridge & Sons, 1871

——. *The Amateur's Greenhouse and Conservatory*, W.H. and L. Collingridge, revd edn, ed. T.W. Sanders, *c.* 1895

——. *Familiar Garden Flowers*, 2nd series, Cassell and Co Ltd, *c.* 1880

———. *Rustic Adornments for Homes of Taste*, New edn, Groombridge & Sons, 1870

Hingston Fox, R. *Dr John Fothergill and his Friends*, Macmillan & Co, 1919

Hobhouse, Penelope. *Plants in Garden History*, Pavilion Books Ltd, 1994

Jacques, David, and van der Horst, Arend Jan. *The Gardens of William and Mary*, Christopher Helm, 1988

Johnson, Thomas. *Gerard's Herball*, 1633

Key, Hazel. *1001 Pelargoniums*, B.T. Batsford, 2000

Llanover, A. (ed.). *Autobiography and Correspondence of Mary Granille, Mrs Delany*, 6 vols, Richard Bentley, 1861

Llewellyn, Jean, *et al. Check List and Register of Pelargonium Cultivar Names*, Parts 1 and 2, Australian Geranium Society Inc, 1978, 1985

Llewellyn, Jean, Hudson, Betty and Morrison, Gordon C. *Growing Geraniums and Pelargoniums in Australia and New Zealand*, Kenthurst, Australia, Kangaroo Press, 1981

Longstaffe-Gowan, Todd. *The Gardens and Parks at Hampton Court Palace*, Francis Lincoln, 2005

MacGregor, Arthur. *Ark to Ashmolean, The Story of the Tradescants, Ashmole and the Ashmolean Museum*, Oxford, Ashmolean Museum, 1988

Malet, M. and Verlot, B. *Culture Pratique des Pelargonium*, Paris, E. Donnaud, undated

Marsach, Robyn. *My Garden, Letters of Mary Russell Mitford*, Sidgwick & Jackson, 1990

Masson, Francis. 'An Account of Three Journeys from the Cape Town into the Southern Parts of Africa, addressed to Sir John Pringle', *Philosophical Transactions*, LXVI, Kew, 1776

Miller, Diana. *Pelargoniums, A Gardener's Guide to the Species and their Hybrids and Cultivars*, B.T. Batsford Ltd, 1996

———. '*Pelargonium* "L'Elegante"', *The Garden*, September 1996, p. 560

O'Brian, Patrick, *Joseph Banks, A Life*, Collins Harvill, 1989

Pavord, Anna, *The Naming of Names*, Bloomsbury, 2005

Pearson, Charles E. *Essay on the Pelargonium and its Cultivation*, Nottingham, Chilwell Nursery, *c.* 1900

Rude, George. *Hanoverian England*, Stroud, Sutton Publishing, 2003

Scott-James, Anne, *The Cottage Garden*, Penguin Books, 1987

Shellard, Alan. *Geraniums for Home and Garden*, Newton Abbot, David and Charles, 1981

Sweet, Robert. *Geraniaceae, The Natural Order of Gerania*, 5 vols, 1820–30

Taylor, Jan. *Geraniums and Pelargoniums, The Complete Guide*, Marlborough, Crowood Press, 1994

——. *Pelargoniums for Colour and Variety (Crowood Gardening Guides)*, Marlborough, Crowood Press, 1990

van der Walt, J.J.A. and Vorster, P.J. *Pelargoniums of Southern Africa*, 3 vols, Cape Town, South Africa, Purnell & Sons S.A. (Pty) Ltd, 1977–88

Van Pelt Wilson, Helen. *The Joy of Geraniums*, New York, M. Barrows and Company Inc, 1964

Walker, G. and Walker, A. *A Colour Guide to Pelargoniums*, Ormskirk, Grange Publications, undated

Warner, Marjorie F. 'The Morins', *National Horticultural Magazine*, July 1954, p. 168

Weaver, Pat. *Pelargoniums (Collins Aura Garden Handbooks)*, Marshall Cavendish Ltd, 1988

Webb, William J. *The Pelargonium Family*, Croom Helm, 1984

White, John W. *Geraniums IV, The Grower's Manual*, Geneva, Illinois, Ball Publishing, 1993

Wijnands, O. *The Botany of the Commelins*, Rotterdam, A.A. Balkema, 1983

Wilkinson, Anne. *The Victorian Gardener*, Stroud, Sutton Publishing, 2006

Willson, E. (ed.). *Fancy-leaved Pelargoniums, Peter Grieve and After*, British Pelargonium and Geranium Society, 1990

——. *West London Nursery Gardens*, Fulham and Hammersmith Historical Society, 1982

Witham Fogg, H.G. *Geranium Growing*, John Gifford Ltd, 1973

Wood, Henry J. *Pelargoniums, The Grower's Guide to 'Geraniums' and Pelargoniums*, Exeter, Henry J. Wood Publications, 1987

Woodbridge, Kenneth. *The Stourhead Landscape*, The National Trust, 1995

Periodicals

Amateur Gardening

Curtis's Botanical Magazine

Geraniaceae Group News

Henderson's Illustrated Bouquet

Philosophical Transactions

Proceedings of the RHS

RHS Journal

Richmond and Twickenham Times

The Journal of Botany

The Linnean

The Botanists' Repository

The Cottage Gardener

The Floral Magazine

The Floral World and Garden Guide

The Floricultural Cabinet

The Florist

The Garden (RHS)

The Garden (William Robinson's)

The Gardeners' Chronicle

The Gardener's Magazine (Shirley Hibberd's)

The Gardener's Magazine (John Claudius Loudon's)

The Gardening World

The Times

Nursery catalogues

Barnfield Pelargoniums, 2006

Bruant's Catalogue, 1913

William Bull's Catalogue, 1867, 1873, 1876

Caledonian Nursery, 1950s

Cannell's Floral Guide, 1866, 1868, 1870, 1880

Fibrex Nursery, 2006

John Fraser, Lea Bridge Road, 1866-7

Henderson's Catalogue, 1869, 1870, 1878, 1880

Rollisson's Plant Catalogue, 1877-8

Brian and Pearl Sulman's Nursery, 2006

Sutton's Amateur's Guide to Horticulture for 1896

Charles Turner, Royal Nurseries, Slough, 1849-71, 1885

Vernon Geranium Nursery, 2006

Index of Pelargoniums

bel Carrière, 168
rotanifolium, 91, 242, 252
erifolium, 103
etosum, 34, 42, 70, 252
ldisonii, 143
donis, 138
Happy Thought, 170, **170**, 172
jum multiflorum 191, **191**
chemilloides, 42, 252
de, 232
fred, 143
ice Spenser, 171
ine Sisley, 208
ma, 143
inum, 254
ny Hogg, 140
ais (Segalas), 115, **pl. 16**
gel, 10, 220, 221, **221**, 227, 235, 236
gelina, 221
julosum, 103
tler, 125, 248
ifolium, 77
ple Blossom (Rosebud), 171, **171**, 172
ricot, 211
ctic Star, 229, **229**
lens, **76**, 77, 92, 118, 242
gus, 167
el, 242
tar of Roses, 241
traction, 134, 140, 144, 151, 154, 155
drey, **pl. 16**
rea marginatum, 168
rora Borealis, **pl. 10**
rora's Beam, 119
rora's Unique (Unique Aurora), 87, 130, 210, 211

Avalanche, 140, 144

Balcons, 235
Baronne A. de Rothschild, **pl. 16**
barringtonii, 87, 91, 173
Basilisk, 138
Bath Scarlet, 77, 135, 138
Beaton's Indian Yellow, 157, 162, 179, 203, **pl. 9**
Beaufortianum, 103
Beauté de Poitevine, 201
Beauté de Suresnes, 174, 202, 208
Beauty of Blackheath, 143
Beauty of Oxton, 190, **193**
bedding, 3, 4, 6, 123–46, **149**, 177, 222
bentinckianum, 29, 138
betulinum, 50, **51**, 221, 254
bicolor, 55, 100, 118
Bijou, 143
bipinnitifidium, 118
bird's egg, 201, 234
Black Vesuvius (Red or Salmon), 197, 198, **198**, 231
blandfordianum, 75, 241
Bolero, 237
bowkeri, 91, 255
Bridal Wreath, 167
Brilliant, 138
Brook's Purple, **pl. 16**
Bruant, 201, **203**, 204, 227, 228
Brunswick, 246
Burgenland Girl, 227
Burning Bush, 151

cactus-flowered, 200, 201, 216, 222
caffrum, 91, 255, **pl. 2**
calamistratum, 88
Cape Scarlet, 138

'Cape varieties'
generally, 98, 100, 109, 115, 127, 161, 179, 211
at shows, 118, 181, 186
Capitan Jolivet, **pl. 16**
capitatum, **7**, **26**, 27, 37, 42, 51, 220, 241, 254
Captain Flayelle, **pl. 16**
Captain Raikes, 190
Carefree (F1) 235; (Unique) 237
carnation-flowered, 200
carnivorous, 195
carnosum, 36, 37, 92, 242
Cascade, 235
Cassandra, 114
Catford Belle, 221, **221**
Cavalier, 114
Centurion, 114
ceratophyllum, 52
cerinum, 138
Cerise Unique, 130, 134, 140, 151, 202
Chancellor, 143, 194
Charles Gounoud, **pl. 16**
Charles Turner, *see* Souvenir de Charles Turner
Chinese Cactus, 229, 231
Chinese Dragon, 201
Chocolate Peppermint, 73
Christine, 138–140, 143, 144, 189
Citriodorum, 92, 241
Claret Rock (Unique), 242
Clorinda, 216, 242, 246, **246**; Golden Clorinda, 246
Cloth of Gold, 143, 156
clypeatum, 165
Coccinea/um, 127–9
cochleatum, 103
Commander-in-Chief, 76, 89, 92, 100

Index of Pelargoniums

Commines, **pl. 16**
Compactum, 134, 150 (multiflorum),
212
Compte de Hainaut, **pl. 13**
Comtesse de Grey, 232
concinnum, 88
Concolour Lace, 246
Congestum, 88
Conspicua/um, 127, 128, 210, 241
Copthorne, 246
cordifolium, 70, 254
cordiforme, 103
Coronation, 76
cortusifolium,52, 247, 252
coruscans, 88
Cottage Maid, 143, 151, 154, 155
cotyledonis, 69, 92, 253
Countess, **pl. 16**
crassicaule, 52, 252
Crenaeflorum, 89
crenatum, 77, 134, 135, **137**;
(mollifoliatum) 138
Crimson Nosegay, 157, **157**
Crimson Unique, 143, 210, 211
crispum, 68, 221, 222, 235, 241, 254
Cruenta, 114
Crystal Palace Gem, 156
cucullatum
description, 21, 22, 50, 173, 254
history, 21, 27, 36, 42, 242, 246
hybridising, 76, 87–9, 91, 94, 99,
100, 103, 107, 124, 138, 169,
214
Culford Beauty, 151
cuneiflorum, 87
Cybister, 134, 136, 143
cynosbatifolium, 89
Czar, 182

Daedelum, 103
Dagata, **pl. 16**
Dandy, Variegated or Little, 199
Daveyana/um/*davyanum*, 87, 92, 100,
124, 128, **pl. 7**
Deacon, 230, 232; Deacon Lilac Mist,
230, **230**
Decora, 235
Decorative, 176, 177, 186–91
Defiance, 87, 88, 92, 128
dennisianum, 91

denticulatum, 50, 51, 211, 241, 248,
254
Diadem/*atum*, 143, 210, 211, 242
(*rubescens*) 143, 173
Dianthiflorum, 88
dichondrifolia, 255
Distinction, 198
Dolly Varden, 161
domesticum, 214, 240
double, 172–4, 216
Drakae, 103
Duchess, 143
Duchess of Bedford, 194
Duchess of Edinburgh, 189, 194
Duchess of Gloucester, 103
Duchess of Sutherland, 99, 136, 128,
143, **pl. 12**
dumosum, 221
dwarf, 10, 199–201, 216, 220, 222,
230

echinatum
'Cape variety', 109, 161, 241, 242
description and history, 53, **54**, 55,
252
hybridising, 90, 91, 118, 212, 247
Edward Perkins, **pl. 15**
Efulgens/ence/*fulgens*, 100, 138, 276
eggshell, 234
E. Herbert, **pl. 16**
elegans, 252
Elegant, 140
Emperor, 131
Emperor Nicholas, **pl. 16**
Emperor of the French, 153–5
Empress of the French, 153
Endsleigh, 241
Eugenia, 184
Eve, 143
exornatum, 88
exstipulatum, 68, 90, 255

F₁ hybrid, 234
Fair Emily, 241
Fairest of the Fair, 184
Fair Helen (Ellen), 88, 183, 241
Fair Rosamund, 89, 220, 242
Fairy Queen, 89
Fancy, 21, 51, 110, 114, 118, 120,
122, 162, 169, 186

Fiat, 201, 228, 229
Fiery Chief, 229
filicifolium, 69, 220, 241
fingered–flowered, 229, 231
Fire Dragon, 200
Flagrans, 124
Flesh Pink, **pl. 16**
Fleur Poitevine, 207
Flexuosum, 90, 118
Flower of the Day, 143, 151, 202
Flower of the Spring, 139, 140, 143,
201, 217, 218
Formosa/um, 229, 231
fothergillii, 43, 45, 46, 134, 135, **13**
fragrans, 90, **90**, 242, 255
Freak of Nature, 169, **169**, 172
'French', *see* Spotted
Frewer's Nosegay, 135
Fright, 174
Frogmore (Scarlet), 132, 203
frutetorum, 235, 252
fruticosum, 254
fulgens, *see* Efulgence
fulgidum
description, 37, **37**, 254, **pl. 1**
origin and history, 36, 41, 42, 92
94, 100
hybridising, 76, 77, 86–8, 107,
115, 118
F.V. Raspail, 208, 213, **pl. 16**

Galilee, 226
Garibaldi, **pl. 13**
Generalissimum, 88
(General) Tom Thumb, 132–4, 139,
140, 151, 174, 202, 203, 208
233
Geoffrey Horseman, 195, **195**
gibbosum, 34, **34**, 35, 37, 42, 91, 2
glabrifolium, 138
glaucifolium, 77, 91
Gloire de Clermont, 202
Gloire de Nancy, 174, 208
Gloryanum/*glorianum*,129
glutinosum, 69, 241, 248
Golden Banner, 140, 144
Golden Cerise Unique, 130, 151, 15
Golden Chain, 124, 140, 151, 154,
156
Golden Fleece, 143

olden Harry Hieover, 156
olden Tom Thumb, 151, 153, 154
old Pheasant, 154, 155
andiflora/um/folium, 77, 90, 220, 254
andis odorata, 211
randissima/um, 99, 124
rand Slam, Lavender Grand Slam, 228
atum, 243
aveolens, 69, 75, 220, 241, 242
eytonense, 254
ossularioides, 53, 241, 254
lielma, 114
ustav Emich, 223

arkaway, 140
arlequin (Beck's), 116, **117**, 230; (striped Ivy-leaved), 231, 232
arry Hieover, 208
derinum, 165, 214
enry Jacoby, 213, **pl. 16**
gh Admiral, 76
ghfields, 227
rsutum, 241
M. Stanley, **pl. 16**
areanum, 89
nora, 114
rseshoe, see Zonal
rtense Parent, **pl. 13**
rtorum, 214
owarth Ashton, **pl. 10**
la, 237
mei/Humei, 99, 124
W. Longfellow, 140
bridum, 135

escens, 86–8, **87**, 92, 99, 115, 131, 211, 218
ogen, 170
plicatum, 173
arnatum, 252
dian Yellow, see Beaton's Indian Yellow
nocence, 167
quinans
    description, 29, **29**, 30, 133, 252
    hybridising, 86, 94, 115, 123
    origin and history, 30, 36, 42
instratum, 89

involucratum, 76, 99, **pl. 18**
    ('Incarnatum') 89, 99
ionidiflorum, 242, 255
Irene, 227
Isabella, 103
Islington Peppermint, 55, 236, 246
Italia Unita, 151
Ivy–leaved
    hybridisation, 129, 132, 151, 184, 217, 226, 231, 232, 235
    origins and classification, 23, 70, 98, 163–8, 222
    uses, 144, **163**, 186, 235

Jealousy, 170
jenkinsonii, 89
Jesse, 102
Joan of Arc, 120
Joe, **pl. 15**
jonquillinum, 79
Judd's Rose Unique, 130

kewense, Silver Kewense, 236
King of Denmark, 217
Kingston Beauty, 194
Konig Albert, 167

La Belle Alliance, 121
laciniatum, 74
La Destinee, 208
Lady Bess, 171
Lady Clinton, 88
Lady Cullum, 154, 155
Lady Curzon, **pl. 15**
Lady Ilchester, **pl. 16**
Lady Mary, 241
Lady May, 171
Lady Plymouth, 241
    (Variegated) 242, **242**
Lady Scarborough, 241, 243, 244, **244**
Lady Washington, see Martha Washington
La France, 168
lanceolatum, 70, 72, 103, 254
Lara, 247
lateripes, 164, 168, 252
Lave, **pl. 16**
lawrencianum, 77
Lee's Variegated, 150

L'Elegante, 165, **165**, 166, 168
Le Nain Blanc, 199, 209
L'Enfer, 197, 198
Leopold, 194
Lilac Banner, 140
Lilac Nosegay, 135
Lilac Unique, 126–9, 210
Lilliputian Zonals, Lilliput, 199, 208
Lion Heart, 143
Little David, 143
Little Dear, 201
Little Gem, 241
Little Trot, 200
L. Nootens, **pl. 13**
lobatum, 24, 34, 76, 77, 92, 255
Lord Kitchener, 226
Lothario, 241, 242, 243
Louisa Smith, 143
Lucius, 171
Lucy Grieve, 154, 155

Macbeth, 210
macranthon/Macranthon, 89, 90, 100
Maculatum, 86
Madame Amalie Baltet, 174
Madame Bruant, 207
Madame Crousse, 168, 217, 233
Madame Emi(l)le Galle, 226
Madame Fournier, 200
Madame Layal, 236
Madame Lemoine, 208
Madame (Mons) Nonin/Ninon, 211, 241
Madame Roseleur, **pl. 16**
Madame Salleroi/n, 199, 200, **200**, 209
Madame Tasson, **pl. 13**
Madame Thibault, 174, 208
Madame Vaucher, 143, 169, 170, 189, 202, 203
Magenta, 143
Mangles' Variegated, 143, 159, 199, 200, 209
Marechal MacMahon, 156
Margherite, **pl. 15**
marginatum, 149
Maria Isabella, 88
Maria Massinon, **pl. 13**
Martha Washington, 228
Mephistopheles, 198

Index of Pelargoniums

Mexicana (Mexikanerin), 232
Mexican Beauty, 231, 232
micro-miniature, 232
Midas, 194
Miller's Variegated, 150
Millfield Gem, 168
miniature, 10, 199, 232
minima, 199
Miss Burdett-Coutts, 161, **pl.10**
Mons Ninon, *see* Madame Nonin
Monstrosum, 173
More's Victory/*moreanum*, 87, 88, 92,
    124, 128, 183, 242
Moulton Gem, 242
Mr Coombes, **pl. 15**
Mr Wren, 234
Mrs Benyon, 154, 155
Mrs Cannell, 168
Mrs Dumbrill, 221
Mrs J.C. Mappin(g), 201, 218
Mrs H. G. Smith, 221
Mrs Kingsbury, 211, 242
Mrs Lewis Lloyd, 194
Mrs Parker, 174
Mrs Pollock, 154, 155, **155**, 202, 217
Mrs Quilter, 156, **156**
Mrs Taylor, 129
Mrs Vernon, 135, 159
Mrs W.A.R. Clifton, 217
multiradiatum, 90, 91
myrrhifolium, 254
Mystery, 237

New Life, 168, **168**, 171, 204, 234
nodosum, 90, 91
Noisette, *see* Rosebud
Nosegay
  generally, 46, 77, 134–138, 162,
    175, 178, 179, 204, 227
  hybrids, 157, 159, 169, 170, 172,
    181, 186, 208, **pl. 12**
Nosegay Queen, 134
nubilum, 89
Nymph (The), 102

oak-leaved, 68, 69, 102, 211
oblongatum, 170, **pl. 3**
odoratissumum, 36, **36**, 37, 42, 56,
  90, 255
oculate(d), 201, 207

Orange Nosegay, 170
Ossian, 134
ovale, 55, 68, 103, 252
Oxford, New, 88, Old, 88, 89
oxoniense, 88

paintbox, 234
palmatifolium, 230
panduriforme, 68, **68**, 69, 254
pansy-faced, 235
papilionaceum, 35, **35**, 36, 42, 254
Paton's Unique, 211
Patricia Andrea, 228, **228**, 229
Paul Crampel, 207, 213–15, 217, 226
peltatum
  description and origins, 23, 23, 30,
    42, 70, 94, 214, 252
  hybrids, 164, 165, 167, 209
peltatum elegans, 166, 167
pencillatum, 241
Peppermint Candy, *see* New Life
peppermint-scented, 72, 73
Peter Grieve, **pl. 10**
Pheasant's Foot, 125, 211, 241, 248
Philemon, 209
phlox-flowered, 234
Phlox New Life, 171
Phyllis, 211
Pink Bonanza, 228
Pink Nosegay, 143
pinnatum, 241
piperitum, 72
platypetalon, 103
Pluto, **105**, 108
poinsettia-flowered, *see* cactus-flowered
Polka, 237
Prince of Orange, 211, 241
Prince of Wales, 283
Prince Regent, 100
Princess Alexandra, 167
Princess of Prussia, 134
Princess of Wales (coloured leaf), 153,
  153; (Regal), 189, 194
Princess Royal, 138, 139
Punch, 140
Purple Nosegay, 135
Purple Unique, 124–7, 130, 140, 241;
  see also Rollisson's Purple Unique
purpureum, 86; (Superbum) 88,
  89

Queen of Queens, 143
Queen of the Fairies, 106
Queen of the Hellenes, **pl. 15**
Queen's Favourite, 151
Queen Victoria, 107, 115, 190
quercifolium, 68, 69, 87, 88, 127, 24
  248, 254; *minor*, 211; *quercifolia*
  coccinea, 143
quinatum, 71
quinquelobatum, 230, 252
quinquevulnereum, 75, 118

radens, 254
radula, 70, 75, 211, 220, 241
Rainbow, **pl. 16**
Ranunculaeflora plenissima, 208
rapaceum, 241
Red Black Vesuvius, *see* Black Vesuviu
Red Nosegay, 135
Red Rambler, 172
Regal
  description, 193, 195, 214
  hybridising, 220–2, 228, 235–7
  origins, 21, 22, 37, 51, 186,
    189–96
Regina, 227
Renate Parsley, 55, 236, 246
renifolium, 53
reniforme, 72, 90, 91, 252
Reticulatum, 233, **233**
Rienzi, 178, **179**
Rival, 89, 103
Rob Roy, 89
Roller's Satinique, 237
rollissonii/Rollissonia, 91, 99,
  125
Rollisson's (Purple) Unique, 125–9,
  126, 209, 219, 242; *see also*
  Purple Unique
Rosamund, 114
Rose Bengal, 221
Rosebud, 171, 172
Rose d'Amour, 127, 129
Rose Queen, 139, 140, 143, 144
Rosy Circle, 146
Rosy Morn, 212
Rouletta, 231, **231**, 232
Rubens improved, 143
rubescens, **pl. 6**
rutaceum, 91

llen, 233
lmon Vesuvius, 171
  see also Black Vesuvius
nguineum, 115
nspareil, 184
ndens, 236
arlet Pet, 88, 128, 241
arlet Rambler, 172
arlet Unique, 128, 130, 209,
    209–11, **210**, 241
ented-leaved, 161, 210, 211, 218,
    220–2, 239–46, 248
hizopetalum, 90, 91, 255
ntillans, 86
utatum, 165
een Rival, 159
irley Ash, 221
ottisham Hero, 243
ottisham Pet, 246
ow
  hybridisation, 169, 173, 186, 222
  origins, 21, 51, 118–20, 161, 215,
    216, 218
  rubland Pet, 130, 242, 243
  rubland Rose, 242, 243
  rubland Scarlet, 202
oides, 255
elly's Pride, 200
eil, 170
ferino, 221
ubile, 103
ohia Cusack, 152, **152**
uvenir de Charles Turner, 184, 217
uvenir de Mirande, 207
arkle, 234, **234**
ciosum, 99, 103, 132
ctabile, 99
endide, 55, 236, 252
hosum, 50, 54, 254
otted', 120, **121**, 122, 162, 169,
    177, 180, 184
otted Gem, 54, 212, 241
physagroides, 229, 230
lla, 134, 136, 138, 140, 143, 144;
    Stella variegata, 159
ellar, 116, 229, 230, 231
nopetalum, 252

striatum, **81**, 86, 89
Striped Vesuvius, see New Life
suffusum, 103
Sunset, 140, 154, 155
Superbum, see purpureum Superbum
Sussex Lace, 233
Sweet Memory, 237
Sweet Success, 237
'Swiss', 227
Sydonie, 143
Sylph, 120

T.A. Dickson, 194
tetragonum, 70, 242, 253
The Boar, 235
The Crocodile, 232, 233
The Moor, 194
The Shah, 221
Thomas Moore, 140
tinctum, 89
tomentosum, 55, 72, **73**, 236, 242,
    254
Tom Pouce, 202
Tom Thumb, see General Tom Thumb
Touchstone, 243
Trentham Rose, 143
tricolor, 55, **55**, 56, 68, 72, 100, 236,
    252
Triomphe de Gregovia/Gergoviat/
    Gergonia, 174, 208
Triomphe de Paris, 143
Triomphe de St Mande/Maude, 189,
    194
triste, 13–21, **14**, 24, 34, 42, 92,
    248, 255, **pl. 4**
Tristram Shandy, 143
tulip-flowered, 228, 229

Unique
  plant name, 107, 125
  type
    generally, **126**, 209–11, **209**,
        237, 241, 242, 244, 245, 248
    origins and history, 37, 51,
        124–31, 162, 227
    see also under specific names
Unique Aurora, see Aurora's Unique

Unique Diadem, see Diadem
variegatum, 56, 148
veitchianum, 92, 173
Vesuvius, 171, 189, 197; see also
    Black Vesuvius
Victory, see More's Victory
violareum, 236
viscossimum, 248
vitifolium, 36, 37; Vitifolia, 143, 254
Volonte Nationale, 194
Voodoo, 237

yeatmanianum (grandiflora/um), 99,
    100, 124
youngii, 89

Wellington Hero, 138
West Brighton Gem, 171
Westdale Appleblossom, 171
White Distinction, 198
White Mesh, 232
White Perfection, 143
White Unique, 127, 130, 210,
    241
White Vesuvius, 171
Willoughbyanum, 183
Willsii rosea, 167
Wilmore's Surprise, 173, **173**
Wonderful, 171

Zonal (Zonate)
  bedding, **3**, 125, 136, 138–45,
        145, **149**, **pl. 5**
  Dauthenay's classification, 202–9
  florists' type, 176–181, **179**
  hybridisation, 46, 132, 134,
        148–156, 169–71, 172–4, 234,
        235
  origins, 24, 29, 98, 214
zonale
  description and qualities, **22**, 23,
        109, 195, 214, 252, **pl. 14**
  hybridisation, 77, 115, 123,
        133–5, 181, 202, 204, 208, 236
  marginatum,148
  origins and history, 23, 34, 42
zonquil, 230

General Index

Where alternative spellings for plant names exist, all variations are given. Illustrations are referenced in **bold** type.

Abbott, Peter (b. 1923), 210, 245, 248
Aiton, William (1731–93) 59, 82
Aiton, William Townsend
(1768–1843), 82
Amateur Gardening, 217, 223, 226
Andrews, Henry C. (1794–1830)
Botanists' Repository, 72–5
generally, 79, 86, 99, 103, 134,
135, 138, 164, 199, 221
Geraniums, 75–7
Arndt, Milton, 230, 232
Ayres, W.P., 132, 133

Bailey, Liberty Hyde (1858–1954), 214
Banks, Sir Joseph (1743–1820), 42,
44, 46, 47, 54, 64–6, 71, 72,
186
Beaton, Donald (1802–63)
generally, **127**, 136
plants, 127, 128, 130, 135, 157,
159
Shrubland Park, 139, 151, 243
Beaufort, Duchess of, *see* Somerset,
Mary Capel
Beck, Edward (1804–61), 109–119,
111, 146, 175, 183, 184, 218,
230
Bentinck, Hans Willem (William), Earl
of Portland (1649–1709), 24–9,
28, 39, 40, 41
Beurier, Henri, 174, 207
Blandford, Marquess of, 75
Boos, Franz, 51, 59
Botanical Magazine, see *Curtis's
Botanical Magazine*
Botanical Register, 72, 82

Botanists' Repository, see Andrews,
Henry C.
Both, Ted, 229, 230, 232
Boucharlat, M., 128, 207
Brenan, Miss E. A. V., 241, 242, 248
Bruant, Paul, 199, 201, 207–9
Bull, William (1828–1902), 189, 190,
192
Burchell, William James (1781–1863),
52–4, 91
Bute, 3rd Earl of, 47, 62
Bute, Lady 53, 54

Candolle, Augustin Pyramus de
(1778–1841), 68, 93, 251–4
Cannell, Henry (1833–1914), and
Cannell's Nursery, **158**, 159,
168, 170, 171, 173, 197, 201,
212
Cannell's Floral Guide, 128, 129, 171,
172, 174, 194, **210**, 222, 226
Cavanilles, Antonio José (1745–1804),
58, 59, 148
Cavendish Holles Hartley, Lady
Margaret, Duchess of Portland
(1715–85), **38**, 39–42, 44, 47
Chelsea Physic Garden, 33, 34, 42, 60,
70, 82, 120, 175
Clifford, Derek (1915–2003), 167,
221, 226, 227, 244, 245
Clifton, R.T.F., 202, 245, 252
Clifton, W.A.R. (d. 1962), 216, 217,
222, 223
Colt Hoare, Sir Richard (1758–1838),
84, **85**, 86–90, 93, 100, 103,
136, 246, 253

Colvill, James (c.1778–1832), and
Colvill's Nursery, 71, 80, 82–[?]
86, 87, 90, 91, 115
Commelin, Caspar (c. 1667–1731) a[?]
Jan (1629–92), 23, 24
Compton, Henry, Bishop of London
(1632–1713), 25, 29
Cornut, Jacques, 14, 18, 19
Cottage Gardener, The, 127, 135, 136[?]
140
cranesbills, 4, 16, 19, 34, 52, 57, 7[?]
Cross, John E., 172, 199, 221–3, 24[?]
244
Curtis, William (1746–99), 34, 59–[?]
61, 67, 70–2, 93
Curtis's Botanical Magazine, 52, 59, [?]
70–2, 252

Dauthenay, H., 200, 202–9, 227
Davey, Thomas (1758–1833) and
Davey's Nursery, 87–9, 100
Dean, Richard (1830–1905), 209,
210
Delany, Mrs Mary (1700–88), 40–2
Dennis, William (1785–1851) and
Dennis's Nursery, 84, 88, 89,[?]
91, 92, 99, 103, 129
Denny, Dr John (c. 1820–81), 159,
170, 172, 175, 177–180, 18[?]
185, 186
Dillenius, John Jacob (c. 1684–1747[?]
35, 36
D'Ombrain, Revd Henry Honywood
(1818–1905), 120, 136,
159
Dryander, Joseph (1748–1810), 66

klon, Christian Friedrich
(1795–1868), 93
wards, Sydenham Teast
(c. 1769–1819), 72
odium, 7, 67

oral Magazine, 120, 136, 155
oral World (and Garden Guide),170,
178
oricultural Cabinet, 99, 100, 106,
108, 109, 124, 131
orist, The, 114, 116, 118, 119, 145,
147, 157, 159, 177, 189
rists
market, 95, 187–9
pelargoniums, 98, 100, 102–9, **104**,
116, 118, 120, 124, 132, 248,
249
shows ands societies, 8, 95–7, 114,
191
Zonals, 176–8, 180, 187
ster, Edmund, 106, 109, 120, 184
ster, E. B., 186
thergill, Dr John (1712–80), 42, **43**,
44, 45, 135

ines, Mr, 106, 119, 128
rden, The, 129, 168, 184
rdeners' Chronicle
Beck, Edward, 110, 112
florists' flowers, 102, 103, 107, 114
history and development of
pelargoniums, 109, 114, 118,
129, 132, 133, 160, 165, 174,
209, 216, 218, 226, 233, 240,
244
market florists, 189
Pelargonium Society, 185
Shrubland Park, 140
variegation, 147, 149
rdener's Magazine (Hibberd's), 169,
172, 178, 180, 183, 184, 211,
248
rdener's Magazine (Loudon's), 72, 92,
189
rth, Revd Mr, 106, 109, 120
ranium, 2, 7, 8, 13, 18, 19, 34, 58,
67, 73, 102, 119, 240
distinguished from pelargonium, **5**, 6
rose', 218, 220

'scarlet', 98, 124, 131, 132
see also Index of Pelargoniums
Gordon, George, 114, 167, 168
Grieve, Peter (1811–95), 148–56,
150, 159, 174, 176, 209, 233
Groom, Henry, 106, 147

Hally, Mr, 151, 159
Hamilton, Emma and William, 40, 71
Hartsook, Frances, 227, 237
Harvey, William Henry (1811–66),
122, 214, 251–4
Henderson, Andrew, and Henderson's
Nursery, 107, 121, 125, 130,
138, 166, 172, 183, 200
Henderson's Illustrated Bouquet, 134,
138, 148, 156, 170
Hermann, Paul (1646–95), 21, 31
heronsbill, 7
Hibberd, Shirley (1825–90)
florists' flowers, 184, 185
pelargoniums, 132, 138, 144, 145,
167, 168, 171, 180
RHS lecture, 16, 17, 98, 99, 150,
151, 172, 173
Hibbert, George (1757–1837), 71, 74
Hope, Frances Jane (d. 1880), 129, 219
Hosking, Albert (c. 1874–1938), 199,
218
Hove, Antonio Pantaleo, 52
Hoyle, George W. (c. 1801–72), 118,
118, 184

Jacquin, Nikolaus Joseph von
(1727–1817), 57
Jenkinson, Robert H., 76, 77, 86, 89,
91, 253
Johnson, Thomas (c. 1600–44),
14–16, 18, 19

Kennedy, John (1759–1842) and his
nursery, 51, 73, 84
Kew, Royal Botanic Gardens
generally, 27, 52, 59, 71, 210, 223
plants from, 54–6, 236, 241, 243
theft from, 80–3
Sir Joseph Banks at, 42, 46, 54
Kinghorn, Francis Rodney (1813–87),
130, 139, **139**, 150, 151, 176
Knight, Joseph (c. 1777–1855), 71, 82

Knowles, Edna, 244, 245
Knuth, Reinhard (1874–1957), 214,
251, 254, 255

Lake, Sidney, 227, 232
Langley-Smith, Arthur (d. 1953),
220–2
Le Coq, Henry, 173, 207
Lee, James and Lee's Nursery, 42, 51,
72, 73, 75–7, 84, 173
Lemoine, Victor (1837–1911), **166**,
167, 173, 204, 208, 213
Nursery, 174, 189, 197, 200, 201,
207
Lettsom, Dr John Coakley, 45, 62
L'Heritier de Brutelle, Charles Louis
(1746–1800), 59, 63–70, 73,
84, 93, 164, 165
Lindley, John (1799–1865), 114, 115
Linnaeus, Carolus (Carl von Linné)
(1707–78), 48, 58, 63, 74, 251
Liverpool, Earl of, 76, 88, 99
Loddiges, George, 82, 86
London, George (d. 1714), 27, 29, 30
London, Henrietta, 27, 30
Loudon, John Claudius (1783–1843),
72, 149

magazines, botanical, 59–63;
horticultural, 97, 98
Masson, Francis (1741–1806), 46,
48–51, 70, 186
Masters, Maxwell T. (1833–1970),
159, 175
Miller, Philip (1691–1771), 33, 34,
63, 70, 149
monsonia, 7, 67
Moore, Thomas (1821–87) 120, 175,
185, 246

Niven, James (1774–1827), 51, 71

Parkinson, John (1567–1650), 17, 19,
20
Paul, William (1822–1905), 88, 128,
130
Pearson, Charles E. (1856–1929),
175; Pearson, John Royston
(d. 1876), 175, 176, **177**, 183
Pelargonium Congress, 159

General Index

'Philo', 109, 112
Portland
   Duchess of, *see* Cavendish Holles
     Hartley, Margaret
   Earl of, *see* Bentinck, Hans Willem
pyramid, 'geranium', 144–6, **145**

Redouté, Henri Joseph, 67
Redouté, Pierre Joseph (1759–1840),
   63, 67
Ridgway, James, 72, 82
Robinson, William (1838–1935), 184
Rohde, Eleanor Sinclair (1881–1950),
   223
Rollisson, William, and Rollisson's
   Nursery, 91, 92, 125–7, 129,
   183, 190

Salter, John (1798–1874), 126–8,
   199
sarcocaulon, 7
Schmidt, William E., 228, 232
Scholl, George, 51, 59
Sherard, James (1666–1737), 35
Sherard, William (*c.* 1658–1728), 31,
   35, 36
Sisley, Jean (*d.* 1891) 180, 208
Sloane, Sir Hans (1660–1753), 33
Society,
   Australian Geranium, 247
   British and European Geranium,
     233, 247
   British Pelargonium and Geranium,
     226
   Geraniaceae Group, 247
   Linnean, 57

North-West Geranium, 233
Nottingham Horticultural and
   Botanical, 175
Pelargonium, 175–86
Royal, 57, 64, 65
Royal Botanic, 119
(Royal) Horticultural
   generally, 71, 102, 128, 171,
     175, 179, 185, 201, 236, 244
   lectures and articles, 16, 241
   shows, 109, 112, 114, 115, 165,
     182, 216
   trials, 125, 165
   South Australian Pelargonium and
     Geranium, 230
Solander, Daniel (1733–82) 42
Somerset, Mary Capel, Duchess of
   Beaufort (1630–1714), 30, 31,
   35, 164
Sonder, O.W., 122
Sowerby, James (1757–1822), 67
Steudel, Ernst Gottlieb (1783–1856),
   93
storksbill
   Countess of Liverpool's, **pl. 6**
   Davey's, **pl. 7**
   generally, 7
   Large-bracted, **pl. 8**
   Lord Yarborough's, 124
   Queen of Portugal's, 129
   Sir Abraham Hume's, 88
   Streak-flowered, 81
Stringer, Revd Stanley T., 230, 231
Sweet, Robert (1782–1835)
   classification, 251–4
   Geraniaceae, and plants in it, 79, 84,

   90–1, 99, 103, 115, 125,
     128–9, 134, 138, 165, 173,
     229–30, 243–4
   life, 79, 80, 83, 93, 246
   trial, 80–3
Thunberg, Carl Pehr (1743–1828),
   48, 49
Thurtell, Captain Charles, 104, 108
Tradescant, John (*c.* 1570–1638) an
   Tradescant, John (1608–62),
   13, 15–18, 248
Trattinick, Leopold (1764–1849), 9
Troyte-Bullock, Miss M.C., 241–4, 2
Turner, Charles (1818–85), 116, 18
   184, **185**, 189, 199

Vandes, Countess de, 71, 75
variegation in pelargoniums, 147,
   148, 163
Veitch, James (1792–1863) and
   Veitch's Nursery, 71, 92, 173

Walt, Prof. J.J.A. van der, 236, 252
Weltje's Nursery, 236, 252
White, Henrietta, 219, 220
Willdenow, Carl Ludwig (1765–181
   92, 93, 148
William (III) of Orange, 24–6, 29
Willmott, Ellen (1858–1934), 219
Wills, John (1832–95), 167
Wynne Rushton, Gerald, 218–20,
   240, 241

Young, Charles and James, 89, 92

Zeyher, Karl Ludwig (1799–1858),